GRANTA

12 Addison Avenue, London W11 4QR | email editorial@granta.com
To subscribe go to www.granta.com, or call 845-267-3031 (toll-free 866-438-6150)
in the United States, 020 8955 7011 in the United Kingdom

ISSUE 121: AUTUMN 2012

EDITOR	John Freeman
DEPUTY EDITOR	Ellah Allfrey
ARTISTIC DIRECTOR	Michael Salu
ASSOCIATE EDITOR	Patrick Ryan
ONLINE EDITOR	Ted Hodgkinson
EDITORIAL ASSISTANT	Yuka Igarashi
PUBLICITY	Saskia Vogel
ASSISTANT DESIGNER	Daniela Silva
FINANCE	Geoffrey Gordon, Morgan Graver, Craig Nicholson
MARKETING AND SUBSCRIPTIONS	David Robinson
SALES DIRECTOR	Brigid Macleod
SALES MANAGER	Sharon Murphy
TO ADVERTISE CONTACT	Kate Rochester, katerochester@granta.com
IT MANAGER	Mark Williams
PRODUCTION ASSOCIATE	Sarah Wasley
PROOFS	Sarah Barlow, Katherine Fry, Juliette Mitchell, Jessica Rawlinson, Vimbai Shire
PUBLISHER	Sigrid Rausing
CONTRIBUTING EDITORS	Daniel Alarcón, Diana Athill, Peter Carey, Sophie Harrison, Isabel Hilton, Blake Morrison, John Ryle, Lucretia Stewart, Edmund White

MINISTÉRIO DA CULTURA
Fundação BIBLIOTECA NACIONAL

Published with support from the Brazilian Ministry of Culture / National Library Foundation.
Obra publicada com o apoio do Ministério da Cultura do Brasil / Fundação Biblioteca Nacional.

Granta em português

PUBLISHER	Roberto Feith
EDITOR	Marcelo Ferroni
EDITORIAL ASSISTANTS	André Marinho and Vinicius Melo
PRODUCTION MANAGER	Marcelo Xavier

Granta, ISSN 173231, is published four times per year by Granta Publications, 12 Addison Avenue, London W11 4QR.

The 2012 US annual subscription price is $48. Airfreight and mailing in the USA by agent named Air Business Ltd, c/o Worldnet Shipping Inc., 156–15, 146th Avenue, 2nd Floor, Jamaica, NY 11434, USA. Periodicals postage paid at Jamaica, NY 11431.

US POSTMASTER: Send address changes to *Granta*, Air Business Ltd. c/o Worldnet Shipping Inc. 156–15, 146th Avenue, 2nd Floor, Jamaica, NY 11434.

Subscription records are maintained at *Granta* Magazine, c/o Abacus e-Media, PO Box 2068, Bushey, Herts WD23 3ZF.

Air Business is acting as our mailing agent.

Granta is printed and bound in Italy by Legoprint. This magazine is printed on paper that fulfils the criteria for 'Paper for permanent document' according to ISO 9706 and the American Library Standard ANSI/NIZO Z39.48-1992 and has been certified by the Forest Stewardship Council (FSC). *Granta* is indexed in the American Humanities Index.

ISBN 978-1-905881-63-5

"Building Stories"

A new Graphic Novel by Chris Ware

author of "Jimmy Corrigan, the Smartest Kid on Earth."
(Winner, 2001 Guardian Book Award; Top 100 Books of the Decade,
The Times, and included in the 2002 Whitney Biennial.)

Jonathan Cape, October 2012.
260 pages. (Some assembly required.)

ISBN 978-0-224-07812-2   capegraphicnovels.tumblr.com

CONTENTS

Foreword

This is the first edition of *Granta* dedicated to Brazilian writing. It is being published in the English language at a time when Brazil has attracted global interest on a variety of fronts: the surging economy, sports and culture. Brazil will host the next World Cup and the 2016 Summer Olympics, and Brazilian music is as vibrant today as when bossa nova swept the world in the 1950s. Yet, when one considers literature, what is written and read in Brazil at this moment is still largely unknown outside the country. The lack of will to translate the work of our best new writers is beginning to change, and we hope that this issue will speed that momentum along.

The work of the twenty young Brazilian writers selected as the Best of Young Brazilian Novelists is deeply rooted in their experience and culture, even if it may not be reflected in the manner expected. The stories here do not convey an image of an idealized, tropical nation.

This is a generation less interested than those that have preceded it in the question of a Brazilian identity. For many years this identity was often defined through a return to the land or to the 'authentic' Brazil, where the search for cultural origins could be made outside the corrupting influences of the world at large. Young Brazilian writers are not especially concerned with parsing what derives from within and what comes from outside. Sons and daughters of a nation that is more prosperous and open, they are citizens of the world, as well as Brazilians.

Many of the pieces are set in cities and take place outside easily identifiable Brazilian settings. Laura Erber's main character travels to a remote part of Romania searching for the works of a dead artist. Ricardo Lísias describes a chess player's descent into madness, over the course of repeated (and progressively more farcical) international trips. Leandro Sarmatz writes about an actor trying to escape Nazism in Germany.

These young writers are also less interested in explicitly political issues such as inequality and ideology, which permeated much of the

7

writing of their parents' generation. They experienced the Brazilian military dictatorship (1964–85) through the lives and stories of their elders. Born after 1973, they were very young during the struggle for freedom that consumed Brazilian society in the early eighties. Their work is a reflection of the political and economic developments of later decades.

Still, the dictatorships that shaped the history of South America are present in these stories as an indirect consequence of the oppression in neighbouring countries. The families of four of the twenty selected authors left their native land and emigrated to Brazil in the seventies, exiles from repressive regimes.

Carola Saavedra was born in Chile in 1973, the year of the military coup, and her father, an engineer specializing in hydroelectric power plants, moved to Brazil in 1976, attracted by the so-called 'economic miracle' of the seventies. Javier Arancibia Contreras was born in Salvador, Bahia, but is the only Brazilian-born son of a Chilean family of five brothers. As in the case of Saavedra, his parents moved to Brazil after Pinochet took power in Chile.

Julián Fuks is the son of Argentinians who fled the dictatorship in 1977, and his story of a family dinner at which one of the guests, a retired army officer, becomes the focus of tension, is largely based on personal experiences – an encounter his parents had with a member of the Argentinian military government during a family wedding in the 1990s.

It's the same story with Miguel Del Castillo, one of the youngest authors in this collection, whose father left Uruguay in 1976, fleeing as well from a violent dictatorship. His story describes family members arrested by the repressive forces and, as in the work of Fuks, is based on fact.

Contemporary Latin American literature looms large for this generation – even among those born in Brazil – with influences that range from Borges to Bolaño. It can be seen in Lísias's slightly surreal story, or in the parallel, fragmentary structure of Emilio Fraia's piece, or in Sarmatz's descriptions – more literary than historical – of Germany under Hitler.

Taken as a whole, the twenty texts form a surprising mosaic of styles and themes. They are remarkable for the vigour and craft of their prose – the aptness of details, the search for a coherent language, the development of character. The stories speak of personal loss and family relations (Vanessa Barbara, Michel Laub), the alienation of large urban settings (Chico Mattoso), moments of childhood (Antonio Prata, Luisa Geisler), and trips where anything can happen (Antônio Xerxenesky, Carol Bensimon). Tatiana Salem Levy and J.P. Cuenca, two writers who live in Rio de Janeiro, express very different perspectives on the same city.

This selection includes authors who range from the most well-known writers in Brazil to the ones who have published only a few stories in anthologies and are now working on their first collections. Laub is working on his fifth novel, and in 2011 won the *Bravo!/ Bradesco* Prize. Levy won the São Paulo Prize for Literature for her first novel, which has been translated into five languages. Daniel Galera has written three novels, a volume of short stories and a graphic novel. He is the winner of the Brazilian National Library's Machado de Assis Prize.

Among the lesser-known authors, Vinicius Jatobá is established as a literary critic and is currently finishing his first novel and a book of short stories; Cristhiano Aguiar published a collection of stories in 2006. The oldest of our authors were born in 1973. The youngest, Geisler, the author of a collection of short stories and a novel, both of which won the SESC Prize for Literature, was born in 1991.

In recent years, *Granta* has acquired a global dimension, with editions in other countries and languages: there are Spanish, Brazilian, Italian, Swedish, Norwegian, Bulgarian and Chinese editions. The fact that the English, Spanish and Chinese editions of *Granta* have committed to publishing translations of *The Best of Young Brazilian Novelists* will guarantee that the work of these authors reaches close to 80,000 readers in Latin America, Spain, the United States, the United Kingdom and China – a heretofore unheard of audience for these young writers.

Granta em português was first published in Brazil in 2007. The first issue was a translation of *The Best of Young American Novelists 2*. Since then, we have published issues with themes such as travel, family, sex and work. We select pieces published originally by *Granta* in the UK as well as new material by Brazilian authors. In recent editions, *Granta em português* has also published pieces that first appeared in the Spanish and Italian versions of the magazine, thus expanding the possibilities of translating new and exciting authors from other languages. The magazine is currently on its tenth edition.

The Best of Young Brazilian Novelists was conceived at the end of 2010. Our idea was to make a selection of twenty authors born from January 1972 on: that is, writers younger than forty at the time the issue was published in Brazil. They needed to be prose writers, writing in Portuguese and publishing in Brazil, and with at least one story published.

We assembled a team of seven highly qualified, independent judges, active in different strata of the literary world. Beatriz Bracher is the author of three novels and a story collection, and worked as a literary editor from 1992 to 2000; Italo Moriconi is a literary critic and poet, and teaches Brazilian and comparative literature at the University of the State of Rio de Janeiro (UERJ); Manuel da Costa Pinto is a journalist and critic, columnist for the newspaper *Folha de S. Paulo*; Cristovão Tezza is a writer and former university professor, author of the novel *The Eternal Son*, winner of the most important Brazilian literary prizes and a finalist for the International IMPAC Dublin Literary Award in 2012; and Samuel Titan Jr is a professor of comparative literature at São Paulo University (USP), and the editor and translator of Flaubert, Canetti and Capote, among other classic and contemporary authors.

Granta in the UK suggested a sixth judge, Benjamin Moser, an American writer, editor, critic and translator, author of *Why This World: A Biography of Clarice Lispector*. His 'outsider' point of view enriched the judging process. The seventh judge was Marcelo Ferroni, editor, writer and one of the coordinators of this issue of *Granta*.

The project was officially launched in July 2011. We received 247 valid submissions by our deadline of October 2011, which were judged over the following months. At the end of February 2012, each of the seven judges drew up a list of names, and met in a hotel in Rio de Janeiro to agree on the shortlist. The Brazilian edition was published in July 2012, a year after the call for submissions.

Over the past two decades, few Brazilian authors have been published abroad. There are several reasons for this. Brazilian literature is sometimes seen as difficult, and the language barrier is significant. Few people outside Portugal and Brazil read Portuguese; hence the gap between the vitality of Brazilian literature and its presence in the world. The writer Jorge Amado, when speaking of the potential of Brazil, said we are a continent rather than a country. The work of these writers is part of the diversity and scope that Amado perceived. We expect they will go on to produce works that will be essential to an understanding of Brazilian literature, and to ensuring a wider presence for it in the world in the coming decades.

Roberto Feith and Marcelo Ferroni
Translated by Nick Caistor

BULGARIA   ARRIV

ITALY   ARRIV

BRAZIL   ARRIV

SPAIN   ARRIV

CHINA   BOARD

NORWAY   BOARD

SWEDEN   BOARD

TURKEY   BOARD

AN INTERNATIONAL

CONSPIRACY

OF GOOD

WRITING

Granta has editions in Spain, Italy,
Bulgaria and Brazil. The magazine
will soon be launching in China,

Norway, Sweden and Turkey.
Read the best new writing –
from around the world.

GRANTA

THE MAGAZINE OF NEW WRITING

GRANTA

ANIMALS

Michel Laub

TRANSLATED BY MARGARET JULL COSTA

MICHEL LAUB
1973

Michel Laub was born in Porto Alegre and currently
lives in São Paulo. He is a journalist and the author
of five novels. His latest book, *Diário da queda* (2011), received
the Brasília Award, the *Bravo!*/Bradesco Prize and the Erico
Verissimo Award. It is being translated into Dutch, French,
German and Spanish, and is forthcoming in English in the
UK. 'Animals' ('Animais') is a new story.

When I was eleven years old and living in Porto Alegre, my dog Champion was killed by our neighbour's Dobermann.

Our neighbour was a Korean, the owner of a biscuit factory, and his house was subsequently demolished to make way for an apartment block. The same thing happened to our house and to the whole neighbourhood, which had a lot of empty building plots and broad pavements you could skateboard along.

The maid usually took Champion for his walks. On the day he died, he was sniffing around in a bush and, when the maid wasn't looking, he managed to slip out of his collar, run off and stick his nose through the railings surrounding the Korean's garden. The girl had worked for us for one or two years, but after that I never saw her again, and from the age of eleven until now I have never owned another dog. The only other pets I had were a hamster, a duck, a cat and a second cat.

I was given the hamster after Champion died. I used to enjoy cutting up bits of carrot for him, changing his bedding and watching him run in his wheel, and I only stopped playing with him when he began biting the fingers of anyone who tried to pet him. He had a ritual of swallowing the cubes of carrot, then disappearing underneath his little blanket and regurgitating it all, scrabbling at his mouth with his paws as if he were scratching himself. One time, a bit of his gut came up with the food, and when I went to clean out his cage the following day the hamster was lying there stiff and cold.

V

It was my father who told me about Champion's death. He came into my room, sat down on my bed and, after explaining what had happened, asked me not to tell my sister because he didn't want to upset her before the ballet performance that night. My sister is two years younger than me and had been going to ballet classes since she was little. Every year we had to go and watch some thirty or so children prancing about onstage. I could stand it for about ten minutes and then I would go and wait outside at the exit, and one time my father did the same. The theatre was in Praça da Matriz, and we stood on the steps talking and looking across at the cathedral, the Legislative Assembly and the Courts of Justice.

VI

Two years ago my father died of pulmonary fibrosis, a kind of progressive scarring that damages tissue, gradually reducing lung function. Once the first symptoms have been detected, the survival rate is around five years. It began with my father having difficulty going up the stairs, then he started using a walking stick, then he couldn't stand and finally he had to have an oxygen cylinder beside his bed. In his last months, he needed a nurse to care for him. I used to go for walks with the two of them, pushing his wheelchair. We'd go to an ice-cream parlour and sit at the table outside, in a street lined with trees, my father almost glowing with health from the corticosteroids he was on. At the funeral the rabbi gave a speech, and made a small cut in the clothing of each family member, and sang the prayer for the dead before the coffin was lowered into the grave, and everyone present picked up the trowel and dropped a little earth onto the lid.

VII

In 1937, when my father was six, he and his mother had to leave Germany because of the Nazis. His father – my grandfather – emigrated to Israel with the older daughter. My father only saw his sister again in 1970 when he went to visit my grandfather. Despite being in hospital with terminal cancer, my grandfather refused to see someone whom he considered a *turned page*. All because my father, when still a child, had failed to reply to letters sent to him in Brazil. My father only told me this in 2007 when I was already living in São Paulo, during a brief conversation we had while waiting for a taxi on Alameda Itu.

VIII

My father was an engineer. He worked on a number of large projects: the refurbishment of the market in Porto Alegre, the Metro in Recife and a hospital in Sierra Leone. In May 1992, more or less as he had on the day Champion died, he came into my room to tell me about a friend of mine. My friend had been into skateboarding like me and we were very close until our final year in school. When I was thirteen, we were both mugged by a street kid who threatened us with a penknife and demanded that we give him our knee pads and our gloves. I just stood there, but my friend ran off, as he would in 1992, when he was attacked by a mugger as he was getting out of his car. He was shot three times in the back. My father said: Something bad has happened. I went to my friend's house that same night, my dad went with me, and my friend's father opened the door to us and we stayed with him for nearly half an hour. There was a constant flow of visitors – acquaintances and relatives. My friend's father was in his stocking feet. His shirt was hanging out, his tie loose, and when he saw me he said almost apologetically: What can I say?

IX

That night, my dad and I went to a snack bar. We ate cheese and roast beef sandwiches and I drank a beer. My father started talking, recalling a day about five years earlier when I came home with a duck, given to me free at an agricultural fair. The friend who died was staying with us at the time. We gave the duck some water and some corn, and it strutted up and down in the garden, and my friend was fascinated, and because his mother was always giving me presents and I didn't much care for the duck anyway I asked my friend if he'd like to keep it.

X

The duck's name was Donald. The name of the friend who died was Marcelo. The name of another friend who died, this time in 1987, when he got caught in a fishing net while surfing, was Victor. On the day of the accident Victor, Marcelo and I were in the water, the beach was Capão da Canoa, it was about five degrees and we were near the sewage outlet. You can walk for miles along the beaches in Rio Grande do Sul and the landscape never changes – lifeguard huts, scrappy bits of grass, an old horse that keeps stopping to graze and getting beaten because it won't pull the cart. Given the position of the rope tethering the net – we found the rope later on in the sand – and the direction of the current, which was pulling towards the south, it was clear that the net had passed underneath me and then underneath Marcelo before either getting entangled in Victor's leash or caught on the tail of his board or around his leg, I never knew for sure. He was carried unconscious to a first-aid station. Salt water dribbled from one corner of his mouth. They tried artificial respiration, then applied electrodes to his chest, first shock, second shock, a guy in a white coat counted the seconds. Later, someone said he'd done it all wrong, that he hadn't even placed him face down or expelled the water from his lungs or removed his wetsuit to allow his chest to expand more easily, but I think Victor was already dead when he was brought out of the sea.

XI

I was staying at Victor's house. We had arrived the evening before, had eaten sausages for supper and played canasta until we went to bed. I went back to Porto Alegre at two o'clock the next afternoon, with my dad at the wheel, he and my mum having driven straight to Capão da Canoa when they heard about the accident. On the day Marcelo died I thought about that journey, Lagoa dos Patos, the toll station, the hour and a half drive to Porto Alegre, and I had that memory vividly in my mind when I left Marcelo's house I told my dad this in the snack bar, but he told me not to think about it. These things happen. Sometimes they make no sense at all, he said, and now I realize that I never talked to my dad about his childhood, the school friends who had perhaps stayed behind in Germany, some or all of whom would have ended up in concentration camps, or about the memories he had of the streets and the town and the country that was laid waste in the years that followed.

XII

My father didn't attend synagogue. He took no part in any charitable activities associated with the Jewish community. He showed no interest in religious topics, never quoted from the Bible, never prayed or said whether or not he believed in God. In almost forty years I never so much as heard him mention the word, and when the rabbi made a speech at his funeral praising him as 'a man who lived his Judaism every day' I couldn't recall a single episode in his life that justified such a comment.

XIII

After my father died, my mother was left alone. His death came in the wake of a particularly grim period of her life, during which she had also lost her best friend. My sister had a Labrador puppy whose life was devoted to drooling, trashing the apartment, stealing food and barking at night, and my mother came to enjoy looking after him and taking him to a square frequented by other dogs and their owners or trainers. My mother likes to talk about my father but there's nothing morbid about this, not at all, and I like it too because every now and then her memories include something I didn't know or had forgotten: the time he won a prize from the Engineering Council, the time he decided to have a barbecue and to fan the hot coals with a hairdryer, the time he made me a little theatre out of modelling clay because I was having nightmares about giant otters.

XIV

In 1977, a sergeant saved a child in the zoo in Brasília. She had fallen into the enclosure containing giant otters, and the sergeant leaped in after her and was attacked and later died in hospital when the bites he had received became infected. The incident was featured on the TV news for days afterwards, and one night my dad called me into his room, where he had placed the 'theatre' on the bed with a towel as the curtain and behind it various dolls. He had made them all himself. The story always began with giant otters, about the babies they had and how they swam on their backs when eating fish. My dad told the story over several nights, explaining that giant otters are only aggressive when they feel threatened and that, besides, such creatures were unknown in Porto Alegre. I would watch this show before going to sleep and my mum says I never again woke up screaming.

XV

My father taught me to drive, to swim, to use a soldering iron, and together we rigged up a primitive lighting system by fixing four sockets to a piece of wood, each with a plug attached by a cable to four light bulbs positioned at various points in the garage which could be turned on and off to create our very own ghost train effect. He went with me to have my MMR jab. My first trip on a plane was with him. He opened a bank account for me and taught me my first words in English and bought me magazines full of stories about the Wild West, stories that encouraged me to read and, later on, to become a writer.

XVI

When I was thirty-one, my father rang me one Friday to tell me that an old university friend of mine, recently appointed public prosecutor in Santa Rosa in the state of Rio Grande do Sul, had been shot six times by a drunken policeman. For many years, he had been one of my best friends. During the year I spent in London, I stayed in the same place he had stayed. Like me, he had done his military service, and like me, he had considered becoming a diplomat. We read the same books and throughout our time at university we both often talked about giving up law and trying another profession. We worked together in the same practice before I became a journalist and moved to São Paulo. The murder was reported in all the newspapers and was talked about for weeks afterwards. A street in Porto Alegre was named after him, another Marcelo. The funeral took place late on Friday afternoon, and I didn't go because I had something important to do at work, or because I wouldn't have had time to catch the plane, or for both those reasons or neither, but my father offered to go in my place.

XVII

A year after my father's death, I was in Porto Alegre for the unveiling of the headstone. In attendance were cousins from Florianópolis and Vitória, from France and Israel. The ceremony took place on a cold Sunday morning. The black cloth was removed from the grave marker and a few small stones placed on it, and then we went to a *churrascaria* for lunch, and since several of my cousins already had children every single person at the table asked me if I had any plans to start a family. Whenever I attend these family gatherings, I always notice how people interact with their children, one cousin spoon-feeding her eight-month-old baby, another kicking a stone back and forth with his son. The closest I came to being a father was when I was married. But the marriage ended, and I didn't give the matter of having children any more thought, and now I can only respond to the kind of questions I was asked at the restaurant with some banal, jokey comment.

XVIII

The first cat I had was run over. The second one I lost when my wife and I split up. On the day my wife left I went to a bar on Avenida Roosevelt, then to another bar on Augusta, then I crossed the road and went into a club where there was a show on, then to another club and another show, then to a bar that had a jukebox and where you can breakfast on chocolate milk and brandy, and that was my life every night for the next three years. It lost me a job. It was the reason why none of my subsequent relationships worked out. I never again spoke to my ex-wife, or to any of the other girlfriends I'd had, or to the majority of the friends I'd made over a period of forty years, at school, university or work, and about whom I now know nothing, where they live, what they're doing, or if they're even alive.

XIX

The photo on my father's headstone was taken when he was about sixty, the smile is fairly typical of him, but when I'm alone and try to remember him no specific pose or expression comes to mind, neither does his voice, because people's voices change with age and in the last twelve years of his life we spoke more often on the phone than face to face. In the novels I've written, I've portrayed my father in different ways: as a Jew marked by the memory of the war, as a secondary character in that story about the fishing net, as a man who gives his son the worst possible news just before a football match. All of these are true and false, as is always the case with fiction, and I've often wondered why I keep writing about him and if, when I'm older, I'll get my real memory of him mixed up with the memory I've set down in those books: the facts I chose to include or exclude, the feelings I did or didn't have, who my father really was and the kind of person I did or didn't become because of that or despite that or entirely independently of that, this story which, for various reasons, begins at the ballet performance that took place after Champion's death.

XX

My father was sitting next to me. The theatre was packed, then everything went dark and shortly afterwards a solitary spotlight lit up my sister alone on the stage, dancing the part of Little Red Riding Hood.

XXI

My sister found out about Champion when we got back home. The Dobermann had torn off half of Champion's snout, and the maid described how his body, with his jawbone protruding from his cheek, seemed to hang limply from the other dog's mouth. First aid for dogs is much the same as it is for people: you lay them on the ground, make sure the airways are unobstructed and apply pressure to the wound. When he was put in the car, Champion was very still, wrapped in a blood-soaked towel, and at the veterinary surgery, after the vet had checked his pulse and the temperature of his paws and the colour of his gums, he told my father there was nothing they could do for Champion and that it would be best to have him put down.

XXII

When he came back from the vet's, my father went straight to the Korean's house. None of us had ever been there. They had an enormous living room, with a swimming pool and a basketball court out back. By then, the Korean knew what had happened and he told my father it was our maid's fault. After all, she was the one who had let Champion slip out of his collar. The dog should never have been allowed that close to the fence, we should have kept a more careful eye on him, the Korean said, and one day I heard my father on the phone and I stood behind the door listening to him telling the whole story in detail, before, during and after the Dobermann attacked Champion, and then he was saying: I mean, shit, what the hell was I to do? That was the first time I'd ever heard his voice tremble. It almost tailed off in a whisper. But he never said anything more about the incident, and all I have left of Champion are a few scraps of memories: the bowl he ate his food from, the plastic snake he was always chewing, his dark, wet fur after we had bathed him, the night of a football match when we sat up with him, my father and I, until the fireworks had stopped.

XXIII

There are many ways for a dog to die. It can catch rabies, distemper or canine parvovirus. Or hepatitis or cancer. It can get shot or eat some poisonous plant. Or else, one humid day in the garage, when no one else in the house is stirring, you take a glass bottle, wrap it in newspaper, and stamp on it several times until the fragments of glass are so small as to be almost invisible. Then you pick those pieces up one by one and stick them into a chunk of raw meat until it's really heavy and has the texture of sand. Then you go up the steps, through the living room, open the door, cross the garden to the neighbouring fence, as close as the shrubs will allow, and you lob it – that favourite dish of any dog anywhere any time – onto the other side.

XXIV

My sister cried all night for Champion. My father went into her room several times, and his steps sounded heavy, as if he were dragging his feet, and I remembered our conversation earlier that evening, his asking me to be strong, saying that we had to protect my sister, that I was a big boy now, the older brother, and that's what older brothers had to do. There's no point being angry, he said. You should never hang on to anger. An angry person will never be the master of his own life, said my father, but at the theatre the wolf appeared onstage and my sister mimed her questions about the size of his ears, his big eyes, his huge mouth, and throughout the rest of the show all I could think about was the Korean. The Korean's house. The few occasions I'd seen the Korean leaving the house and setting off to work in a suit, and what I would do the next time I saw him. And what he would do when he saw me. And if I would make a point of looking him in the eye, knowing I knew that he knew. And never again, not when Victor or Marcelo or the other Marcelo died, not even when my father died or at the unveiling of the headstone, perhaps because I didn't cry on any of those occasions, not a single tear, a whole life without shedding a tear, no, never again did I feel as I did on that night at the ballet performance: sitting in the fourth row, my dad in the half-light, and me looking at him and fixing his profile in my mind, his nose, his jaw, his eyes and his expression, the clearest image I have of my father, with me so close to making a decision and him waiting for the wolf's answer. ■

GRANTA

VIOLETA

Miguel Del Castillo

TRANSLATED BY AMANDA HOPKINSON

MIGUEL DEL CASTILLO
1987

Miguel Del Castillo was born in Rio de Janeiro. His father is Uruguayan and his mother is from Rio. While studying architecture at PUC-Rio, Del Castillo worked as editor of the culture and architecture magazine *Noz*. In 2010, he moved to São Paulo, where he is now an editor at Cosac Naify publishing house. He received the Paulo Britto Award for Poetry and Prose for his story 'Carta para Ana' and is currently at work on his first collection of short stories, from which 'Violeta' is taken.

I

M iguel Angel was one of my father's cousins, a Tupamaro who disappeared during the military dictatorship in Uruguay. I was named after him. For many years I was unaware of my family history, of the twenty-two years my father spent in Montevideo before moving to Rio, Miguel Angel and the rest of it. I learned Spanish on my own, as nobody bothered to teach it to me.

I like to think that Miguel Angel feared nothing: looked at himself in the mirror every morning, took his guns, and made two or three coded phone calls

– *Now the bird flies off alone*

sipped his maté, bade farewell to his daughter Ximena, entrusting her to my father, and set off to find his comrades in arms. Violeta, Miguel Angel's mother, was taken prisoner more than once because of her son's subversive activities, her head inside water barrels, the soldiers provoking while undressing her

– *She doesn't look all that old after all*

gripping her tightly, telling her that her son had been captured, that they were torturing him nearly to death but still he wouldn't reveal anything, so she'd better spill the beans. Until one day one of Miguel Angel's female comrades was brought into the prison and she and Violeta decided that, should the girl succeed in getting out before her, she would find her family and ask them to write to Violeta in an agreed code, to inform her regarding her son. Two days after her release, this woman bumped into my father

– *I can't believe I found you, I've got something to tell you*

and she explained how, since Violeta spent her time in prison sewing, they had agreed that sending her some needles would indicate Miguel Angel was well and that a skein of wool meant he was going to leave the country. My father wrote to his aunt to announce the birth of her grandson, Pablito, and that baby clothes would be useful, which was why he was sending the wool and needles

– *Now the bird flies off*

and Violeta jumped with joy, the guards could not understand, even after reading the letter once twice three times, why Violeta was dancing naked around the prison

– *She doesn't look that old*

my father, a student at the military school, enquiring at every military headquarters about a lady called Violeta, Miguel Angel had left the country, the skein of wool, Chile still free of dictatorship

– *I can't believe I found you*

and Violeta, back at home, sewing, Chile then under a military regime, a news blackout. I assume at this point Miguel Angel must have already been captured, the water barrels, the silence.

I visited the old house where my grandmother and Violeta lived for most of their lives, in Prado, where I ate grapes off the vine stretched over the pergola in the backyard, in a grey part of Montevideo far from the centre. Miguel Angel wanted his Montevideo to be free of the military, my grandmother was nervous about yet another police inspection into her home

– *My son how long is this going to go on, please don't get mixed up in this business like your cousin did*

my father attempting to calm her down, saying that he knew nothing, that he had no intention of becoming involved, my sister's mother was pregnant, the move to Rio

– *Now the bird*

my grandmother comforting her sister, telling her that they would find Miguel Angel just as soon as that military nightmare came to an end, that he must be either in Chile or perhaps in Bolivia, he had always been clever, even if at times somewhat coarsely spoken, my new wool coat

– Son when I arrived from Uruguay we no longer had any news of my cousin

(I was listening carefully)

Violeta's Alzheimer's, the visits to the old people's home, Ximena collecting the benefits for the children of the disappeared, the afternoon cup of tea, my grandmother

– Viola do you remember when Miguel Angel was little and used to say he'd grow up to be the captain of a big ship?

my great-aunt nodding her head in agreement, adding milk to the tea

– Son when I arrived from Uruguay we no longer

the house in Prado, the pergola in the backyard, the sweet grapes, the Alzheimer's

– Viola do you remember when Miguel Angel was little

my baptism in the parish church of São Conrado, the heat of Rio de Janeiro, I grew up intermittently hearing the Spanish I struggled to emulate

– Son

on the plane returning to Rio, dinner was gnocchi with tomato sauce, not a patch on what my grandmother used to prepare

– Viola you remember when Miguel Angel

I landed at Rio's international airport and called a taxi, the driver was from the south of Brazil, his maté right there

– Where are you coming from chief?

he had been to Uruguay and Argentina too, of course, it was winter in Rio de Janeiro, it was exceptionally cold, and my wool coat was in the boot of the car.

II

When he enrolled in the School of Fine Arts, Miguel Angel was probably unaware of what awaited him, the military coup, the life of a revolutionary. In Chile he became a chauffeur for the Finnish Embassy, and extradited Uruguayans to Chile with the help of his Finnish girlfriend, the dictatorship there by then, too, I imagine that was why he went to Argentina, to the Victoria del Pueblo Party, to prison. Soon he was on one of the death flights: they were all political prisoners on that plane, the launch chute opening, then all of them gyrating through the air, what went through his head at that moment

(Violeta, the house in Prado, his daughter?)

my father

– I was always ashamed of having studied at the military school, my cousin was the one who opened my eyes

crying as he related this to me, I told him not to be ashamed, I said that at times we really don't see things for what they are

(descending in free fall)

my father opening the cupboard containing the photo albums, hoisting the flag at school

– My cousin was the one who opened my eyes

now in Rio, calling his mother, all was well and she could soon go and visit him, the journey was cheap by bus, all she had to do was to follow the coast road up through Brazil, preferably during winter because of the heat, Miguel Angel gyrating through the air, the distant plane, Violeta's phone call

– *Chiche your cousin has disappeared*

and then her travelling across Chile and Argentina looking for her son, about to embark for Bolivia, and my grandmother

– *Viola don't go, can't you see that Miguel Angel isn't there any more*

giving up on trying to convince her, putting more milk in the tea

– *Chiche your cousin*

(falling at an ever-increasing speed)

– *Chiche*

I used to visit the house at Prado and sit on the swing, watching for ages the pergola offering shade dotted with small spots, Blacky the puppy at my heels, Violeta

– *Miguelito don't be afraid, she doesn't bite*

she spoke a rapid and convoluted Spanish but this much I understood

– *Miguelito don't be afraid*

her curved nose, the tickles and me begging her to stop, my grandfather, Totito, had a cupboard full of junk, stuff he used to make swords and shields for me

– *Touché*

crouching down so that we could fight as equals, throwing himself on the floor, he was toppled and I really was the bravest knight who had ever been seen or heard of in our backyard. I remember seeing him there, playing cards with Violeta's husband, after they'd sold the house, the walking sticks leaning on the white armchair

– *Viola don't go*

they moved to Pocitos but luckily Violeta's old people's rest home was nearby, on the days they brought her home she would sit sewing in the corner of the living room, the Alzheimer's, and always the same questions

– *Telma where is my son?*

always

– *Telma*

and more milk in her tea

(in free fall, the sea always drawing nearer

– *Touché*)

Months later they found some bodies in the bay of Cabo Polónio but Miguel Angel was still missing, I returned to Uruguay and Violeta at the airport

– *Miguelito*

glad to see us, tickling me

– *Miguelito*

I saw a photograph of her at the age of twenty, leaning over the windowsill, boots up to her knees, she would have been out riding that day, lifting her face to the strong winds of Lavalleja, my father closing the album, storing it back in the cupboard

– I was always ashamed

the sea of Montevideo, I never understood why almost no one goes swimming there, they just hang out on the sidewalk, by the shore, drinking maté, maybe because they had seen the bodies washed up onto the beach at Cabo Polónio, maybe because of the brown water, when I go to the rambla and see the empty beaches I feel a pang, the sea empty, people on the shore looking out towards the horizon as if they could see something, as if the waves could bring them someone

they'd not seen in a long time, as if they were
 as if they longed to dive in but somehow couldn't manage to.

III

Returning from Uruguay was always different from returning from any other country. Once inside the plane, I kept my eyes fixed on that empty prairie, an immense plain stretching as far as the horizon. I gazed at that green desert, thinking how that could be possible.

Before, on the way to the airport with my uncle in the car, I would slowly scan the historic houses of the old centre, the port, the market, the rambla filled with people drinking their early-evening maté. I think the trip lasts for more or less an hour. Looking through the plane window at the runway, I consider the melancholy this country has always evoked in me, but why? It does not seem to be about the buildings in the old centre, nor the late-afternoon sun on the red stone benches of the rambla. Perhaps it should be put down to the people and everything I had already been told, that's just what Uruguay was like, and then those days when the tango singer Zitarrosa was still alive etc., or maybe the ex-Tupamaros. Perhaps it's those restaurants with their elderly waiters, it's drinking grapefruit juice from glass bottles. I picture Miguel Angel eating with Violeta in one of those restaurants, saying how one day he would become a ship's captain, her placing the order with one of the old waiters

  – A roll and two small white coffees

(the husband would be coming very shortly). My father opening the albums, the military school, the shame. I bear this melancholia with me, and I can't and don't want to let it go. My eyes stay fixed on the immense vacant plain surrounding the new airport at Carrasco. The death flight, Miguel Angel toppling through the air. On take-off, I can't stop myself from crying, as once again I gaze down on the

enormous patchwork of plantations with their different shades of green. I could return, yes, to Violeta waiting for me at the airport
   – *Miguelito*
and she would tickle me until I couldn't stand it any more.

IV

W ho was Violeta? I think about it while I walk through the front garden of the house at Prado, where she and her husband lived side by side with my grandparents, and with Marta, Violeta's daughter, at the back with the twins. I think if we get to know someone only when we are still children, the memory we have of that person is different. As if we had not been able to understand enough and needed to know something more, something beyond a child's comprehension. And which is brought to light when someone, years later, tells us about it.

I also remember the sun coming in through the kitchen at the Prado house, my grandmother preparing Milanese steak and Russian salad, the backyard out there so inviting. Before going into the rest home, Violeta would come to us talking loudly and laughing, laughing uproariously at something, which then gave rise to guffaws from all. My grandmother and she were like Martha and Mary: while one of them supervised the sauce cooking on the stove, the other would stay around the table with us, making everyone laugh with her jokes. Violeta loved to play 'arm-measuring': as her arm was obviously longer, her hand reached up to my armpit, which always gave rise to another round of tickling. I remember few of the things she told me directly, but I do remember her loud laughter perfectly.

Once Alzheimer's had set in, the silence grew more and more. Soon she would just smile, but never laugh out loud. That silent laughter made a strong impression on me, she seemed to want to laugh at something, but couldn't exactly recall what. That was why she kept a ready smile on her face, and that was how she used to look at us when we arrived at her rest home.

The day she died I was unable to go to Uruguay. My father did, he called me from there, very sad. I think that had I gone I would have asked them to use make-up to recreate that smile on her lips. It would have been the ultimate silent laughter. I learned that the cemetery where she was laid resembled a public garden, as large and leafy as a park. ∎

GRANTA

BLAZING SUN

Tatiana Salem Levy

TRANSLATED BY ALISON ENTREKIN

TATIANA SALEM LEVY
1979

Tatiana Salem Levy is a writer and translator.
She was born in Lisbon and now lives in Rio de Janeiro. Her debut
novel, *A chave de casa* (2007), won the São Paulo Prize for Literature
and was a finalist for the Jabuti Award and the Zaffari & Bourbon
Award. It has been translated into French, Italian, Romanian, Spanish
and Turkish. Her second novel, *Dois rios* (2011), is forthcoming in
Germany, Italy and Portugal. Levy co-edited *Primos: histórias da
herança árabe e judaica* (2010) and is also author of the book-length
essay *A experiência do fora: Blanchot, Foucault e Deleuze* (2011).
'Blazing Sun' ('O Rio sua') is a new story.

After living abroad for seven years, I arrive in Rio de Janeiro in late December, in the middle of summer. The walls and furniture of my flat are hidden beneath a layer of mildew. If it weren't for the green paths traced by the mould, I'd say that the interval separating my departure from my return never existed. The strong smell almost drives me away, but I persevere, and enter. I leave my suitcases in the hallway and open the window, my big glass window, its wooden frame painted white.

Muggy air envelops my face; there isn't a hint of a breeze. Beads of sweat rapidly squeeze through my pores, cross the barrier of skin and trickle down my body, leaving me drenched. It's been years since I've sweated like this. It's been years since I've felt my clothes stick to my body as if I were standing in a downpour.

Finally and immediately, I understand why I have returned. My body understands; the same body that always protested against Europe's harsh air with dry legs, straw-like hair, nausea, dizziness, difficulty breathing. In a sweat, it recognizes itself. Much faster than I had imagined, my blood stirs, aroused by the month of December. Then I realize, sitting on the sofa moistened by my sweat, why I have returned: because here, in Rio de Janeiro, my body feels at home.

~

A few days earlier, I awoke, reluctantly climbed out of bed – it was cold and grey outside – and when I saw you lying on the sofa with a book over your face, I thought: It's time to go back.

Is something wrong? you asked me. No, I answered: I just miss it. I want to spend a little time there. Ah! you sighed, as your face twisted into a lopsided expression, I see. You didn't say anything else, just lit a cigarette and started pacing the room in circles. We both tried to cling to the word *time*. Just a little time.

~

Our parting was silent. We smiled, pretending to believe we would be reunited. Now, slouching on the sofa in my old flat, I perspire: it's never easy to trade one love for another.

~

We came to Rio together only once. I vividly remember your enchantment with every last detail of the place. I was at the peak of my anti-Rio phase, while you, on the other hand, were delighted by everything. Why didn't we ever come back? Is coming here without you a betrayal? Is that what you think, that I'm betraying you? No matter how hard I cast about for the redeeming word, all I can say is: only solitude makes sense. Solitude in this city that overnight shouted out that it was missing from my life. Me, of all people, who has always made people my home. Suddenly I hear the rumbling voice of a city, like the voice of a former lover that comes to life again with the violence of things stowed from sight. (What if I regret my decision? If I change my mind, will you still be waiting for me under the bear-fur blanket?)

~

First thing to do: scrape the mould off the solid surfaces, free up the flat's pores. I came here to breathe.

~

In the summer, the minutes leading up to a storm have a greasy thickness about them. The plants give off a strong, sweet smell. The black sky announces that the world is about to be turned inside out.

Before the storm is the very definition of disaster: nothing has happened yet; everything is about to happen soon, very soon. The imminence of tragedy in its extreme beauty: few things are more beautiful than the instants that precede momentous things, the second before a passionate kiss, before a marathon runner crosses the finish line, before a rainstorm hits Rio de Janeiro.

Before the water comes crashing down, Rio teems with activity, people make a frantic dash for it, birds disperse in a flurry, cockroaches scurry, monkeys leap from branch to branch, all seeking shelter, a roof of any kind. The city suddenly begins to palpitate when the humidity reaches an unsustainable level, when you know that the hot, heavy, sticky weather is about to come undone in a downpour. And if you are lucky enough to be somewhere safe, you will soon see nature's strength unleashed, supreme, reminding us of how fragile and fleeting we are.

That is why, in December, when the smell of approaching rain reaches my nostrils, I am filled with genuine joy: the joy of things that are about to happen.

~

Between one bout of cleaning and another I head out into the streets. The buildings are ugly; the pavements, potholed; the heat, inhuman; and, nevertheless, it is what I need: to feel like going out.

~

You shook as we took the cable car up. I, on the other hand, was filled with enthusiasm. Sugarloaf Mountain is the only tourist attraction I visit each time as if it were the first. I love to see the world from up high. From Morro da Urca, halfway up, when I see the mantle of water washing over the rocks, I feel like a traveller discovering Brazil. I imagine myself five hundred years ago, anchoring a small ship in Guanabara Bay and being struck with awe as I take in the still-pristine landscape. I don't envy the Amerindians who were already here so much as the Portuguese who arrived and discovered an inhospitable, scandalously beautiful world.

~

Almost a week of cleaning: there is no more mildew on the surface of things, but I still can't get the musty smell out of them.

~

When anxiety gets the better of me, and with it doubt and nostalgia, I head downstairs to seek relief and dive into the swimming pool in the summer storm. The children laugh at the thunder that rumbles and lights up the sky as if it were day.

~

Theory regarding the cheerfulness of Rio's inhabitants: sweat lubricates the muscles; it makes us move.

~

You insisted: you just had to go to a Rio funk dance. Men, women, mothers, brothers, friends, strangers in a continuous curved line down to the ground. With their legs slotted into one another, showing that that was what they were made for, they slotted together. Sweat wasn't an inconvenience, just another fluid.

Just don't ask me to like Carnival, I told you.

~

The heat here is so great that it has melted away the 'h' that the Portuguese still retain. The seriousness of the 'h' blocks direct access to *umidade*, the Brazilian version of humidity that hasn't got time for this letter that goes up before it comes down. Everything bursts out, without permission. Fluids run even from solid objects. Houses melt, papers drip, photographs discolour.

But the Portuguese *humidade* contains the 'h' of 'humus' and the 'h' of 'humour'.

Humus: the remains that retain water, keep the soil wet, the earth damp. The decomposition of remains is also what gives life to everything else. It creates the broth. The earth feeds on its dead; the present, on its ghosts. *Humidade* suggests memory swallowed and transformed. The adjective *húmido* has more history than *úmido*, more vestiges. It doesn't arrive on a straight path: it has to take detours, go around things, but it gathers moisture more intensely.

Humour: a liquid or semi-liquid organic substance. In natural history, it was believed that the human body contained four such fluids: blood, phlegm, choler and black bile. A healthy man (good-humoured) was he who maintained a balance between the four. In a sick man (bad-humoured), the balance was disrupted. Health was directly related to the bodily liquids. (Could the good humour of Rio's inhabitants stem from there? From their moist bodies?)

~

The books are all on the floor, and the cloth by my side: the obstacles to resuming an interrupted story, to restarting a life left behind.

~

Things I don't like in Rio: the water that drips from the buildings in the city centre when summer is at its peak.

The sea is serene at first. Waves form, looming bigger and bigger until they are frightening, until they drag me from wherever I am – from the sand, from the beach promenade, from the sea itself. First I see the white of the foam, then an enchanted world, brimming with sea horses, anemones and corals, then everything goes dark. I wake up sopping wet, the blanket in a tangle, my pillow on the floor, and I ask myself: Why aren't you here?

~

I used to buy flowers every Friday. I would remove the previous week's arrangement from the vase and replace it with the fresh flowers. My little wonder, my quota of moisture in that dry land.

Here, the flowers are abundant; they are large-lipped and catch the warm, sticky rain that the sky pours on them. Here, I don't buy flowers.

~

I'm going to buy a plane ticket, you say. I'm going to join you in Rio. No, I say, drily, as if the European air were able to pass through the telephone line. Each thing in its own time.

~

I leave home at ten o'clock at night, dressed in white, and head for Copacabana. For the first time I'm going to spend New Year's Eve on my own. I walk along the lakeside until I get to the Corte do Cantagalo, and then down to Copacabana, arriving shortly before eleven. The beach is crowded, a vast carpet of yellow sand dotted with white. I carry my sandals in my hands and let my feet sink into the moist sand, strewn with offerings.

The afternoon was sultry, and now heavy clouds menace the city. I circulate among the people, brush past strangers' bodies. Looking down I see thousands of naked feet in the sand, among lit candles, boats and giant flowers. I have my own: four white gladioli.

Before I toss them into the water, I sit facing the ocean. I've never seen Copacabana so crowded, and I have never felt so alone. But my solitude doesn't trouble me. It would be beautiful, I think, if for one moment the people lining the waterfront fell silent and the sound of their breathing was indistinguishable from the coming and going of the waves.

I get up and head for the sea. One by one, I throw the gladioli to the *orixá* of salt water. The first three are for my dead, so they will know they are always with me. Last of all, I throw one in for you.

The people start preparing the champagne, holding hands, anxious. I join a circle of strangers, who invite me over when they see that I am alone. There is a countdown and, suddenly, fireworks in the sky. Immediately afterwards, as if they have been politely waiting for the spectacle to end, the black clouds pelt down on us, mixing with the champagne, sweat and salt. Then, locals and tourists rally the vaguest certainty, with astonishing conviction: the year to come will be the best of their lives.

~

The solid weight of the humidity: in 1770, the Marquês do Lavradio observed that the inhabitants of Rio de Janeiro were inordinately lazy.

~

The air saps voices of their enthusiasm; they are drawn out, slow, quiet, almost a whisper. The people of Rio economize on words: they don't greet one another in the lift, or when they get on the bus; they don't say excuse me before walking between two people, or sorry when they bump into someone; they rarely say please or thank you. When I first arrived back, coming from a country where words build things and define relations, I thought everyone was rude. Later I understood: Rio's inhabitants speak with their bodies. With their bodies that collide, slide, cross, brush up against others. They greet one another and say excuse me, sorry or thank you with their lethargic, flexible bodies, with their flesh and hair that rub against one another without modesty or disgust, their hugs on first meeting, even if they are sticky with sweat.

Today, comparing the two places, I'd say: Words don't always contain the truth, but the body never lies.

~

I awake with a start. The emptiness on the other side of the bed. Difficult choice: air or hand?

~

Theory regarding the cheerfulness of Rio's inhabitants: sadness exits through the pores.

~

Etymologically, melancholy means black bile. Bad humour, the body overflowing with black moisture. Unlike the other three humours enumerated by Hippocrates – choler, phlegm and blood – black bile doesn't exist. It is merely fictional.

~

The people of Rio don't accept sadness. They don't know how to live with pain. Not feeling well? Take a dip in the sea, crack open a cold beer, go dance samba in Lapa. Sadness: only with music, only in community. Sadness: only with cheer.

That's why I left, why I went away for so many years: nothing is more contradictory to happiness than the obligation to be happy. The requirement that one be cheerful in Rio can be as oppressive as the grey sky in Paris, London or Berlin. Everything in excess becomes banal. And I wasn't able to be happy having to be happy all the time.

~

The posture of one who is melancholic: sitting, hunched over himself, head tilted, chin in one hand, he stares downward, lost in the void. His body paralysed, petrified, his soul immersed in memories and regrets.

How is one melancholic in Rio de Janeiro? You lower your head, but on your right side a hill rises up, majestic; on the left side, scandalous nature makes its presence felt; in front of you, the infinite line of the sea. You try, but your right eye stubbornly wants to see the landscape; the left is drawn to the greenery. And you know that if you happen to lift your head and look at the horizon, there'll be no way out: you will smile.

One must, therefore, find the melancholic corners of the city, those in which you can look down without being sucked in by the landscape (but where?).

~

On the other end of the line, the shaky, faltering voice, slightly stammering, asks: Are you trading me for a city?

~

I'm sorry, but I never did learn to live in such aridity. The chapped skin was ageing me. Little by little it is recomposing itself. Beads of sweat work like stitches, and I think: I am going to survive.

~

Theory regarding the cheerfulness of Rio's inhabitants: people walk to the beach in bikinis and swimming trunks. They share the pavement with men wearing suits and ties and women in high heels.

~

On the telephone, I beg: Please wait a little longer.

~

When uncertainty strikes, I get up and walk over to the window. A dense fog covers Corcovado in white, splitting it in half, separating the foot of the mountain from the top. Christ the Redeemer floats, and I chat with him, a habit that in times past filled many a solitary night in this flat.

~

My organs were becoming equally arid and dry, atrophied. Little by little, the moist air expands them again. I cycle through Flamengo Park and have the curious feeling of being almost happy.

~

Don't ask me to talk as if time hasn't passed, I tell you. At the other end, I feel the weight of my selfishness: for you, time is intact, monolithic, waiting for someone to give it a shove.

~

The beach has always been my refuge. The sea, my home away from home. When I was very young, I liked to dive under and hold my breath. That was how I forgot the outside world and imagined that a mermaid would lead me with her warm hand to a colourful universe, full of anemones and creatures of the depths, where I would no longer need to breathe.

I also liked to stretch out along the seashore while my sister covered me in wet sand, leaving only my face exposed. I would stay in this position, unmoving, until the tide rose and the waves licked my body.

~

I set the rules: from one end of Copacabana to the other, only on the black paving stones. If my foot slips and touches a white one, I have to go back to the start. Between one leap and another, cool air rushes up my legs, reinvigorating me.

~

The phone rings and I don't answer it. Today I put my suitcases in the wardrobe.

~

Theory regarding the cheerfulness of Rio's inhabitants: bodies always on display. Women are constantly flattered. Men whisper smutty things when a woman goes past in a pair of shorts and, instead of a kick, they get a smile.

~

Tonight the Carnival theme song is to be chosen at the Salgueiro Rehearsal Hall. I am here to cheer for a samba composed by a friend. My body is just another cell in an enormous fabric, a uniform blanket of skin and fluids. Impossible not to kiss someone, says a friend. Here you only breathe collectively. I try to inhale the rarefied air but can't. Panic begins to set in and I think of the organized bodies on the other side of the Atlantic, until there isn't enough oxygen for my brain, my limbs loosen and I give my body permission to be part of an anonymous mass and mingle with other bodies until it finds one that really appeals to it.

~

When I return home the only guilt is the guilt of not feeling any guilt.

~

On the telephone, you tell me my voice is different. It's the humidity, I say. It purifies the voice.

~

Things I don't like in Rio: the bold cockroaches that scuttle out of drains during summer.

~

Sitting in the only bar overlooking Arpoador Rock, I order a caipirinha. It is a little after 7 p.m. and the pavement and sand are still bustling, even though it is only Wednesday. The sun is about to sink from sight. The sea is placid and reflects the red of the horizon, while more and more people gather on the rock. Whales used to be harpooned from there not all that long ago. Whales that now only put in rare appearances in these parts, causing wonder and commotion among the locals. I hear laughter around me, other people's conversations, I see people going past on bicycles, others drinking coconut water while sitting on a cement bench or at a plastic table. Rio de Janeiro in the summer says many trite but true things. It says, for example, that complicating something as simple as life is useless; that cultivating pain is a waste of time; that all is worthwhile even if the soul is small.

When the sun sets, my glass is empty. People flock to the rock, as if they have come to watch the final judgement, and once the blazing sphere has dipped into the sea everyone claps, whistles and gives thanks. And I, who always thought this spectacle unbelievably ridiculous, find myself clapping along with everyone else, immersed in anonymity, happy to have rediscovered my enthusiasm. When we are done and people finally disperse and start heading home, I think that I don't need you in order to have you with me after all.

~

The telephone hasn't rung for days. Perhaps you want to avoid the answer that is so light and simple for me, but so cruel for you: Yes, I have traded you for a city.

~

If it were possible to choose a perfect ending for Rio de Janeiro, I'd say: a tsunami on a summer Sunday. Anyone on the beach in Ipanema or Leblon would see the ocean pull back as far as the Cagarras Islands. Anyone in Copacabana would see Guanabara Bay dry up all the way across to Niterói. The sea peeling back its own flesh, leaving exposed and airless, for a few seconds, its deepest inhabitants. Then this same ocean would return as a giant wave, covering its creatures once again, but also covering those who are not of the sea. We would all be dragged under, swallowed by the water. Unhurriedly, but magnificently, the ocean would engulf the entire city, its buildings, its forests, the people, the animals. Only the tops of some of its hills would be left uncovered: Morro Dois Irmãos, Corcovado, Sugarloaf, Pedra da Gávea.

Anyone here would have the right to one last image: Rio de Janeiro submerged by the sea itself. Limpid Rio, translucent beneath the water, the extreme beauty of the disaster.

With the years, centuries, millennia, the ocean would expand even further until it found a trace of sand on which to rest. And Rio de Janeiro would be a mere vestige of a marvellous city, lost in the ocean's depths, inhabited by fish and corals, which would make its debris their new abode. ■

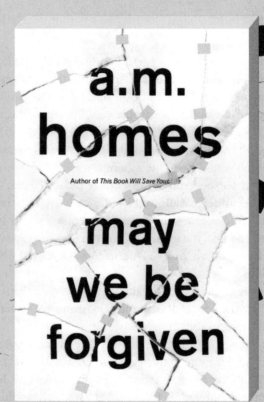

GRANTA

EVO MORALES

Ricardo Lísias

TRANSLATED BY NICK CAISTOR

RICARDO LÍSIAS
1975

Ricardo Lísias was born in São Paulo,
and holds a PhD in Brazilian literature from São Paulo
University. He is the author of one short-story collection and four
novels, the latest of which is *O céu dos suicidas* (2012). His work has
been translated into Galician, Italian and Spanish. His writing has
also been published in the magazine *piauí* and in issues
2 and 6 of *Granta em português*. 'Evo Morales' is a new story.

The first time I had coffee with Evo Morales, he had not yet been elected president of Bolivia, and I was a long way from winning the title of World Chess Champion. My mother was coming back from Australia, where she had been to visit my brother. She was returning to Brazil on a connecting flight from Buenos Aires. Shortly before her scheduled arrival, I discovered that her flight was going to be almost two hours late. I decided to have a coffee to pass the time. At the counter, when I was about to order a second cup, I noticed a strange figure beside me.

A short, stocky man wearing a poncho typical of the indigenous peoples of South America was trying to chat up the waitress. Obviously uncomfortable, the girl managed to disappear. The man was left with no alternative, and so asked me where I was flying to. I explained I was waiting for my mother and asked him: And you, are you from Peru?

I saw he understood Portuguese well. No, replied Evo, I'm Bolivian. As if sensing my curiosity he told me he was hoping to run for the presidency of his republic, and had come to Brazil to meet the leaders of some social movements. Evo seemed particularly impressed with the Landless Workers' Movement. I recall that he smiled when he mentioned one of their camps, which he had visited.

I asked two or three more questions, and then we said goodbye. It was time for Evo to board his plane. When I told my mother the story, she said that she also seemed to meet some weirdo whenever she flew. Being in an airport brings it out in people.

Two years later, I was shocked when I saw Evo Morales on television. My friend had become the first indigenous president in the history of Bolivia.

2

The second time I met Evo Morales was in the transit area of Charles de Gaulle Airport in Paris. I was on my way to Moscow, where I had to take an internal flight to the tiny town of Khanty-Mansiysk to compete in the Chess World Cup. My illustrious friend was returning from a meeting in France.

Evo recognized me and signalled to me from inside the cafe. When I went in, after congratulating him on his victory in the election, I joked that he had one of the essential requirements of a chess player: a good memory. Evo laughed and replied that he didn't even know how to move the pieces. I promised to teach him the next time we met. My friend was delighted, and said that, as soon as he came into office, he hoped to give the sport as much support as possible in Bolivia.

I realized how good I felt in his company, and all at once that made me sad. Now that he was the president of Bolivia, he was only going to travel in a private jet. Evo laughed and told me that Bolivia was in no position to permit such luxuries. Only countries like Brazil could afford privileges like that, he said.

He wanted to know more about my profession. I explained that I had started to play chess as a child because, according to a psychologist, practising a sport would help me overcome my shyness. I was a very lonely child – I couldn't make friends at school, and preferred to spend my time playing shut up in my room. But if I had to go out to play chess, I would have to come into contact with other people.

My parents first tried football, and then basketball, because of my height. It was my grandfather, a Lebanese immigrant who made his fortune setting up mills and selling textiles, who first taught me how to play chess. He soon realized I had a great talent for it. Later, I began to take classes, and at nine I took part in my first competition.

Evo showed great interest in my story and, when we said goodbye, he wished me luck and told me that at our next encounter he would like to learn how to play. I think he meant it seriously.

3

The flight to Moscow was uneventful. On my computer I checked a few openings I was planning to use against my first opponent, a young Romanian who seemed very promising but who would find it difficult to match me. I had a great deal of sympathy for him, perhaps because he reminded me of myself during my early days as a grandmaster.

I slept for the rest of the trip and woke to find the Russian capital on the left-hand side of the plane. It did not take me long to meet up with my coach Mark Dvoretsky in the exit hall. I was going to spend three days with him before flying on to Khanty-Mansiysk.

Despite knowing I would not find him there, every five metres or so I looked round to see whether I could catch a glimpse of Evo Morales. Twice I thought I had recognized him, but soon realized I was mistaken. My two encounters simply showed that Latin Americans are everywhere, even in the freezing car park of Domodedovo airport in Moscow.

Seeing that I did not feel like chatting, Dvoretsky said nothing in that garbled English of his that makes him seem even more friendly, apart from asking if I had put on weight. When I expressed surprise, he explained that it looked as though my cheeks were a little rounder.

In his apartment, before I finally collapsed into bed, I saw it was true that my cheeks had grown a bit fatter. But I didn't pay much attention to it. The next day, Dvoretsky said it must be my swollen cheeks that had helped me make such great progress since our last training session. According to him, my powers of analysis would develop still further. It would be hard not to win the Chess World Cup. At the end of the day, despite the cold, I insisted that we go out to have coffee somewhere.

4

Evo Morales was not in the cafe Dvoretsky took me to. Bitterly disappointed, I decided to make the best of it and channel all my energy into the World Cup. There were seven rounds, with two games in each round.

I became convinced I would win after my two-nil victory over the genial Vassily Ivanchuk, the Ukrainian chess legend. Anyone who understands sport knows that confidence is essential. In addition, winners are all aware of a special kind of feeling: at some point in the competition, we know we are going to win. It's very different when you lose. Each time I've lost, I've only found out the moment it happened.

After Ivanchuk, I won against an out-of-sorts Topalov, and in the final I faced the Armenian Levon Aronian. The first game was very tense. I managed to save a weak endgame and earn a draw. In the second, when I had white, I had no problem consolidating my position, and slowly ground out a victory.

That night back at my hotel, I phoned my family, who were really happy for me. My sister had seen the result on the Internet, and my mother, who has always done everything she can to help me, burst into tears. Afterwards, I sent three or four emails to the people in Brazil who always support me, took a call from Dvoretsky, and finally found myself alone.

Once you get used to it, being alone is no longer sad. It's like feeling cold, for example: you simply have to get used to it. Those with experience know that the ideal (both for the cold and for loneliness) is to slip under the duvet until you fall asleep, or, on the contrary, to get up and move around. That night, I decided to venture out into Khanty-Mansiysk in search of a cafe.

5

The hotel porter was surprised when I said I wanted to go out: the cold, he explained, is almost unbearable, and we could serve you in the hotel, in the restaurant or your room. When I insisted, he showed me how to find the only cafe in town.

It wasn't far off, but there was not much to admire on the way. Apart from freezing temperatures, there are strange sounds in the Russian winter at night. I almost ran.

The cafe was not exactly empty, but I can't say I met many people there either. Two old men were playing chess in a corner, three others must have been discussing some shady business (there are quite a few arms traffickers in Siberia) and an unlikely young couple was canoodling at the bar.

I ordered soup, which came served with an enormous quantity of bread. When I was halfway through it, I saw on TV that they were announcing my victory in the World Cup. I know a bit of Russian, so I was pleased when the presenter praised the patience with which I had won my last game against Aronian. No one in the cafe noticed I was the champion. Only the man behind the counter was watching the TV set. Then Vladimir Putin's face replaced mine on the screen. Loneliness also makes our victories melancholy. Sometimes I can scarcely believe I'm the best chess player in the world.

6

Between the World Cup and the Candidates Tournament, I had three months to prepare. Dvoretsky invited me to stay in Moscow. He is the best trainer in the world (that goes without saying), but I decided to return to Brazil. In the Paris airport I had a coffee at each place it was served, but I never came across Evo Morales.

On the flight to Brazil I ran into a girl who has been pursuing me since the days of school contests. Naturally, she congratulated me effusively on my victory in the World Cup. When we arrived at the airport in Brazil, she suggested we share a taxi. I considered the idea of inviting her to spend the rest of the night with me, but decided against it.

After spending two weeks in São Paulo, I chose, on the spur of the moment, to spend the rest of my preparation time in Buenos Aires. Three days later, I went round the whole of Ezeiza airport twice. I did not see Evo Morales. I began to think I had been right about the presidential aeroplane. He would be in the VIP section of the airport.

Disappointed, I returned to Brazil a few days later. I realized I had wasted almost a month going up and down the continent. Even though I was the favourite in the Candidates Tournament, it wasn't going to be easy: my opponents, who were among the strongest players in the world, had the habit of playing even better when what was being decided was the right to take on the world champion. I was ranked number one, but I still had to win the official title. Vladimir Kramnik was still the king.

I spent the next two months holed up in Brazil. As usual I decided not to take any assistants with me. I felt pretty confident leaving for Mexico, where the event was taking place. I felt even more certain of victory when I saw Evo Morales waving to me from the airport arrivals hall.

7

M y great friend Evo Morales and I chatted for almost two hours. After congratulating me, he said in a very good-natured way that my cheeks seemed to have grown fatter. I laughed. In order not to upset him, I decided not to respond, but Evo is the guy with the chubbiest cheeks I've ever seen.

We talked a bit about my victory in the World Cup. I was happy when he told me he had heard about it. I noticed that one of his assistants also seemed very interested in our conversation. That's because he knows how to play, Evo explained. I told them how the games had gone, explained my strategy, and said how confident I was that I would win the Candidates Tournament.

Evo nodded. I'm going to have a friend who's a world champion! I realized that it was true, I did feel very good in his company. If I do manage to challenge for the world title, I'd really like you to come to at least one or two of the games, I said. OK, but isn't Lula going to feel jealous?

I replied without the slightest bitterness that Brazil has never supported chess. In fact, with the exception of football, we have never had a grass-roots structure for any sport. Evo frowned, looked serious and asked how was it possible then for me to become one of the strongest players in the world.

I explained that in chess, above a certain level, it is individual talent that counts. But how do you reach that level? I remember I felt no shame replying that my family was rich. My grandfather made a fortune out of textiles. All at once, Evo cast a thunderous glance at his assistant. His round cheeks went bright red. In São Paulo, a lot of Bolivians work in slave-like conditions in factories like the ones he had. But my family doesn't run that kind of business. Nowadays, we live from investments and buying and selling properties, I insisted. When he said goodbye, Evo again wished me good luck and said he would like to see me help create a grass-roots structure for chess in Bolivia.

8

I won the Candidates Tournament without great difficulty. Contrary to my expectations, it was Alexei Shirov who gave me the most trouble. At one point, I even thought I was going to lose. I have not analysed the game calmly (I still haven't even put it up on my computer), but I think that when time was running out, he was winning. Then, with five seconds to make three moves in, Shirov made a mistake and ended up losing two pawns in one go.

I noticed after the tournament that my cheeks really had become a bit fatter.

When I returned to Brazil, I got news that a European telecommunications company wanted to sponsor my preparations for the World Championship. My only obligation would be to spend the last month of training in Spain. I accepted at once and asked Dvoretsky to accompany me both for the preparation and the contest.

In Brazil, I gave two or three interviews, and then concentrated on my preparation. Kramnik has never been an easy opponent for me. Since he had the advantage of keeping his crown if there was a tie, my training needed to be intense. But I didn't want to neglect my promise to Bolivia, and so I sent an email to what I thought was the right address on the official presidential website. When I got no reply, I decided to send a telegram to Evo at the presidential palace in La Paz.

FRIEND EVO WON CANDIDATES TOURNAMENT CHALLENGING CHAMPION CHEEKS GROWING ALL TIME WANT CREATE CHESS STRUCTURES BOLIVIA DISCOVER CHAMPIONS TOGETHER FRIEND COME SEE TITLE CONTEST GERMANY JUNE SEE YOU COFFEE YOUR GREAT FRIEND

Two months went by and he did not answer. So I decided to go to Europe for a week to get a bit of rest.

9

Dvoretsky approved of my journey. It was to be a week's rest, a visit to Madrid and then Paris. I insisted we had to suspend my training schedule for ten days rather than seven, and he grudgingly accepted this as well. I disembarked at Barajas airport in Madrid at eight in the morning. All the cafes were very full. I looked for Evo Morales in each of them. By midday, I thought I had better have a bite to eat, and give my friend time to disembark. While I waited for him to leave his plane, I checked my emails. At two in the afternoon I looked for him again, but he wasn't in any of the airport cafes. I searched the restaurants, the shops and even the toilets. The worst of it was a pain that I began to feel low in my chest. I made arrangements to fly to Barcelona at seven in the evening because I had heard that was where

Evo had gone. But by eleven, and remember I have an excellent memory, I began to think we had perhaps missed each other. Evo Morales is my friend, I explained to the guard at the departures gate, but he said I could only go in with a boarding ticket, and at the proper time. I went back to the desks, but Evo did not appear. So I was only going to meet my best friend in Paris. But my ticket for the French capital was via Madrid. And it seemed to me I had been heading for Barcelona to have a coffee with him. But something must have come up, so he said we should meet in Paris. There are lots of flights between Barcelona and Paris. That night I discovered several of them. I got a ticket for four in the morning, which made me a bit anxious. But Evo is a true friend: no doubt he would be waiting for me in Paris. Just in case, I looked for him again in Barcelona airport. On the screens I saw there was a flight to London before mine to Paris. After mine, the next flight was for Rome. I remember that I thought to myself: no, not London or Rome. I'm going to meet my best friend in Paris!

10

E vo, I guess you didn't receive the telegram I think I sent you last week. I told my mother exactly what she should do, but she must have made a mistake. Now I'm going to write you a longer letter. My mother has promised to send it with DHL: that way it will reach you more quickly. It's also safer. I suppose we must have missed each other in Paris. As a friend, you'll understand. I had a problem in Barcelona, and the airport people insisted on sending me to Rome. I seem to remember I refused, but the confusion delayed my departure. You must have been worried. I tried to warn you, but the information service at Barcelona is not the best. Evo, you know how much I enjoy the coffees we have together. It would take something very serious to make me miss the opportunity to chat with you. As an athlete, I've always taken part in competitions, and met many people. I can't complain that I'm lonely. But we don't often meet real friends. I haven't forgotten, I swear, about the promise I made regarding chess in Bolivia. First I have to get out of here. Then I'll get in contact with you again. Evo, my friend, you'll be pleased to see me with my cheeks lifted. They were growing very fat. My mother had me interned for an operation on them. Nothing serious; nothing for you to worry about. There's no need to come and visit me. Not unless you think it's really necessary. Of course, I wouldn't say no, but I'll soon be out of here, shortly after the operation, I think. Then, Evo, we can have that coffee together and talk over the question of chess in Bolivia: I haven't forgotten that. If you're in great haste to set things up, perhaps a visit might be useful: we could start to think of what needs to be done when my operation is over. But there's no hurry. I don't want to put you to any trouble. And there's one more thing. I know that with a friend like you I don't have to stand on ceremony, but the coffee in here is disgusting. As you'll understand, this is no airport, but of course a chat with you would be fantastic, wouldn't it?

11

Dear Evo, I know I wrote not long ago and that probably you don't have much time to reply to letters. That's natural for the president of a republic. I decided to send you another letter so that you wouldn't be concerned – I'm not sure I was clear enough in my first one. I didn't mean to imply that a visit would be inconvenient. Quite the opposite. My intention was to say that you shouldn't be worried if you arrived at some airport or other and could not find me. I'll be staying here until my cheeks have been operated on. They became very swollen, and so my family decided it was time to do something. If it were up to me, I would not have bothered. Between you and me, I think they're exaggerating. But after our missed meeting in Moscow I decided not to contradict them. As it is, I can relax here. To tell you the truth, it's a very quiet place, in spite of some of the other patients also waiting for operations who can be pretty unpleasant, in my view. But above all, you don't need to worry, my friend. If you would like to come, a visit would be fantastic. I can remember our first conversation as if it were today. I don't know whether I made it obvious enough that I really liked La Paz. And how impressed I was by your humility. The president of a republic travelling on a commercial flight! I'll never forget what you said: you must come back some time. You have to see the historic centre of Potosí. We were about to land at São Paulo. And I promised I would return as soon as possible to Bolivia to visit all the places you had been describing to me. You'll have to forgive me if I haven't done so as yet. I intend to fulfil my promise as soon as I get out of here. Strangely enough, yesterday my mother brought me a poncho very similar to the one you wear. I'll keep it for my return to La Paz. I miss our conversations a lot, and the coffees we had. Between us (between friends), the stuff they serve here is awful.

12

D ear friend, everything is as it was. There's no date for my operation, and my mother says I'll possibly have to wait a bit longer. Fine. I don't really care if I have to stay in here. To tell you the truth, I'm worn out. I have a room of my own and can go wherever I like. Even into the garden. I'm only not allowed out into the street. I don't have much inclination to talk to the other patients. As soon as I say I have problems with my cheeks, they all stare at my face. Then they say it looks as though they've grown even chubbier. As if I needed to be told. Some of them find it hard to talk. They're probably waiting for operations on their throat or tongue. I'm sure as well that a few patients are here for psychiatric reasons. I feel sorry for them. But that's not the cause of the enormous weight I have below my chest. Sometimes it makes me feel I don't want to get out of bed. The other day I found it hard to breathe. Perhaps it's the effect of being kept isolated. As you know, my friend, I was never a solitary person. Throughout my life I've taken part in all kinds of competitions, and have travelled all over the world. I get on so well with people that sometimes I can even strike up a friendship in airports. My mother and the rest of my family always come to visit me, but they don't stay long. They often look at me in an odd way. My brother still calls me Grandmaster. Are you there, Grandmaster? But I think he has changed. I don't want to worry you. It's going to take a while, but they can't leave me in here forever. As soon as I've had my cheeks operated on, I'll go straight to La Paz. I'll send you a mail telling you when I'm arriving and the flight number.

13

Dear Evo, I feel slightly better today. I decided to get out of bed. My mother says I have to see the doctor soon. Perhaps at the end of this week. Or next week, I can't remember. I don't go out that often now. In winter, the garden is not so pretty. And we're not allowed out into the street. That must be because of those patients who are in here for psychiatric reasons. I came to have my cheeks operated on. I never thought a simple piece of plastic surgery would need such a long rest period. I spend most of the time stretched out. That's what I mostly do. Not merely to relax. Sometimes I wake up with a heavy weight in my chest. At first. Whenever it gets really bad, I have trouble breathing. That's why I prefer to stay horizontal. If I fill my lungs very slowly, I can manage to breathe regularly. But only if I concentrate quite hard. Well, that's never been a problem for me. I'm not bothered in the slightest at spending the whole day stretched out, since they don't let us out into the street and now in winter the garden isn't so pretty. But I can see this upsets my mother as well. While I'm on the subject, I want to make it clear that I perfectly understand that you can't manage to reply to me. I'm not offended. I realize it's better to chat in an airport, but they don't let us out into the street here. No, I'm not offended. But listen, my friend, you've got the chubbiest cheeks in the world: if they tell you that you have to have them operated on, well, the coffee here is dreadful but, in compensation, we'd have plenty of time to talk.

São Paulo, 4 December 2009

Dear Evo Morales,
Were you offended because I said you had chubby cheeks? I'm sorry. It's because I always thought good friends should be sincere, isn't that right? If I offended you, Evo, I apologize. I never denied that God gave me chubby cheeks as well. But you, Evo, you're the chubbiest-cheeked person in the world. If you're thinking of having an operation on them, my friend, listen: they don't let us out into the street in winter, and now that it's winter, the garden is the same as the street, Evo the Great. Will you be offended if I call you that? The Great Evo, Mister Chubby Cheeks. Evo Morales, the chubbiest cheeks in the world. Evo Morales. Evo Morales. Evo Morales. The Great Chubby Cheeks. Chubby Cheeks. Mister Chubby Cheeks. Yes, Evo, perhaps you should have an operation. But I wouldn't wish that on my worst enemy, still less on a friend like you. It won't be so bad, though, if you come. My mother says they are going to fix the date soon. And as I was saying, Mister Chubby Cheeks, you'll be in good company here. You're not going to feel lonely. Of course, I know there are lots of people with chubby cheeks in the world. I myself am one of them. Have I ever denied it? But not like yours, Evo. But as I've learned here, people with chubby cheeks are never aware of it. Alone, alone, no one ever complains of being lonely. As you know, I've never felt lonely, have I, Evo the Great? Evo, I was never a lonely person, but here there's no chance of a chubby-cheeks feeling lonely. Still less you, the King of Chubby Cheeks, the Great Mister Chubby, the chubbiest-cheeked person ever to enter an airport, ever to have a cup of coffee, the Great Evo. I can guarantee that nobody feels lonely in here, Evo, especially with those chubby cheeks of yours. Don't take offence, Evo: you've got the chubbiest cheeks in the whole wide world. ■

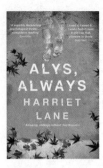

Alys, Always by *Harriet Lane*

Frances is a lowly sub-editor whose routine existence is disrupted when she happens upon the aftermath of a car crash and hears the last words of the driver, Alys Kyte. When Alys's family makes contact, Frances is given a tantalising glimpse of a very different world: one of privilege and possibility, and Frances dares to wonder whether she might become a player in her own right . . .
Weidenfeld & Nicolson £7.99 | **PB**

Wenceslas – A Christmas Poem by *Carol Ann Duffy*

A new poem celebrating the magic of Christmas from the Poet Laureate, and beautifully illustrated by Stuart Kolakovic. In reimagining the carol of King Wenceslas, Carol Ann Duffy's new poem offers merriment and festive cheer, but also celebrates what is truly important: the simple acts of kindness that each of us can show another. A perfect stocking filler.
Picador | **HB**

Little Raw Souls: Stories by *Steven Schwartz*

'How vividly Steven Schwartz describes his characters and how cunningly he wields the knife edge of suspense. I loved entering each of the worlds he creates – a grandfather fighting for his grandchildren, a man misled by a hippy couple, a woman who falls asleep at the airport, a teacher who holds his class hostage . . . These are wonderful, immensely enjoyable stories.' – Margot Livesey
Autumn House Press $17.95 | **PB**

Calunga and the Legacy of an African Language in Brazil by *Steven Byrd*

Calunga is an endangered Afro-Brazilian language spoken by a few hundred older Afro-Brazilian men, for specific, secret communications. A hybrid language with African vocabulary items embedded in an essentially Portuguese grammar, its formation can be seen as a form of cultural resistance. Steven Byrd examines *Calunga*'s historical and linguistic context, sociolinguistic profile, and its lexical and grammatical outlines.
University of New Mexico Press $55.00 | **HB**

GRANTA

EVERY TUESDAY

Carola Saavedra

TRANSLATED BY ALISON ENTREKIN

CAROLA SAAVEDRA
1973

Carola Saavedra was born in Chile and moved
to Brazil as a child. She has lived in Spain, France and Germany,
and currently lives in Rio de Janeiro. She is the author of the story
collection *Do lado de fora* (2005), and the novels *Toda terça* (2007),
Flores azuis (2008) and *Paisagem com dromedário* (2010), which won
the Rachel de Queiroz Award for Best Young Author.
'Every Tuesday' is an extract from *Toda terça*.

'I lied to you the other day, you know.'

'Lied?' said Otávio in that surprised voice that always sounded false coming from him.

'Yep, when I was telling you about the cinema, remember?'

'Yes.'

'I said there was nothing else to tell, but it was a lie.'

I was silent for a moment as if making a short pause to muster up courage.

'So tell me, Laura, what is it?' said Otávio, in an understanding tone.

Otávio didn't care if I lied; he was convinced that all lies were just another version of the truth. He had explained to me that the mere fact of my having chosen one lie over another was already enough to make it a confession, a revelation. For example, if I lied that I'd eaten a cheese sandwich, I had made a choice, seeing as how I could have lied in countless other ways, saying that it was a tomato or tuna sandwich. Which meant that no matter how many subterfuges I found to hide behind (the cheese, for example, or even the sandwich itself), I would always be revealing myself. Bottom line: there was no way out.

Nevertheless, every now and then I tried.

'There actually was someone sitting near me, two seats along, on my left. When he arrived, the film had already started and I couldn't see his face. But he appeared to be young, dark-haired, I think he was wearing jeans. I couldn't see his face, but I saw his hands, well, I saw his right hand. I looked out of the corner of my eye. His hands were beautiful, strong and delicate at the same time, with thin fingers, like a pianist's. I didn't even pay attention to the film properly, there was something about that man, about his presence. I sat there watching the film without really seeing it, thinking about what he must be like, his tastes, his life, whether or not he studied, worked, that sort of thing.'

'And what conclusions did you come to?'

'Not many. First, I thought he must be sensitive.'

'Sensitive?'

'I think because of the film we were watching. It was poetic, romantic, about a writer in Montevideo who falls in love with a prostitute. She rejects him at first, but then she ends up falling in love with him too.'

Otávio was looking at me with special interest. In a few seconds he would start scribbling in his notebook. I'd give anything to know what he wrote in that notebook, anything at all. But in this he was unbudging; his notes were a professional secret, all of my dreams and fears and failings summed up in a report kept under lock and key in his drawer, confidential, or, the old trick, left carelessly on the table, as if they had no importance: *dreamed she was crossing the Atacama, undefined companion, tendency to lose focus.*

'If you think about it, a man who goes to see a film like that, alone, in the middle of the afternoon, has to be sensitive, don't you think?'

'It's possible.'

'But obviously it wasn't just that, otherwise it could have been anyone at all next to me and I would have fallen in love with him anyway. No, he had something different, special, something that came from his presence . . . Oh, I don't know, Otávio. I can't explain it.'

'You said "fall in love", Laura. Are you telling me you're in love with this man?'

'Did I say "fall in love"?'

'Yes, you did.'

'Well, what matters is that I wasn't able to see the film properly. I spent the whole time imagining what he was like, anxious for the lights to come on. It's funny, for some reason I knew he was good-looking, even though I hadn't seen his face. I was sure of it. Strange, huh? After all, he could have had a limp, been missing his teeth, had burns all over his face. But these possibilities didn't even occur to me. All I could think about was what I was going to do when the lights came on: go after him, follow him into the foyer. But then I decided that fate would take care of it for me.'

'Fate?'

'Yes. I thought: if he left straight away, without even glancing at me, I'd forget about him, I'd assume that that was how it was meant to be, but if he stayed there, headed for the bookshop or went to get something to drink at the coffee shop, then it'd be a sign.'

Otávio was doing his best to appear neutral, but he was clearly finding it all very suspicious.

'A sign? And what would this sign indicate?'

'It would indicate that there was something between us, a story that was about to begin, and that he knew it too, and even if he didn't it wouldn't matter because you can't escape these things. Don't you believe in destiny? I do. I believe in fortune-tellers, astrology, almost everything. It's silly to believe, I know, but it's also silly not to. I believe there are signs that life gives us, signs we should take seriously, that are trying to tell us something.'

'It's possible . . .'

It's possible was one of Otávio's favourite expressions. Whenever he didn't want to commit to anything, agree or disagree, he'd trot out his 'it's possible'. It irritated me, but I preferred to ignore it.

'So anyway, I decided that and then sat there waiting for the film to finish, and when it did, he got up before I did and headed out. I stayed put, giving him time to make up his mind, because I didn't want to rush out after him. I didn't want to force fate, you know? I wanted things to happen naturally. I sat there, waiting calmly, then I went to the ladies' room, tidied my hair, touched up my lipstick. I looked at myself in the mirror and thought I didn't look too bad. I actually looked quite nice, because I normally don't think I'm pretty . . .'

I glanced down at the colourful rug, my legs, my feet, my high-heeled sandals, my recently painted toenails. I continued:

'I actually think I'm a bit ugly, my face, I don't know, it's too round, it's always bothered me. It doesn't matter if I lose weight, my face always stays round. I've actually thought about getting some lipo done, you know? The other day I read that in the past, before there was any lipo, women would have one or two molars pulled from each side to make their faces thinner, more delicate. I read that Marlene Dietrich did it, though I've never thought she was all that amazing. Her face is a bit weird, asymmetrical, but anyway, who am

I to criticize Marlene Dietrich's face, me of all people, who's never been pretty, or at least I've never thought I was . . .'

At that moment I paused, waiting for Otávio to disagree, to tell me that I was beautiful, that thinking I was ugly was just a symptom of my insecurity, my lack of self-esteem. Except he didn't say anything; he just sat there in his armchair, silent and elegant as always. Otávio is a good-looking man; it's a shame he is so convinced of it. He remained quiet and I couldn't help myself, I ended up asking:

'Otávio, do you think I'm ugly?'

Otávio smiled, a smile that could just as easily have been admiration or mockery.

'No, Laura, of course not. You're a very attractive woman.'

Attractive. Big deal. 'Attractive' was a word that, coming from Otávio, had no meaning at all. He no doubt said it to every woman who sat on that sofa. *Louise, you're a very attractive woman, Rita, you're a very attractive woman, Dolores, you're a very attractive woman,* always with that same smile plastered across his face.

'Yes, but attractive isn't necessarily pretty, a person can be attractive and horrendous at the same time.'

'You're attractive and very pretty, Laura. You know that.'

Yes, I knew it, how could I even question it? It was evident that I knew. I had only asked to provoke him, that's what he thought, just to hear him say: *No, Laura, you're gorgeous, Laura, you're irresistible, Laura, you're the most beautiful woman ever to have set foot in this office.* Perhaps he thought I was in love with him. It was likely; who wouldn't fall in love with a man like Otávio? I let down my hair, which had been up in a ponytail.

'Of course I don't know. If I did, I wouldn't need to ask.'

'We often ask questions in the hope of getting a specific answer.'

I ignored the comment and kept talking.

'Anyway, what matters is that I looked at myself in the ladies' room mirror and thought I looked pretty; at that moment, let's be clear. Then I went to the bookshop. He was there, in the foreign fiction section. He was tall with slightly wavy hair, brown, it wasn't long, but it wasn't really short either. I estimated that he must be about my age. I didn't want to get too close, I didn't want to be so obvious. I went to the art section, chose a book about Portinari and stood there leafing through it. I was really waiting for a chance, for him to look at me, to notice me. He had taken a book off the shelf and was reading it, engrossed, as if he was at home. Half an hour, and he kept on reading. He didn't even seem to have noticed I was there; in fact, he didn't seem to notice anything or anyone. I gave up. I told myself, I'm going to wait five more minutes and if he doesn't see me, I'll leave. The five minutes passed and I ended up buying the Portinari book, just to gain time. I talked to the shop assistant in a loud voice, oh, what a stroke of luck to have found this book, I've been looking for it for some time, Portinari. The sales assistant answered something or other that I can't remember, while the man from the cinema just stood there, unmoving, as if I didn't exist. I ended up paying for the book and leaving. At that moment I hated him, but at the same time I could have fallen in love with him . . .'

Otávio looked interested.

'And why do you think you could have fallen in love with him?'

'I'm not really sure, but I was certain I could have fallen in love with him, in fact, I could have done the craziest things for him. Isn't it strange how you can fall in love with a stranger like that?'

'A stranger may well function as a projection screen.'

'Projection screen? Otávio, we're talking about love, not cinema,' I said jokingly. Otávio didn't seem to find it terribly funny; he'd never had much of a sense of humour.

'Laura, if I have understood correctly, you don't know anything about this man. You haven't even spoken with him, right?'

'Right.'

'So he can be whoever you want him to be, you can project all kinds of desires and expectations onto him.'

Otávio was speaking didactically, as if I was a simpleton who had never heard of projection or repression or whatever. Sometimes the anger I felt towards him became uncontrollable.

'Oh, honestly, if that were the case, I could fall in love with any stranger who crossed my path. I could project all of my desires onto the popcorn seller on the street corner, the guy in the supermarket, even a telemarketer's voice.'

Otávio still didn't find it funny. I could see that he was about to lose his patience, his pinched lips almost disappearing into his mouth, his body looking as if he wanted to get up and leave. Controlling one's emotions required effort, even for someone like Otávio. In his case, however, the effort always paid off: after a few seconds his body would be still and his face paralysed in a charitable expression. After all, people like him had to be understanding; they could never allow themselves to be carried away by emotions, incompatibilities, personal divergences. His solution was to ignore what I had said.

'Laura, what do you hope to find in this man?'

Oh, I had hoped for so many things: that he would pull a bunch of flowers out of his sleeve, that he would recite a poem in French to me, that he would kiss my hand when he greeted me and help me put on my coat when I left the house, that he would lay down a red carpet for me to walk on without dirtying my shoes, things like that.

'I don't know what I was hoping for, probably nothing.'

'Nothing?'

Otávio was still using that didactic tone of voice of his, but I decided to make peace with him in spite of it and do as he wished, which unfortunately was very different to what I wished.

'Well, maybe I was hoping the desire would be mutual. Isn't that what everyone hopes for?'

'Often.'

'Except that desire is rarely mutual, is it? Take my case for example: Júlio's wife wants Júlio, who in turn wants me, I want the guy in the cinema, and the guy in the cinema probably wants his neighbour or the woman at the news-stand. Who knows? It's not fair, is it? Not to mention the possibility that I might be completely wrong. Maybe Júlio's wife couldn't care less about him and wants her personal trainer. As for Júlio, well, maybe the person he really wants is the secretary on the fifth floor. Who knows?'

'Does that bother you?'

Otávio's eyes gleamed. I thought I detected a glimmer of malice.

'Does what bother me?'

'That Júlio might want the secretary.'

'No, not in the slightest.'

It was clear that Otávio didn't believe me.

'The last time you were here you told me you were seeing each other less often.'

'That's true, in the beginning, in the first few years, he used to come almost every day, that is, whenever he could, sometimes on the weekend, when his wife would drive up to Itaipava and he'd find an excuse to stay here in Rio, blaming it on work. He doesn't do that any more, he only shows up every now and then. Not that his generosity has changed at all. He still pays my university fees, rent, electricity, water, gas, condo fees, an allowance for my personal expenses. An undeniably generous allowance, I must say. He keeps paying without asking any questions or making any demands, without my having to explain what I do with it. And, to top it all off, he worries about me, you know, he worries so much that he asked me to come here and talk to you. It was Júlio who asked me to come. You know I wouldn't have come on my own initiative. He's a wonderful man, don't you think? Who wouldn't like to have someone like him: caring, concerned, capable of doing anything to see me happy? I'm a lucky woman, don't you think?'

'You told me your sexual frequency had also changed.'

'Yes, our sexual frequency.' I made a face. Otávio remained serious.

'Tell me a little more about that.'

'About what, how often we have sex?'

'Yes.'

I became serious again.

'Oh, there's not much to say, I've already told you, we hardly have sex at all. In the beginning, that is, during the first few years we used to have sex all the time, it was normal, then with time it became less and less, until more recently it's become minimal, twice a month at the most. Do you think that's normal?'

'It depends on the couple, Laura. For some it's more than enough, for others it isn't much.'

'I don't know, for a lover it's a bit on the light side, don't you think? Because if he's like this with his lover, imagine what he must be like with his wife.'

Otávio laughed. I thought it was funny too. That rarely happened, for us to laugh together, Otávio and I. I liked it. It made me feel, even if it was a false impression, as if we were just two good friends sitting around chatting, having a good time.

'And does that bother you?'

'Our sexual frequency?'

'Yes.'

I thought about the best answer for a few moments. I did that sometimes.

'Yes, and no. On the one hand, it doesn't bother me in the slightest, since I don't feel like having sex with Júlio. In fact, I don't feel like having sex with anyone. On the other hand, sometimes I think: I'm twenty-eight, they say women reach their sexual peak at thirty, and for someone who is almost at her peak, I'm not doing all that well. I think: if this is my peak, what's it going to be like when I turn forty and start the downhill slide?'

'And what makes you think the downhill slide starts at forty?'

'Oh, Otávio, no one needs to tell me. I know it.'

'You're wrong. Ageing doesn't mean going downhill, much less at forty.'

'Pardon me, I wasn't being fair, ageing is wonderful, I can hardly wait for my first grey hairs to appear.'

'Very well, Laura. Let's leave this subject for later. Now let's go back to what we were talking about, which strikes me as important. You say you don't feel like having sex with Júlio or anyone else. What about the man from the cinema? Would you have sex with him?'

Otávio always came out with this kind of question, it was in his manual. I observed him closely. Would I have sex with him? Quite probably, right there if he wanted to, just so he'd jot it down in his little notebook, just so he'd write in his report: conjugal sexual frequency, once a month; therapeutic sexual frequency, once a week. Me lying on that sofa, naked.

'Oh, I'd have sex with him, right there on the sofa, I mean in the cinema, if he wanted to.'

I stared at him with a smile on my face. Otávio looked away. It was the first time he had ever looked away. A small victory. I straightened my skirt and kept smiling. ∎

GRANTA

LETTUCE NIGHTS

Vanessa Barbara

TRANSLATED BY KATRINA DODSON

VANESSA BARBARA
1982

Vanessa Barbara is a journalist, translator and writer.
Her publications include *O livro amarelo do terminal* (2008),
winner of the Jabuti Award, the novel *O verão do Chibo* (2008),
co-written with Emilio Fraia, and the children's book *Endrigo, o
escavador de umbigo* (2011), illustrated by Andrés Sandoval. She
recently published a translation of *The Great Gatsby*. Barbara also
edits the literary website A Hortaliça (www.hortifruti.org) and is
a columnist for the newspaper *Folha de S. Paulo*. 'Lettuce Nights'
('Noites de alface') is an extract from her forthcoming novel.

When Ada died, the wash hadn't dried yet. The trousers' elastic waistbands were still damp, socks swollen, T-shirts hanging the wrong way out. A rag was left soaking in the bucket. Rinsed recycling bins in the sink, the bed unmade, open biscuit packets lying on the couch. Ada had gone away without watering the plants. The household things were holding their breath and waiting. Since then, the house without Ada has been nothing but empty drawers.

Otto and Ada were married in 1958, just as the town was transitioning between mayors. They bought a yellow house and decided not to have children, no dogs or cats, not even a pet turtle. They spent almost fifty years together: cooking, assembling massive puzzles of European castles and playing ping-pong on the weekends, until arthritis set in and made the game impossible. In the end it was nearly impossible to tell the difference between their tone of voice, their laugh, their way of walking. Ada was thin with short hair and liked cauliflower. Otto was thin with short hair and liked cauliflower. They wandered up and down the hallways and took out the rubbish together. Ada dealt with the various household details and did most of the chores while Otto followed her around telling anticlimactic stories. They were such good friends that Ada's death left a silence in the hallways of the yellow house.

As time went on, Otto learned what to do with dead light bulbs but still didn't have the heart to change out of his pyjamas. And so he stayed that way, wrapped in a plaid blanket even on hot days, missing Ada and taking care of household tasks, couch stains, dirty dishes. He was a quiet widower, reserved and hard-working. He saw his wife in these chores and it made him feel like never leaving the house. He had groceries delivered from the corner store and medicine from the pharmacy, led a peaceful existence and didn't bother anyone.

The delivery boys cultivated this silence respectfully: they'd knock on the door as if they were entering a monastery, have Otto sign receipts and ask how he was doing for the sake of asking. They liked to turn their heads upward and remark: Looks like it's going to rain later, better take the clothes off the line, it might cool down a bit and you'll have to change out of those pyjamas. The weather's crazy. How's your sciatica? Otto would nod, half distracted, thinking about how the delivery boys acted differently when Ada was still around. Ada used to answer the door and would immediately have the boy from the pharmacy sitting down. Nico would open his backpack to show her something, and the two of them would go on chattering about very important subjects, so that sometimes Nico would end up forgetting to deliver their ointments, aspirin and blood-pressure medication.

Ada kept all the neighbourhood's secrets. She knew every single neighbour's life story and recounted them to Otto at dinner in a near whisper: Nico made next to nothing at the pharmacy; what he really wanted was to be a professional swimmer; he lived with his mother and spent all his free time at the gym. He swam very badly but had made up his mind to cross the Strait of Dover – even if it meant he had to go part-time at the pharmacy.

Whenever he laughed, he resembled a monkey, his mouth gaping wide open but without making a sound. Then one day he dived into the pool, and when he came up for air, he was laughing like that. 'Everyone laughed,' Ada recounted. 'He went down again, came up and was still laughing. Everyone was laughing. But then he went under and didn't come back up again. He hadn't been laughing, he'd been drowning and nearly died.' The moral of the story: 'If you laugh with the same face as when you drown, better change your ways.'

Ada was central to the neighbourhood. She was the one who organized the block parties, who solved everyone's problems and found work for those who needed it – even those who didn't want help ended up with some odd job as a bagger at the market, caught off guard like someone who answers the door to a visitor on a Sunday morning.

After Ada's death, the neighbourhood went into mourning for three days, during which time not even Teresa's dogs barked. The postman stopped delivering the mail strictly out of a sense of propriety, since he usually made his rounds belting out songs like

'Boy, Was That Guy Ugly', and no one turned their radio up all the way, no one shouted into their cellphone, no one used their blender at two in the morning to whip up an avocado mousse. After this mourning period, the town returned to its usual commotion. Alone in that huge house, Otto became even sadder: every time the knife sharpener passed by, it reminded him how Ada wasn't there any more; no longer would she jump up from the couch or rush to lean out the window, waving vigorously and laughing through her nose. Now, whenever Teresa's dogs got out, he'd close his eyes and try to imagine Ada tripping over herself as she ran out into the street, shouting for everyone to save themselves while they could, absolutely terrified of the wild canines crashing into gates and leaving behind a trail of fleas, until Teresa caught up to them and restored order with the well-aimed swipe of a plastic bottle.

Otto had only really interacted with his neighbours through Ada and now was left stranded in that sea of collective insanity. He decided to go on sitting in the living room, with the blanket on his knees, silently watching the days go by. Without Ada there to explain all the stories, things happened incoherently. But little by little, Otto started overhearing a conversation there, a blender here, and began to understand his neighbours.

For example: there was the night the newly-weds watched a foreign film. It was a documentary about a mother camel, Ingen Temee, who gives birth to an albino camel. But she doesn't take to her offspring and rejects it, so that the albino calf cries for the rest of the movie. In a heart-warming twist, a boy named Little Ugna decides to set off for the village to find a violinist who will play a beautiful song so that the mother camel will love her calf. It works. Little Ugna is very clever. Then Little Ugna's father tells the people gathered how camels used to have horns, but one day they lent their horns to the deer to wear to a party. That's why to this day camels always stare fixedly at the horizon (even while chewing cud), waiting for the day they'll get their bony ornaments back.

The newly-wed young man slept through the documentary; you

could hear him snoring, and the girl got a bit upset, but watched the whole movie. When it ended, she went to bed and didn't speak to her husband the next day. Otto heard the man trying to get her to say something. 'So, the albino camel was sad the whole time?' But she washed the dishes without responding. 'Little Ugna managed to find a violinist?' But no sign of an answer. Eventually her anger subsided, as usual, and everything ended in a theatrical fight in which she screamed 'Drop the knife!' while he squirted lavender water at her. A couple of lunatics, Otto concluded, thinking back on ping-pong afternoons with Ada – the dented balls, extreme paddle manoeuvres, Otto shouting that it didn't count because the ball had hit her finger. You can't score when it hits your finger. It was one of the few rules they followed in ping-pong.

Something else that Otto noticed in those first few weeks was that Teresa's house was being invaded by a nocturnal army of cockroaches. In the middle of the night, while lying in bed, he could hear his neighbour killing insects with her flip-flop. She'd already tried exterminating them in the living room, judging by the smell, but it hadn't really worked because the pests adored Roach-B-Gone – he could almost hear them licking their chops and flocking in hordes to the house next door. All the better for him, who could muster neither the same readiness nor the same gusto for squashing them with a paper towel as when he used to say 'Hand me your flip-flop' while Ada fled behind the curtains.

At this point, Otto no longer went out into the backyard unless it was to hang clothes on the line. That was where Otto and Ada used to spend afternoons lying in the sun, reading cookbooks and doing crossword puzzles. Ada was always looking for the definitive recipe for breaded cauliflower, one in which it wouldn't fall out of the breading when you fried it and that would keep it glistening and crispy. She never found it. She used to stretch out her legs 'to get my fat rolls nice and toasty' and go on talking about the lawn, the plants, the tulip bulbs she'd got as a gift from Teresa last winter. Otto and Ada's yard was the biggest in town, a grassy field full of rusty tools, old buckets and tulips waiting to emerge. Ada loved the backyard. When Otto was with her, he loved it too; on his own, he hated the tulips as much as he hated the neighbours.

With the blanket over his knees, Otto had the sudden urge to go to the kitchen and cook up some tasty cauliflower, but it still felt too soon. So he stayed put, blinking his eyes vaguely. One after another, the sounds, smells and sights of the neighbourhood found their way into his living room (blender, Roach-B-Gone, mad dog), and he passed the time assembling these pieces into stories to tell. ∎

TERESA

Cristhiano Aguiar

TRANSLATED BY DANIEL HAHN

CRISTHIANO AGUIAR
1981

Cristhiano Aguiar is a writer and essayist.
Born in Campina Grande, Paraíba, he has lived in Recife,
Berlin, Olinda, São Paulo and Berkeley. A visiting researcher at the
University of California, Berkeley, Aguiar is also a PhD candidate at
the Mackenzie Presbyterian University in São Paulo. He was editor of
the experimental literary magazines *Eita!* and *Crispim*. Aguiar's first
collection, *Ao lado do muro*, was published in 2006. He is currently
working on his first novel and also on a collection of essays on
contemporary Brazilian literature. 'Teresa' is a new story.

Birds come to rest on Teresa's shoulders, but they do not sing. In the last few days, she has – always in the late afternoons – sat on the steps that lead into the building. Her feet together and hands clasped shut, she watches the street: ears alert to the sounds, to dirty eyes. No one seems troubled by the presence of the animals. The birds move little once they have come to rest. They adorn her face with a fine garland which they have carried hanging from their beaks. When her son arrives, it will already be that time of night when the traffic has started to ease up. He will take her by the hand, lead her to her room, switch on the light, put the only book that was saved into his mother's lap and at last he will say:

'Goodnight.'

The mud, the stones and an open hand. Two dogs are looking for something in the middle of the wreckage. The muzzle of one of the dogs nudges at the muddy fingers. On one finger it is possible to see the wedding ring, which the animal's muzzle is touching now. It sniffs, sniffs, sniffs. Until its mouth opens.

TERESA: 'After Prince Elias was lost from his family during a hunt, God took pity and sent a lion to raise the boy. In his heart the king was sure that his son was still alive somewhere, and so he sent his soldiers out to every corner of his realm. When Elias was already grown into a young man, a patrol discovered the lion's den. The soldiers killed the animal and rescued the prince. However, nobody was able to make him remember to be a person: he didn't relearn to speak and spent his time running around the gardens like the animals. In those days, there were giants. One of them had arrived in the kingdom and was destroying houses, estates, farms. To put an end to the destruction, he demanded that he be given sixty men every month as food. Word came to the king from the Lord via the prophet Nathaniel: he should send his only son to the giant, along with another fifty-nine men. The whole court was outraged, yet the king decided to carry out that divine will. Elias and fifty-nine men were taken to the lair of the monster, who lived in a mountain. As they entered, all of the men apart from Elias trembled and screamed at the arrival of the giant, who had one huge eye in the middle of his forehead. "Tiny little thing, tiny little thing," asked the monster in a foul voice, "are you not afraid of me?" The prince snarled and threw stones at the giant, who cried: "Last will be your name! Can you not speak?" Because he did not speak, the giant decided that Last wouldn't taste human. He decided to teach him the language of men, before eating him. The giant would devour two men each day, while he taught everything he knew, the learning and the sciences of the world, to Last. Sometimes, when he was unable to control himself, the giant would lick his student, saying: "Are there other little monsters in your land, Last?" When he had eaten the fifty-ninth man, the giant, to celebrate the fact that he was finally going to devour Last, drank two barrels of wine and passed out. Elias, quietly, left the mountain, uprooted a tree and crept back to where the giant lay and, setting light to one of its ends with the bonfire that warmed the giant's lair, plunged it right into his only eye! The monster yelled: "Aaargh! Black-eyed, black-horned, black-mouthed ram! Who has dared to attack me?" as he beat on the walls of the mountain with his huge hands. Elias replied: "You were killed by the name you taught," and he fled the mountain as the giant was buried under falling rocks.'

The mud, the stones and an open hand, buried. Two hungry dogs are looking for something in the middle of the wreckage. Above them, a yellowing mattress is hanging from the electrical cables. Houses in pieces: of one of them, all that remained were one and a half walls of white tiles. The muzzle of one of the dogs nudges at the muddy fingers. On the index finger it is possible to see the wedding ring, which the animal's muzzle is touching now. It sniffs, sniffs, sniffs. Until its mouth opens.

Teresa waited for her husband for three years. Petrúcio left for São Paulo just months after they were married. The brides and wives of these men would wait, garlands in hand. Many feared that they would never return.

Sometimes, new suitors would prowl around the widow-brides. Some of these women would surrender their breasts, in secret, out in their backyards; most of them, however, would remain unmoved – the garlands turned yellow. Teresa remained faithful and continued with her domestic life. She liked, every nightfall, to listen to her grandmother's stories, as she helped her to husk the corn; on Saturdays, she would gather the children in the square and tell tales of the hills, of enchanted princesses and the miracles of the prophets. While her husband did not return, she continued to live with her parents. She helped with the household chores, she sewed, she went to Mass. Each month, he wrote her a slim letter. When those three years were over, Petrúcio returned with some money. He set up a little greengrocer's shop in the centre of town and transformed the yard into a haberdashery store, which you reached by going down the sides of the house, and which he left in his wife's care.

Teresa wondered, sometimes: has Petrúcio changed? As a joke, she'd say: 'Hey, Southerner!' and her husband would return the greeting with a smile that perhaps had a little awkwardness to it. The first week after his return, she asked him polite and appropriate questions about the life he'd had: where had he worked?, where had he lived?, had he left behind any friends? Their relatives behaved in just the same way. It wouldn't be easy to say just what it was that might have changed. His sense of humour, always one of his greatest qualities, was just the same. His voice, only a little different, somewhat accented, something Southern. He remained a good catch: he didn't drink cachaça and he was still a hard worker. Despite this, some people commented that his words and gestures were lacking in spontaneity, as though the past were slowly, but stubbornly, pulling Petrúcio's arms towards a story hidden under the carpet, an unfinished story. Teresa believed it more every day: Petrúcio was pretending. As though he had forgotten himself and was in search of what had been lost on the journey, on the road. Sometimes, she thought he was afraid of something. One afternoon, when she was already pregnant, a car drove around the town and some strangers asked odd questions around the streets. Petrúcio, as it happened, had taken a sudden trip to the nearby towns. He came back a day after the visitors had left and for several days the couple exchanged few words.

Petrúcio liked to spend some of his free time watching the street, sitting at the window. A cigarette in his left hand, the twists of smoke transformed into talons, while his right hand curled and uncurled the hair of his own moustache. His eyes deep in the stones, corners, animals. In those moments, he smoked too much, even for a man! thought Teresa.

Soon after their children had left home, the two of them put themselves on ice; that old, anxious silence of waiting returned, this time transformed, calcified; the silence, after having been smothered by the playing, the rushing about, the crying, the sicknesses and studies of the three sons, returned at full strength when the beginnings of age surprised Teresa and Petrúcio. Alone, again: waiting again.

Teresa usually does the washing-up from breakfast and lunch. She feels that this way she is paying back the charity of her son and daughter-in-law, ever nocturnal and discreet. Next it will be the laundry.

The birds never come into the apartment, they perch on the posts and cables. When she finishes her housework, Teresa retreats into the room at the back: a little mirror in an orange frame; a photograph album, the only one that wasn't taken by the water; the surviving book; the photo of Petrúcio; a photo with the children, cousins, uncles, aunts and siblings.

She sits down on the bed, closes her eyes and remembers. She can't avoid this, it's almost as though she has not yet woken. Closing them allows her to awake in another life, which is not better than this now-life; on the contrary, there is the mud, the hundreds of bodies. Her dreams these past days are upside-down memories, hanging by the heel. At last, when the sun cools and the birds calm their spirits, Teresa will go down the stairs.

In all her years of marriage, Teresa used to serve the dinner plates cold. In the first months after the return from the South, having become so attached to those feelings of missing one another, there were still some discoveries, but it soon became obvious to Teresa that in bed the two of them would never meet. Each body was trying to find a different place. Petrúcio's kisses and his attempts at affection seemed to be expectations that something else, the *real* thing, should be made manifest. While there was still strength enough for sex, Teresa made choices and took the lead. Petrúcio allowed everything to progress without his having to interfere. This is how the invitation came: twice a month, she would light a candle in the living room. The other lights in the house would be out, the boys would be sleeping, the radio clicked off – only the shadows were not asleep. Teresa would lie in bed and wait, her back to the door of the room. Spirals of smoke: between curtains and picture frames, the footsteps would creep towards her.

The stones and the clay shone like the talons of the harpies. Sitting at the window, his moustache full of smoke, Petrúcio moved his eyes over towards Teresa, but only because it's just necessary to move from time to time. That afternoon he'd already given up.

On the wall, a Sacred Heart. She was standing – the blue of her dress was touching the table, which was covered in a flowery yellow fabric. Three little boxes of trinkets rested on top of that table, which also held rings, coins, two pearl necklaces and a photograph album. Teresa, who was stepping through some good memory, a little girl's memory, was smiling. In her right hand she was holding a small pair of scales, which she was trying to balance. Petrúcio, his eyebrows unkempt, followed the scales like a hypnotized snake, as they stopped moving and remained frozen in a space that was divorced from time.

TERESA: 'A great drought. The rivers and lakes had dried out and there were many animal bones on the banks. The prophet-prince Elias had been journeying for several weeks. Covered in dust, the prophet's hands trembled, his face damaged by the heat. Around him, he could recognize nothing but thorns and snakes. Anyone would have succumbed when faced with conditions as extreme as those he had met on his journey, but he was the son of a king and of a lion. When he was close to Sarepta, he saw a woman gathering firewood at the entrance to the city. Elias approached her and asked for water.

'Weeping, she said: "I know you are a prophet. My son died this morning, and I am going to burn him." "No!" said Elias, gripping the woman's wrist. "Take me to your son." Elias went to the room where the boy's body was resting, knelt down and began to pray. After opening his eyes, still kneeling, he caressed the boy's hair, brought his lips close to the boy's ears and began to speak: "If you come back, boy, tomorrow morning you can play again. You will grow, and, apart from a small accident when you'll be rewarded with a little scar on your right thigh, you will turn into a healthy lad and the city will call you up to be a soldier, someone to protect her from her enemies. You will live through three battles, and I shall tell you of two of them now: men, their wives and daughters will perish on the edge of your sword. Your sandals will be stained with blood. You will be married to a beautiful woman, who will betray you with your best friend, but the city will take your part and she will be stoned, while he will be cast out into the desert. After you have returned from the second battle of your life, two young women, at different times, will bare their breasts for you to kiss them. These women will be yours. If you return, boy, you will be able to hear those little birds that you love. If you return, boy, you will bury your kindly mother in the third year. If you return, boy, you will be able to experience that invisible pleasure, which you barely perceive and which you will never mention, not because it is secret but because it is so natural: feeling the day coming down to rest on your shoulders."

'For hours, Elias continued to teach the dead boy what his life would be like, if he were to raise his eyes. The end, however, he kept from him: in a few years, less than ten, after all the things he had recounted had already taken place, Elias's own people would advance on Sarepta and would conquer it. The boy would defend it, but

DISCOVER NEW WORLDS OF WRITING

'An indispensable part of the intellectual landscape' – *Observer*

Have *Granta* delivered to your door four times a year and save up to 38% on the cover price.

Subscribe now by completing the form overleaf, visiting granta.com or calling UK free phone 0500 004 033

*Not for readers in US, Canada or Latin America

UK
£36.00
£32.00 by Direct Debit

EUROPE
£42.00

REST OF THE WORLD*
£46.00

GRANTA.COM

GRANTA

THE MAGAZINE OF NEW WRITING

SUBSCRIPTION FORM FOR UK, EUROPE AND REST OF THE WORLD

Yes, I would like to take out a subscription to *Granta*.

GUARANTEE: If I am ever dissatisfied with my *Granta* subscription, I will simply notify you, and you will send me a complete refund or credit my credit card, as applicable, for all un-mailed issues.

YOUR DETAILS

MR / MISS / MRS / DR ....

NAME ....

ADDRESS ....

....

POSTCODE ....

EMAIL ....

☐ Please tick this box if you do not wish to receive special offers from *Granta*
☐ Please tick this box if you do not wish to receive offers from organizations selected by *Granta*

YOUR PAYMENT DETAILS

1) ☐ Pay £32.00 (saving £20) by Direct Debit
To pay by Direct Debit please complete the mandate and return to the address shown below.

2) Pay by cheque or credit/debit card. Please complete below:

1 year subscription: ☐ UK: £36.00   ☐ Europe: £42.00   ☐ Rest of World: £46.00

3 year subscription: ☐ UK: £96.00   ☐ Europe: £108.00   ☐ Rest of World: £126.00

I wish to pay by ☐ CHEQUE   ☐ CREDIT/DEBIT CARD
Cheque enclosed for £ _____ made payable to *Granta*.

Please charge £ _____ to my: ☐ Visa ☐ Mastercard ☐ Amex ☐ Switch/Maestro

Card No. ☐☐☐☐☐☐☐☐☐☐☐☐☐☐☐☐

Valid from *(if applicable)* ☐☐☐☐   Expiry Date ☐☐☐☐   Issue No. ☐☐

Security No. ☐☐☐

SIGNATURE .... DATE ....

Instructions to your Bank or Building Society to pay by Direct Debit

BANK NAME ....

BANK ADDRESS ....

POSTCODE ....

ACCOUNT IN THE NAMES(S) OF: ....

SIGNED ....

DATE ....

DIRECT Debit

Instructions to your Bank or Building Society: Please pay Granta Publications direct debits from the account detailed on this instruction subject to the safeguards assured by the direct debit guarantee. I understand that this instruction may remain with Granta and, if so, details will be passed electronically to my bank/building society. Banks and building societies may not accept direct debit instructions from some types of account.

Bank/building society account number

☐☐☐☐☐☐☐☐

Sort Code

☐☐☐☐☐☐

Originator's Identification

9 1 3 1 3 3

Please mail this order form with payment instructions to:

Granta Publications
12 Addison Avenue
London, W11 4QR
Or call 0500 004 033
or visit GRANTA.COM

without glory. He would be wounded by one of the first arrows from
the invading army, an arrow that would pierce his right eyeball, throw
him backwards and with all its strength would drag his body towards
death. The prophet placed his right hand on his own breast: how far
should this Revelation go? He fell silent, at last. The boy's mother was
in the living room, waiting. Elias watched, his hands held out over the
body, until the boy moved.

'The whole village celebrated the God of Elias, a God who brings
people back from the dead. However, when they asked him to visit
another man who was lately deceased, a few days later, the prophet
still bore the wounds left by the first miracle. When he reached the
second house, Elias repeated the same ritual, this time at the body of
one of Sarepta's oldest and most important leaders. There was not
much to tell him about the life that he would have, if he decided to
return; there was little he could say about it and the greatest praise
would be just to assert: it exists.

'Hours later, having been expelled from the city, Elias, wandering,
would spend the days that followed trying to understand whether he
should serve the miracle, or the truth.'

The mud, the stones and an open hand, buried. It is no longer
raining. Two hungry dogs are looking for something in the
middle of the wreckage: it's hard to make out if it's a bit of pipe,
palm leaves, wood, bricks, roots; everything has been transformed
into the same tint, a mixture of bone colour, the colour of things
buried. Above the wreckage, a yellowing mattress is hanging from the
electrical cables. Houses in pieces: of one of them, all that remained
was one wall of white tiles, which are now covered in mud, like
everything else after the water, like a thing possessed, invaded the
streets. The muzzle of one of the dogs nudges at the muddy fingers.
On the index finger it is possible, still, to see the wedding ring, which
the animal's muzzle is touching now. It sniffs, sniffs, sniffs. Until its
mouth opens at the moment when the cries can be heard.

The dust rose up from the counter when Teresa put down the books from the library. Petrúcio didn't move. There was nothing to suggest that he had taken any notice of the arrival of the children, led by Teresa out into the yard. The little greengrocer's had gone under years earlier; Petrúcio dragged the haberdashery store along like a second body, behind which he hid each morning, Monday to Friday. Now Teresa was supporting the household with a job at the municipal library and the help of their sons.

After lunch – his wife left food on the table – he would close the shop and head out into town, but his walk, people said, wasn't like the aimless wandering that madmen do. Petrúcio walked like a man who knows where he is going. 'I'm going to get a copy of the front-door key made,' 'I'm going to have a little flutter,' his certain steps seemed to be saying.

At night, he would return home, sit in his armchair and smoke. It was only when he went into the bedroom that he would see Teresa, who read every night before going to sleep. When the book closed – words weakened by sleepiness, transformed into something less than the subtlest of sounds – and the pages bore the only light that was still on in the house, the light of the little standing lamp, only then would Petrúcio turn his gaze away from the ceiling.

Teresa couldn't bear to live in that house any longer, unless the streets were, with some regularity, invited inside; on two Fridays of the month, it was the turn of the children, freed from their day's lessons if they attended those storytellings. Having met them in front of the library, she would lead them to the yard of the house, where they would sit, laugh and swing their arms; as Teresa told the stories, with the books in her hand or from what she remembered having heard as a child, they would settle down. The spirits that haunt the local mythology, the ghosts, the saints, the princesses, the enchanted stones, the dragons and the Moors, the perils of sword and of death and of love, the metamorphoses and wings open in the sky – there would be a multitude to fill the afternoon.

TERESA: 'Elias is an old man now and this is his final miracle. When he reaches a distant village on the edges of the kingdom, a family asks him to meet a man called Trasilau. An honest merchant, he had gone mad with no explanation. A sudden punishment from God, perhaps, who could tell? Could Elias intercede with the Lord to rescue him from madness, that was what the madman's family, abasing themselves, asked him, promising to perform countless Mass sacrifices and songs of praise to the Lord. Trasilau said he was a king and that his own shadow covered the mountains, the roads, the walls of the city – his kingdom, cried Trasilau, was in everything that breathed! Elias left the city and went to meet him under a nearby fig tree. When the prophet arrived, he was dancing naked around the tree, singing chants of praise. His expression was serene. With stones that he'd tied to one another and piled up, he had made two crude constructions that resembled a throne and an altar. Elias ignored that king, tore little branches off a nearby tree and thrashed Trasilau. "Awake, man!" At that moment, the Lord returned his sight to him. Cowering, head hanging low, Trasilau, who could barely contain his tears, gathered up his belongings. As though his dignity had been restored in the blink of an eye – a second miracle – Trasilau, still naked, stood in front of the prophet and said: "Enemy prophet! Why did you take me away from the only kingdom that does not weigh on the heads of men?" Elias did not reply – his body was already rising, like a bolt of light, to the centre of heaven, carried off in a chariot of fire.'

The mud, the stones and an open hand, buried. It is no longer raining. Two hungry dogs are looking for something in the middle of the wreckage: it's hard to make out if it's a bit of pipe, palm leaves, wood, bricks, roots; everything has been transformed into the same tint, a mixture of bone colour, the colour of things buried, the colour of something that compresses, that accumulates. Above the wreckage, a yellowing mattress is hanging from the electrical cables. Houses in pieces: of one of them, all that remained was one wall of white tiles, which are now covered in mud, like everything else after the water invaded the streets, like a thing possessed. The stretch that can be seen on the right is a newborn river filled with bits of cloth and shoes, mixed with hundreds of books; a single, dead, viscous mass. The muzzle of one of the dogs nudges at the muddy fingers. On the index finger it is possible to see the wedding ring, which the animal's muzzle is touching now. It sniffs, sniffs, sniffs. Until its mouth opens at the moment when Teresa's cries can be heard shooing them away from Petrúcio's body. On her knees, she cleans her husband's face with a piece of paper that is dirty, stained, crossed out, blotted, crumpled, torn; shroud-paper.

There, Teresa vomited up the birds.

They rise up into the sky, like vultures.

When she tries to read in her bedroom, in the afternoon, the birds start singing very loud, they abandon their posts and cables and hurl themselves towards the apartment; Teresa puts down her book and runs to close the windows and the veranda doors; still they insist, beat their heads against the glass, scratch, flap their wings, scatter feathers like tears through the air. Teresa gives up on reading, she goes back to her room and lies down.

She cannot concentrate on the television or on the music from the radio. All that remains is the street, the leave-taking of the sun. The neighbours arrive home from work and from the activities that the city demands of them; Teresa, however, does not see them. When her son arrives, before his wife, it's already that time of night when the traffic has eased up. He takes her by the hand, sighs and leads her with all care to the room at the back. He turns on the light, and after Teresa has lain down, he combs her hair. He covers her with a white sheet, puts the book down into his mother's lap and at last he will say:

'Goodnight.'

The birds desert the street. They float happily, swarm-dense, a thick shoal above the town. ∎

THAT WIND BLOWING THROUGH THE PLAZA

Laura Erber

TRANSLATED BY ANNA KUSHNER

LAURA ERBER
1979

Laura Erber was born in Rio de Janeiro,
and is a visual artist and a writer of short stories, essays
and poetry. Her four books of poetry include *Os corpos e os dias*
(2008), which was shortlisted for the Jabuti Award. She has
collaborated with Italian writer Federico Nicolao on the book
Celia Misteriosa (2007) and with artist Laercio Redondo on the
video project *The Glass House* (1999–2008), and has exhibited her
work across Europe and Brazil. Her book on the Romanian theorist
and poet Ghérasim Luca is forthcoming this December. Erber is
currently working on her first novel, *Os esquilos de Pavlov*, to be
published in 2013. 'That Wind Blowing through the Plaza'
('Aquele vento na praça') is a new story.

I didn't go for the dental treatment, or for the gypsy dancing, or for the *țuică*, or for Bran Castle. Nor did I go to settle old scores, to do genealogical searches or to buy rare copies of *avanguardea literarea romaneasca*. I wasn't interested in the breeze over the Dâmbovița River, the nocturnal song of the *strigoi* or the wildlife in the Danube Delta. I went because I was asked to, and I met Martina. The best-smelling locks in the East, the Caravaggio-esque locks of Martina Ptyx. They confused and attracted me. Was it a fetish? Maybe. But none of that matters much now. I went to Bucharest for Neagu's boxes, I met Martina and returned with old Stefan's things.

Last Thursday, at age 66, the Romanian-born artist Paul Neagu, a resident of Holloway, in the north of London, passed away. Born in Bucharest in 1938, he moved to the British capital in the seventies. A fan of bicycling, yoga and swimming, Neagu liked to show off his enviable physical form in arduous performances that he had named *post-apocalyptic rituals*. Still, in the last years of his life he faced many health problems, aggravated by his excessive consumption of coffee and unfiltered cigarettes. In 1989, his sister gave him a kidney. He was stubborn and persistent: the more his illnesses spread, the more monumental his sculptures became. Under Victor Brancusi's influence – and perhaps that of his father, a shoemaker who specialized in women's footwear – he moved from painting to three-dimensional forms. In his famous series of sculptures

Hyphen, he represented the geometric trinity made by a triangle, a square and a spiralling circle. He studied that sacred geometry intensely, to the point of believing that basic forms determine all aspects of life. In 1969, he met Richard Demarco, who introduced him to Tadeusz Kantor and Joseph Beuys, with whom he later became great friends. To get by in London, he taught at various art schools (Hornsey, Slade, Chelsea, Royal College of Art), where artists like Antony Gormley, Anish Kapoor and Rachel Whiteread took his classes. In 2001, he had a stroke that affected his speech, but all the same he continued to work and to communicate his ideas. In 2003, the Tate did a show commemorating the acquisition of an important part of his body of work. Neagu was seen for the last time on the night of the opening with an iridescent silk kerchief tied around his neck.

When my father fell into a coma, Mr Bernard Marmonier sought me out immediately. We met for almost two hours, time enough for me to sell him the shampoo labs my father had invented fifty years prior. Thus Marmonier became the emperor of smoothing, straightening and anti-frizz shampoos. I didn't have the least interest in managing my father's monster. The Marmoniers had been in the hair business for over a century. Mr Bernard was the great-nephew of Dr Marmonier of Marseilles, member emeritus of the Royal Society of Dermatology and Syphilography, author of the first European manual on capillary hygiene, *Soins de propreté et hygiène de la chevelure*.

I commemorated the sale with Nick, my neighbour across the hall, who lived alone with a female poodle. Whenever there was something important to celebrate or mourn, I sought out his company. At the end of the night, Nick's dog had an epileptic attack. I went home but couldn't sleep. I turned on the TV in hopes of dispelling the image of that fluffy animal frothing at the mouth and dragging itself along the carpet, but I couldn't shake the feeling that something terrible or unexpected was about to occur.

I changed my name, turned into an artist, became famous as Philip Honeysuckle. Under that stolen name, I created works of which I am now a little ashamed. The name belonged to one of the five members of the Generative Art Group, a collective created by Paul Neagu in 1972 that included Neagu himself as well as the fictitious members Husney Belmood, Anton Paidola, Edward Larsocchi and Philip Honeysuckle. Some critics believed that those fictional signatures gave Neagu a margin of creative freedom; thus, after he was established, he managed to delve into new languages without having to confront the wild resistance and provincial mistrust of English critics.

'My' Honeysuckle made objects from folded paper – '*povero* origamis from an industrious *povero* guy', Nick used to say – that floated continuously thanks to the work of some super-powerful fans (modified microturbines). After a few years of trips and prizes, I decided to put an end to Honeysuckle's career. Around then, I ran into a childhood friend who had just been hired by Tate Modern, even though his true passion was sixteenth-century Caucasian tapestries and whose greatest desire was to poison the director of the tapestry section at the Victoria and Albert Museum and settle in there with his cigars until the end of time. The only thing I knew about the Caucasus, besides the genocides, came from a Loreena McKennitt song that talked about a nocturnal cavalcade amid lightning, silent trees and the moon. He explained that in Russian, the Caucasus was called Kavkaz, in Turkish it was Kafkas, and that in the place where Zeus chained Prometheus, today there is a huge deposit of precious metals. He thought that the ancients knew or suspected the existence of some powerful material there. 'Kafka mentions a verse of the legend in which Prometheus, after the intense agony of being pecked at by eagles, held himself so stiff that he turned into a rock.' My friend also had theories about the art market. He said that money was going to move, as a matter of fact it had already moved to sports, that he himself had two millionaire friends who now preferred to invest their fortunes signing up contracts for Latin American players. Around eleven, he got sentimental, telling me about his contentious divorce, his daughter's psychiatric treatment, far-fetched stories about his ex-wife who, from time to time, threatened to commit suicide Puccini-style. His speech getting all the more slurred and impenetrable, he finished the night with an exaltation of the public collections of contemporary art. Finally, we toasted to the health of men and children and we said goodbye.

One week later, I received a phone call from this same friend, who wanted to know if I would be interested in working for the Tate's new collections. 'We need people with discretion who can travel on a budget and who know the framework for buying and selling in post-communist countries.' I didn't know the framework, but the idea of travelling to the East at a moment when nothing tied me to anything or anyone seemed grand. The terms were reasonable. I signed the contract and they arranged for me to go to Bucharest to buy Paul Neagu's censored works. 'Next year we'll do an exhibit, *The Unknown East*. Trustworthy sources guarantee that in Bucharest there are still many works produced by Neagu in the 1950s and 60s. They're in the hands of ex-colleagues, ex-lovers and relatives. They're probably simple people who have little or nothing to do with the art world.' They suggested that, before I leave, I meet with Paul Overy, the author of a minor study about Neagu's artistic trajectory. Overy gave me contact information for a man named Stefan Ptyx. 'Mention my name, he should remember.'

The man would be waiting for me at nine in the morning at the entrance to Bucharest's National Theatre, a squat and charmless building, built over the ruins of the old theatre bombed by the Germans in '44. While I was waiting, a young girl with a head full of wine-coloured hair appeared. I immediately liked her pixie ears. She held out her hand to me and said she had come at the request of Mr Paul Overy. She introduced herself as Martina Ptyx and, in rather proper English, said that her father, Stefan Ptyx, was unfortunately too sick and weak to leave the small village in which they lived, about fifty kilometres from Bucharest. She also said that, if I would like, we could go out there together. I would spend the night at the home of a neighbour or, if I preferred, I would return on the last train. We boarded a carriage full of old, wrinkled peasants. It took us more than two hours to get to the small village. During the journey, I asked if she was interested in art. She answered yes, but that she didn't have anything intelligent or interesting to say about the matter, that her father did, her father had many opinions, what a shame that he was now sick and couldn't express himself very well. I decided not to ask any more questions. The train stopped suddenly, and we got off in the middle of a field and continued down a path that ran alongside a garden of beets.

There was something weird about that girl. It was as if at any moment she would start dancing amid the beets, the farmers would make a chorus circle around her and reality would turn into a bad film. By the devotion with which neighbours greeted her, I understood that it wasn't just me, the village was under the same strange spell. How had that hair survived Ceauşescu's shampoos? What did she do in her free time? Did she have any free time at all? From the impression she had given me, she spent night and day protecting her father from domestic accidents, because he had a rare syndrome with a name she couldn't pronounce. As far as everything else was concerned, her story was simple. Her mother had died several years before and since then she preferred watching her father to watching the garden grow. I asked if she wouldn't have more options in Bucharest, but 'the capital stinks' was a difficult argument to refute, even though I didn't know what stink she was referring to. After almost half an hour of walking, we stopped before a wooden house, identical to the eight wooden houses we had passed. The heat, my exhaustion and thirst, and the scent coming off Martina's locks had left me with a mix of euphoria and nausea. I could no longer remember why I had come to that backwater town.

The Ptyx house stank of cats. A swarm of flies buzzed around a milk saucer. At the back of the living room was a figure hunched over a desk piled with books. He looked dead, but he was alive. Our arrival had disturbed the old man, and he began to stir and growl in harmless agitation. Martina tried to calm him down, explaining who I was and where I came from. Either he had not been aware that I was coming or he had forgotten. Suddenly, he straightened up and walked towards me. He held out his hand to greet me, but then continued to walk around the room greeting everything he found before him, 'Good afternoon, wooden table, good afternoon, candlestick, good afternoon, candelabra, good afternoon, flies on the milk saucer, good afternoon, milk saucer, good afternoon, sewing machine, good afternoon, window, good afternoon, Neagu's little boxes'. There on a sideboard was a collection of small paper and plaster boxes, *The Cake Man* and *Anthropocosmos (23-Storey Man)*. Neagu's works didn't have much of a visual impact; their value was in their metaphoric power. In any event, they were the material remains of a time period, of a way of understanding and making art.

Though I had only seen Paul Neagu once in my life, and even then from far away, old Stefan Ptyx's face made me wonder if the two were related. Martina brought some tea and we settled in before the window that overlooked the beet garden. Stefan Ptyx had gone back to his original position at his desk. I asked Martina what he was doing. 'Papa is passionate about Balzac. It's an obsession, ever since he was an adolescent, no, before. He inherited those books from a Mr Barthes who directed the French Institute of Culture of Bucharest, back before the arrival of communism. Papa did the cleaning at the institute's library. He said that my mother was Henriette de Mortsauf de Turnu Severin.' Martina let out a shrill laugh. 'So what is he writing?' 'He's rewriting.' 'Translating?' 'He wakes up, sits down in that corner and spends the day copying Balzac's books.' 'He writes down quotes?' 'No, he rewrites line by line, page by page, every page of each book. He intends to get to the last one, but I'm afraid, I don't want it to end, do you understand?' I looked at Stefan Ptyx, he seemed happy, entirely swept up by the ecstasy of writing, as if there were no one else in the room, or as if a dangerous ghost were forcing him to carry out the drawing of each letter of each word of each phrase.

A Canadian artist once locked himself in a gallery for several months before the public to transcribe every book of the last century that featured a character who writes. A Brazilian artist once spent a year lying on a hammock reading *In Search of Lost Time* with a camera on him. The filmed images were projected in their entirety on the front of Proust's old home, in Illiers-Combray. But that old man Ptyx, who had no apparent ambitions besides the alienating pleasure of manually copying the printed words of his favourite author, seemed to me a far more powerful sight. 'What are you writing today, Papa?' '*Gobseck*, Martina. *Gobseck*.' Martina let out another little laugh and I felt that the two were exchanging a secret.

Perhaps this was an elaborate drama put on especially for idiot visitors like me. Perhaps those boxes weren't even Neagu's, perhaps the old man wasn't hurt or sick, perhaps that wasn't the house where they lived, perhaps they weren't even father and daughter, perhaps they weren't even named Martina and Stefan. What kind of name was Ptyx? It was too poetic a surname to be real.

I tried to find out a little more about the old man's obsession. Martina didn't want to or didn't know how to go into detail. She said only that he did it every day, ever since before he was diagnosed, and that his doctors encouraged it, because they thought it was a good way for him to keep busy. Someone knocked at the door and a female voice whispered something inaudible. The flies had gone from the edge of the milk saucer to the head of *The Cake Man*. Martina closed the door and came back with two containers of *papanasi*. 'I don't know very much, but I know it has to do with the names of people he met many years ago in Piteşti. You have probably never heard of that place, it's a city to the north-east of here, where the Argeş and the Doamnei meet. Whoever goes to Piteşti likes to visit the Vidraru Dam in the mountains nearby; it's a pretty place, you should go. At the very top of the dam is a sculpture by Constantin Popovici, it's a monument to electricity, a Prometheus with his arms raised up, you would like it.' It felt like a good time to start the negotiation. 'Sadly, my time here is very short,' I said. 'Perhaps it would be good to talk to your father about the Paul Neagu works he keeps here.' I looked at the sideboard, and suddenly the boxes didn't have the same appeal. Wasn't the pursuit of the last specimens of the avant-garde in dirty little houses in Eastern Europe the height of fetishism? But this Stefan Ptyx, the way he leaned over the table, his Benedictine monk script, the smiles every time he reached the end of a page, it was hypnotic and simple and I didn't want him to finish. I decided to spend the night in the small village.

The girl who brought over the *papanasi* was named Dimitra and lived with an aunt and her mongoloid brother, Emeric. The two women received me without much friendliness. The kid was playing a game with a cup and ball, and every once in a while he looked at me and smiled as if we had always known each other. I slept in a small, windowless room with a hole in the ceiling covered by dirty plastic. I spent a night of dreamless sleep and woke up to the ploc-ploc of the cup and ball. Dimitra led me back to the Ptyx house. Martina was in the kitchen wearing a white dress with lace cuffs, old Stefan was spilling milk on the saucers, the spirited flies were circling again. I noticed that Neagu's works were no longer on the sideboard; in their place were Chinese zodiac figures. Martina gave me a plastic bag with all of the Neagu objects they had in the house.

She charged the equivalent of three hundred pounds sterling. I paid four hundred and left my contact information, so that she could find me if she should come to London one day. She asked me not to, in any hypothetical situation, ever tell her father about the sale of those 'things'. I asked if I could send the exhibition catalogue that would include photos of those boxes. She preferred not to receive it, but she said that if I wanted to thank her, and if I had time, she would love to receive a book by Paulo Coelho. 'Anything except *Brida*', which she had read enthusiatically during the spring. I tried to say goodbye to old Stefan, but he had withdrawn to his room. Martina accompanied me to the road and pointed out the place where the train would stop.

The return train seemed newer than the one from the previous day. I settled into my seat and let myself be mesmerized by the landscape in motion. I felt my oily hair on the back of my neck, thought of Bernard Marmonier and my father's infallible formulas. I thought about the strange fertility of dwarves, I thought of Nick cleaning his carpet before going to sleep. I remembered my father's last days, deliriously seeing butterflies on the hospital ceiling, I remembered the eulogy and the priest who couldn't stop coughing. I remembered the flies at the Ptyx house and the story of Prometheus turning inward. And, for a second, everything made so little sense that I felt relieved. Not art, not travel, not Pythia at Delphi, not the constancy of mourning, not scandalous visions, not divine manifestations, not mobile wealth or heavy metals, not true genius, not the calculation of pleasure, not the mortal child sucking a lollipop next to me, none of it made up a web of significance. Nothing guaranteed that life was more than a collection of fake men and copied novels. I thought of Paul Neagu making palpable objects for friends he would never again meet. It would be good to see Martina again and know if Stefan Ptyx suffered or smiled upon reaching the last page of *La Comédie humaine*. It would be good to see Martina again without any motive. Even if Martina Ptyx were not Martina Ptyx. Even if Martina Ptyx were a harpie, a barren bandit, a heartless Amelia Sach. 'Must we wait until autumn to make love?' Which character said that?

I got out at Gara de Nord where a group of gypsies competed to read my future. A bluish dust tinted the city. I crossed Unirii Square as if I were climbing Mount Fitz Roy. The bag was about to break, there was so much wind that it was impossible to keep my eyes open. ∎

GRANTA

THE COUNT

Leandro Sarmatz

TRANSLATED BY PETER BUSH

LEANDRO SARMATZ
1973

Leandro Sarmatz was born in Porto Alegre and has lived
in São Paulo since 2001. He is currently an editor at the
publishing house Companhia das Letras. Sarmatz is the author
of the play *Mães e sogras* (2000), the collection of poetry *Logocausto*
(2009) and the short-story collection *Uma fome* (2010).
'The Count' ('O Conde') is taken from *Uma fome*.

When Emil Fleischer, the Yiddish actor, left the Lager after a two-year period in which he suffered privations nobody can ever anticipate, his first thought was to find a decent bed to sleep in. Despite the real blessing it was to be alive, his second thought was to travel back to see a place he dearly loved before it was swallowed up by the death machine: Czernowitz, the city in Bucovina where he was born with the new century. He would go to America only after he had done that.

Did the decision of a man who felt annihilated make any sense? It was, no doubt, absurd. To make internment in the Lager tolerable, Fleischer – a mediocre actor who had grasped the opportunity to earn his living by playing the part of Count Dracula in a series of roadshows of dubious artistic merit – started to fantasize about a new life in America. At night, on his bunk, writhing from hunger, the actor elaborated truly Hollywood-style idylls.

Sometimes he voiced his thoughts out loud, in the black-hole dark of the hut. Some people thought he was boasting, like Berman, the butcher, who'd never ever seen an artist before. Others swore the actor was simply one more lunatic among so many others dumped there prior to being turned into a shapeless pile of twisted bones, like Aronis, the tailor, who usually spoke French but broke into Yiddish in his nightmares.

As for a bed, Fleischer was happy, in those first few days of freedom, with a handful of sawdust laid out for him by a sturdy Polish woman who was working – rather reluctantly – for the Russians. After spending several nights next to a heater and eating countless decent meals, his body was invigorated and the actor felt like a real prince. Besides, he seemed to have an iron constitution. There was a touch of magic in surviving all that.

Now, he needed to get on the road to Czernowitz.

A fluent German speaker – his city of birth boasted a vast, affluent German population – Fleischer also spoke Yiddish, Romanian and a smattering of Polish and Russian thanks to tours in the remotest corners of the East. It was in towns and villages that knew next to nothing about the outside world, unless there happened to be an epidemic or even a pogrom, that the actor was given the name he would be recognized by whenever there were Jewish fans of theatre about. The Count. That tiny scrap of information ('the Count's performing') broadcast along the streets, spread through gossip by women going to the market and whispered in synagogue doorways and *yeshivot*, ensured that a large, attentive crowd would gather around the small, famished troupe: Fleischer, Gabi – a pretty young thing who said she was Viennese but had come into the world in the shtetl in Lakhva – and old Maltchik, who had been the sexton of a synagogue burned to the ground by Cossacks many years ago. Extras were recruited there and then from the audience. And obviously they weren't paid a cent.

Fleischer, a clown and a ham actor, escaped death by the skin of his teeth on at least a couple of occasions thanks to his ability to slip between languages and roles. The first time was after Hitler's invasion of Poland. Not really aware of quite what was happening, the troupe was travelling in their cart along a road when they were stopped by a German convoy. One of the soldiers barked at the Count in garbled Polish, taking him to be a peasant or, who knows, even a Jew. Fleischer, wearing a suit that was so threadbare it wasn't hard to see the frayed edges of each garment, immediately saw his opportunity. In the purest German he cunningly related how he was a travelling salesman who had been held up by bandits, probably gypsies (at that moment the actor spat dramatically on the ground), and that he was on his way home with his wife and father-in-law. Without remotely dreaming what the truth might be, the soldier handed him a few coppers and told him to take care on his journey.

That was a close thing. Gabi and Maltchik were all set to intone the Shema Yisrael.

The second time that Fleischer gave death a miss the troupe was no more, and in the cities where they would have performed, their audience had been swallowed up. Where had they all gone? The

Count found out one summer morning, almost suffocating from the heat and starving to death, in a truck where whole families were travelling crammed in like cattle. It was twelve days since Gabi – who had always had fragile health – had died from dehydration. 'How old was she?' the actor wondered now. 'At most twenty-three, the poor thing.' He had bumped into her five years ago, practically in rags, with a broken arm, by the side of the railway line on the outskirts of Linz. She was running away from what was her first day of work in a brothel. After seeing to her wounded arm and feeding her, the Count taught her the rudiments of the art of acting. In any case, he wasn't exactly a Molière. She was amusing – when she wasn't having one of her turns – and was good at promoting their show.

As for old Maltchik, at least he would not experience any uncertainty: before they even started off, three soldiers kicked him to death, just for the fun of it.

When they got out of the truck in the Nazi camp, his heart frozen, Fleischer had to pass himself off as a worker who might be useful. It was a small lie, but at the time a little fib could mean everything for people like him. Obviously, nobody played with any advantages in that farce, but something about the Count – his foreign accent, his half-slanted eyes, his sleek, dark hair – sparked a quite inexplicable reaction in the fellow staring at him, who found him amusing and selected him for the workers' hut. The actor had survived that day. And the many days that were to follow.

Europe was in chaos immediately after the war. There were often no roads; people were forced to make long detours to avoid endless craters, blown-up bridges, the debris. Railway lines were the same: slow progress, stopping hours, if not days, at some spot on the track to wait for a convoy to come from the other side or for one of the victorious armies to make the necessary repairs.

It was always an effort for Fleischer, penniless and dressed like a buffoonish beggar (clothes he had filched on a night-time foray into a huge warehouse guarded by Russians), to board trains in the stations that separated him from his city of birth. He had to play a different role on each train. He was a virtuoso of forgery. In his favour, he could even produce a clutch of letters of recommendation – written in Russian and English – in which would-be generals made a thousand and one references to the qualities of that actor who 'would no doubt make a name for himself in the cinema'. Given the gravity of events at the time, when everybody was worried about surviving and having something to eat or a place to sleep when night fell, nobody could fathom why generals who had led armies and won a war would waste their time on an actor wandering across Europe. The fact is that Fleischer had almost no serious upsets on his journey.

What kind of star did the Count have? He hadn't worried about Death for a long time or, at least, had tricked her like one of those unscrupulous gallants who wheedle up to rich old ladies and live on their excesses, and then mount a scene of jealousy once in a while – all to guarantee emotional control over their hapless dames. Nothing untoward ever happened to him. He had crossed several countries, gazed upon cities in ruins, processions of defeated men, skeletal orphans and women who cackled as if they were out of their mind, but Fleischer seemed to have been touched by some mysterious higher design. He was immune to that kind of unhappiness.

Had he ever paused to think about any of that? It seems very unlikely because the actor wasn't exactly likely. His sort doesn't usually think about what is happening around them. He seemed to have a kind of instinct or, even, second nature. Almost an attribute independent of his will. Life is there, with all its challenges, for him to do the necessary without embarking on big debates. That's why it's not really surprising that Fleischer did manage to cross a large chunk of the continent and return to the place where he had spent his childhood. There he hadn't been 'Fleischer, the actor', or 'Fleischer, the Count'. He was just Emil, or the seventh and last son – and yet the one who most felt out of place – of a tailor who disappeared from home a few months before the bar mitzvah of his youngest son. What his father did was pure madness, he was thinking, as he drew close to Czernowitz.

In the distance, the actor could now see the chimneys, the plumes of smoke reaching into the sky. He was anxious to reach the outskirts of the city. Who will have survived of his relatives and acquaintances to hear him intone a Kaddish in homage to those who departed?

That night in Czernowitz they were massacring anyone who spoke the German language. ∎

THE DINNER

Julián Fuks

TRANSLATED BY JOHNNY LORENZ

JULIÁN FUKS
1981

Julián Fuks was born in São Paulo and is the
son of Argentinian parents. He has worked as a reporter for the
newspaper *Folha de S. Paulo* and as a reviewer for the magazine
Cult. Fuks is the author of *Fragmentos de Alberto, Ulisses, Carolina e
eu* (2004) and *Histórias de literatura e cegueira* (2007), which was a
finalist for the Telecom Award as well as the Jabuti Award. His latest
novel, *Procura do romance* (2011), was shortlisted for the São Paulo
Prize for Literature and longlisted for the Telecom Award.
'The Dinner' ('O jantar') is a new story.

Ensconced in the entrance hall that grows more and more claustrophobic, Sebastián is an adult, fully grown, a respectable and solemn man. Well-defined muscles, rigid features, a bottle of wine held tightly in his fist. A deceptive outward appearance, for beneath the almost immaculate surface, this respectable man is a wreck, a body in shambles, an adolescent reincarnated with all his insecurities, all his fears renewed. He can imagine a drop of sweat running down his cheek, shattering his aura of tranquillity, undermining the composure of the face that appears in the spyhole.

He doesn't wait for very long, but the person coming to the door isn't announced by the sound of footfall, and the silence deprives time of any measurement. In an instant the darkness is undone by light, and in his eyes, now shut, pale circles of luminosity begin bursting. 'Hola, Sebastián,' a monotonous voice greets him without affection or enthusiasm, and the hand that grabs him by the shoulder is firm and pulls him close, and the lips that smack a kiss on his cheek are crinkled. His eyes now open, his skin bristling, his body leaning a second too long against this woman who is no longer embracing him, the assault on his senses is too diverse to assimilate. He takes a step back to get a good look at her, returns to an erect posture and examines her face in uncertain recognition. He knows this face or will come to know it. The features are those of his mother but with more pronounced lines, the features his mother's face will gain one day, in the near future, except for those unruly eyebrows and the wrinkles radiating from her lips, signs of her famous sternness of character.

'Hi, Auntie, how's it going?' he responds after a long delay, and the awkward timing of the phrase as well as the incongruous tone of joy that betrays a certain childishness are sufficient cause for regret. The bottle of wine passes from his hand to hers without much fanfare, a simple *gracias*, then it's immediately lost among the other bottles on the shelf. She makes a quick gesture with her arm to indicate the sofa where he should sit down, the sofa that was forbidden to him throughout his childhood, because it was a place where only adults could sit, although on occasion, he recalls, alone in that apartment belonging to his ancestors, he had dared to lean back and stretch his legs on those cushions, establishing beneath absent eyes some sort of intimacy with the space.

'Should I sit here?' he asks with diffidence as if her gesture hadn't been clear enough, an excessive diffidence that nullifies even that false intimacy, returning him to the condition of guest, conceding all authority to her. Now isn't the time to be timid, he says to himself before she's responded to his question, and clenching his jaw, he lets himself slump down on the indicated spot with a thump that is heavier than required.

'And your children, your grandchildren, aren't they joining us?' Sebastián asks, avoiding the nasalized vowels of Portuguese, pressing his tongue against the roof of his mouth when pronouncing an 'n', attempting the music of proper Spanish, hoping to erase his own Brazilianness and impress her with his accent.

'No,' she responds, as though surprised, squinting her eyes at him and adding, in her own majestic Spanish, a phrase that sounds hostile: 'I didn't think to call them.'

'And the family, what are they up to?' Sebastián insists, with real interest, wanting to hear news of his cousins for whom he still nurtures some affinity in spite of distance and inherited frictions.

But she effectively eludes him with a modest play on words: 'They're up and about, those who can stand up at all,' alluding perhaps to her youngest grandchildren and becoming entangled in an inopportune literalness.

'Please tell them I send my best.' And so Sebastián finds himself wrapping up that conversation at the wrong moment, saving himself from making any more indirect hints destined to fail.

There is in this woman a total refusal to abide by traditional conventions, that's how Sebastián formulates his first diagnosis. Polite conversation about mutual acquaintances cannot distract her from her seriousness or alter her unruffled countenance or cause her muscles to stretch into a warm smile. To speak of close relatives – one might notice the spasmodic oscillation of the elevated foot of her crossed leg – provokes an impatience that is poorly concealed, a disinterest proportional to the interest the other person demonstrates, almost a disdain for such frivolity. The living room doesn't seem to be a space she really enjoys, at least not as a space for domestic pleasures or as an intimate setting, a place to indulge in trivial formalities.

'So what do you think of Buenos Aires?' she asks – a question that counters his somewhat unsubstantiated theory, and it behoves him to throw away his previous judgements in order to devote himself more fully to the conversation.

'Ah, but what could I think of it? Buenos Aires is eternal like water and air,' he quotes offhandedly, and instantly regrets having done so. 'Here things seem to have perpetuity, reproducing themselves with every decade and at every corner, always the same, always preserving the same peculiar quality.'

When he finishes speaking – expressing poorly an idea that came to him earlier that afternoon while sitting in a century-old cafe on the Avenida de Mayo, leaning over a menu identical to that of previous occasions, under the impatient stare of the very same waiter from similar afternoons – he knows he's taken a risk with his irresponsible analysis. Buenos Aires is her city, terrain favourable to her own analyses, and it's evident that his thoughtless remark will provide her with the opportunity for a dissenting speech.

'I wouldn't be so optimistic,' she responds, already distorting what he meant to say. 'If only we knew how to preserve the values we hold most dear, but unfortunately not a single one of those values can be found in our leaders today. That woman. You know who I'm talking about,' and Sebastián can feel the fury in her voice. 'That woman took over the Casa Rosada, only to ruin everything in an act of petty, foolish vengeance. Sure, now she's rich, she got very rich, she and her husband who didn't die soon enough, but at what price did they build their fortune in the dirt-poor valleys of Patagonia, working as lawyers with who knows what authority? Now they take vengeance on those who once spurned them, persecuting our former leaders, insulting their political enemies merely for their own pleasure, and in the meantime restricting our freedoms and the freedom of the press.'

That severe face of hers changes very quickly from indifference to the most conspicuous anger. Her eyes are fierce, the pupils dilating, and her mouth forms a different mask with every syllable she utters. Her right hand, raised halfway, starts to tremble, and her extended forefinger punctuates every declaration she makes. Sebastián, half repelled and half amazed, notices how easily she stamps her authority on the conversation, how agile her transition to a topic she holds dear and now she's reciting the names of ministers and other leaders, the ones who in her estimation don't even deserve the salary of a subordinate or the position of chauffeur or cleaning lady in the presidential palace. Sebastián's eyes sweep across her face, examining the mutable creases of her skin, the smallest details, and as her voice reaches his ear, it competes with the noises emanating from the dining room, the placement of the china on the tablecloth, the clinking of the silverware and glasses laid out by invisible hands in the next room. Sebastián is barely paying attention to her words, but even so he has no difficulty understanding her anger, seeing that it reflects not so much a critique of the current situation or the nation's politics but rather the spite his aunt feels for not being able to occupy that position herself, the position currently occupied by the woman who is the central target of her attacks.

To be cordial, to be prudent, he refrains from speaking when silence re-establishes itself in the house. Without inviting him to follow, his aunt simply gets up and walks towards the dining room, opening the large doors to reveal a setting already evacuated by the people who have prepared it. He follows her, clicking against the parquet floor with cautious steps, hesitating as to which chair he should occupy, sitting down only when she has taken her place at the head of the table. The display of food, modest and frugal, contrasts with the surrounding opulence: nothing but a lettuce salad with a few tomatoes and aubergine filled with something he can't quite make out, accompanied by a small quantity of water already poured into each crystal glass.

Forgoing any ceremony, she begins to serve herself with the same aplomb with which she resumes her previous litany, speaking now about the shady schemes of the country's new leaders who are blinded by power and supported, naturally, by the ignorant masses. Shady schemes involving the very same names she was listing moments before – opportunistic, dishonest and indecent people – in addition to, shockingly, 'some of the most unseemly members of the Mothers and Grandmothers of the Plaza de Mayo', she goes out of her way to emphasize. Sebastián is silent, and begins to reprimand himself. He's allowing her voice to impose itself on all other voices, on his own ideas or the ideas he might borrow, and his passivity while interacting with the woman sitting in front of him would disturb anyone witnessing this banal conversation.

And so, to upset her or to shatter his own cowardice and redeem his presence at the dining table, Sebastián forces himself to respond to her in a tone that is not feverish, but composed: 'I'm surprised by these rumours you boast of. We've heard nothing of this in Brazil. On the contrary, the people you insist on disparaging still enjoy enormous prestige there, as they do here.'

She takes advantage of the interruption to focus on the small bit of food she had set aside for herself. After a sip of water, she resumes her speech, as if there hadn't been any disruption, completely indifferent to his opinions but not even showing him any disdain, as though he were not worthy of her disdain. Her words initially sound neutral and cold, but little by little they become animated as she grows more and more emotional discussing the misery of elderly men deprived of their last years of life and liberty, helpless gentlemen locked away in their homes and practically denied the right to receive visitors, and all of them destined to a tragic end, forsaken, but for the sense of honour they've maintained, the fortitude that has always defined their character, the pride with which they still wear their uniforms, which are now too long for their arms and legs. Except for a few who are still in good health, they're all terribly feeble, she informs him, and now they're obliged to appear in court in their wheelchairs, and for what?

she asks. Do they have anything to answer for at this point, those elderly officers? Sure, they made some mistakes here and there – it was a war, after all – and sometimes they went too far and committed a few sins just like the others, but don't you think enough time has passed to forgive and forget?

Sebastián can do nothing but seek refuge in his dinner plate, wishing to express through silence his profound disagreement. Is she trying to provoke him? How can she openly defend those torturers, how can she allow herself to be so insensitive when her family, her own sister, was victimized by them? And how does she dare speak such nonsense to his face when those defenceless and forsaken old men were the same ones responsible for the erratic course of his destiny, by-product of his parents' destiny, the same ones who were to some degree his persecutors, as well?

His plate does not provide refuge, so he turns his face away to avoid looking at her directly and in doing so catches a glimpse of someone in his peripheral vision: there, on the sofa of the living room, leaning back and reading a newspaper with a few columns cut out, is one of those men in uniform. He's not young, indeed a number of the hairs in his moustache are grey, but neither is he a feeble old man, there's no crutch or wheelchair by his side. The man bites on the end of the pen he's holding, and his way of biting causes Sebastián to remember a gentleman he saw just once at a dinner long ago, at the wedding banquet of his oldest cousin. He recalls laughter abounding among the guests, but his father refused to smile, and his mother seemed troubled as she tried to calm him. Uneasy, not knowing if he should join in the fun, he decided to find out what the problem was. He discovered that, at a distant table, holding his fork tightly in his right hand, the man with the slightly grey moustache who was clamping down on a big hunk of meat, that man was a general by the name of Jorge Videla.

He resented his father that night and condemned his intolerance. Of what importance was the appearance of some general if that general wasn't even a relative of the bride or groom, if the entire family had gathered together for this event for the first time in a long while, everyone at that moment so lively and at ease? And even if indeed it was he, as they had explained, if that general, whoever he was, happened to be the person responsible for the years they had spent separated from everyone, expelled from their own home, exiled to São Paulo, why couldn't they enjoy themselves now that the punishment had been retracted? Now that his aunt is calmly cutting a slice of tomato and continuing to talk about the mistakes of the current government, exalting the economic vitality of previous decades, now that a man in uniform is sitting on the sofa tranquilly turning the pages of his yellowed newspaper, both man and newspaper obfuscated by Sebastián's dim peripheral vision, at last he understands what his father had been thinking at that party long ago, he feels the affliction his father must have felt, the anguish that must have weighed on him, and he wishes, too late, to escape from that night just as he wishes to escape from this dismal encounter.

He can't stand up, he can't remove his plate or leave the table and let her go on by herself, analysing the failings of a government without any muscle, a government averse to discipline. He's not capable of perpetuating the great insult of making an overly dramatic exit – he can still hear the voice of his mother asking him to be more accepting of the family even when he's all too aware of the antagonisms, even when he sometimes feels uncomfortable, oppressed, subjugated. He can't walk away, he can't allow the man in uniform to take his place at the grand table that belongs to everyone – he can't run off, he can't remain silent. He must clarify that he doesn't agree with anything she's said, he must express in some way his own discomfort, he must make his feelings known immediately: 'They murdered thirty thousand people. Not to mention the tortured, the persecuted, all those kidnapped children, all the forced migrations for which they were responsible. As frail as those officers might appear today, there is a symbolic importance in punishing them. So that they and their followers might understand, as much as possible, the terrible evil they perpetrated.'

His abrasive words, his heated tone and the sudden gravity of his voice take over the surrounding space and in some way protect him, calming him at least for a moment. And for a moment she seems affected by the force of his phrases, shaking her head from side to side, compelled this time to respond to him.

Her response, however, is a summary refusal to give any ground or offer concessions, returning him to the distress he had felt moments before and restoring her inexorable dominion over the room: 'These numbers are always inflated. Only the most rebellious, the most inconsequential, the insubordinate people died. It's the same in Argentina as it was in Pinochet's Chile, or Franco's Spain: a systematic effort to exaggerate the negative aspects. The only reason why the same thing doesn't happen in Brazil is because your military has always been too soft, so there wasn't anything to blame them for. Did some people die here, and in Chile, and even in Brazil? Yes. But the context justified those deaths. When order is being threatened, when there's a country to save . . .'

Sebastián can't go on listening, he is immersed in the torment from which he can no longer escape. To listen to those words is to let himself be trapped again between the walls of terror, to return to the structure of oppression, to its fulcrum, to the site of greater evil, it's to walk once more through the rooms of the Escuela Superior de Mecánica de la Armada, which he visited like a distracted tourist a few days ago, without realizing the effect it would have on him. His guide, a young and very serious woman, explained: the prisoners, hooded, their hands tied behind their backs, would enter through this door. There's another stairway over there that goes down to the torture chamber, but it was sealed up and hidden when this prison was about to be inspected, so let's go through here. Right where we're standing, the prisoners were undressed and subjected to a slow and meticulous ordeal – 'making them sing', that's what they called it. Nothing was off limits, the contorting of arms and legs, blows to the spine, everything was allowed, lacerations, breaking bones, applying electrical shocks, it was all valid, and they used the most diverse instruments. After a day or two, or however much time was necessary, they were all taken here, to the attic, which was extremely cold in the winter and oppressively hot in the summer, and they were locked in large wooden trunks, very similar to coffins. They would spend on average a week here while the information they had provided was confirmed and compared to other depositions, but there was really no limit to the amount of time they could be subjected to this horror. They were fed the minimum, water and scraps of bread, and, to distract them, the radio would be left playing all day long at extremely high volume, hindering their ability to think or to communicate with one another. They would wear the same hood for the whole week, then immediately it would be put on another head – the smell of this hood, the pestilence in the fibres, the nausea it produced, are palpable in the testimony of those few who survived, the prisoners who somehow gained the trust of those in command. If there happened to be a pregnant woman among the prisoners, they'd give her the same food the guards ate, they'd avoid any punishment that might hurt the foetus, they'd beat her only on her arms and legs, they'd pull out her hair, her nails. When she was about to give birth, they'd isolate the mother here, in this room reserved for delivering babies, and on the very same day the child would be taken to another family, handed over to the open arms of a couple not able to have children, a couple on friendly terms with the regime. Afterwards the mother joined a group of prisoners who were taken to the ground floor where they received an injection to make them docile for transfer. Unconscious, they were brought to the vans parked just outside, and then they were taken to a plane about to depart from the Aeroparque two kilometres up the avenue. When the plane was far enough away from the coast, when all that could be seen was blue sky and the wide mouth of the Río de la Plata, the bodies were thrown from the plane, still weakened by the anaesthesia, unable even to feel the vertigo, and one by one they plummeted through the void. Each of those death flights ended with the muffled sound of a body striking the cold surface of water.

She rouses him with the metallic sound of cutlery striking the china, her arms resting on the table now, nothing left on her plate. Her mouth at last seems exhausted of speech, she's satisfied, but there's a quivering in the corner of her lips that disturbs him. She's smiling, that's what he notices, nothing more than a mere reflex, very subtle. She smiles with her chin raised high, but she's discreet, sardonic, and he knows that smile isn't directed at him, it could only be directed at someone behind him, someone he can't see but whose presence makes a shadow, and the shadow grows larger, until it is undeniable. He doesn't need to turn his head, he's certain that there's no one sitting on the sofa now, that the living room is empty, and suddenly he feels two hands settling on his shoulders, two hands grabbing hold of him, softly, but they do not intend to let go of him, two hands that confine him to his chair, and without covering his mouth they silence him, two hands that evoke everything and make everything disappear from his memory, two hands that are gentle but nevertheless they place on his shoulders a tremendous weight. ∎

GRANTA

A TEMPORARY STAY

Emilio Fraia

TRANSLATED BY KATRINA DODSON

EMILIO FRAIA
1982

© Renato Parada

Emilio Fraia was born in São Paulo.
He is an editor at the publishing house Cosac Naify and
has also worked as a journalist for the magazines *piauí*
and *Trip*. He co-wrote the novel *O verão do Chibo* (2008) with
Vanessa Barbara, which was shortlisted for the São Paulo Prize
for Literature, and is currently working on the graphic novel
Campo em branco with the illustrator D.W. Ribatski.
'A Temporary Stay' ('Temporada') is a new story.

The leg with the bum knee drags as he walks. The caretaker runs ahead to shut off the water valves, start up the pump. His only remaining staff are the ageing caretaker and a fat housekeeper who doesn't let a day go by without airing out the rooms, to let some life pass through, as she says.

It's a place of tarnished cutlery, outdated gym equipment, a marble fireplace, filthy cloth napkins. Towards the back of the patio, the unused bar shares the space with a purple hot tub in which people have left behind oars, bags of fertilizer, a tennis net, a pair of Le Coq Sportifs missing their laces. In a low voice, he runs down an inventory: sheets, stacks of plates, chipped teacups, the wooden owls in the entrance hall.

They stand side by side at the edge of the swimming pool, Nilo and the caretaker. They watch the water draining away. Nilo rests his hands on his waist, thumbs hooked in his waistband – the water has left a line of scum on the tiles two feet from the top. We'll know soon enough whether or not he's in there, Nilo says.

Years ago, when he'd first had the pool built, he'd imagined one of those sweeping stretches of water: bright, blue, crystalline. But the water that gets pumped in from the river is murky. At this time of year, it only gets worse, turning muddy from the rains. The caretaker shakes his head and says it doesn't make any sense whatsoever. If he were really in there, sir, the body would have floated to the surface. The caretaker asks something else. The drainage system is chugging at full force and Nilo doesn't hear the question. Nor does the caretaker repeat it. But the judge could easily have gone on a binge. He could have had way too much to drink and fallen in. The caretaker sighs. They go back to just focusing on the water.

The two men stand there, unable to make out anything that looks remotely like the bottom. Under his breath, Nilo runs down the inventory: towels, boots, riding helmets, seed packets. He asks when they're going to plant the pumpkins. The caretaker says they've already been planted, two weeks ago. The racket from the pump disorientates him even further.

It was two weeks ago that all this trouble with the judge first began. Or three. Nilo had been lying in one of the deckchairs, trying to read – a book on the importance of sleep for leading a happy life – when their car pulled up, the retired appeals-court judge and his wife. She was driving. She was frail and nervous-looking. He thought she was awful, not exactly for being ugly, though she was ugly too, but because she seemed high-strung and disapproving. They got out of the car. The wife asked if there was a room available. As they stood on the patio, the shadows of Nilo and the couple lengthened alongside one another, the sun drawing them over the cracked slate of the entryway. They'd come on a friend's recommendation – but it had been a long time ago, and they'd remembered it as they'd been passing through Redenção, which didn't happen very often, the wife added, since they almost never travelled through the rural areas of São Paulo state. They'd gone to a cousin's wedding the night before. Its theme had been 'A Thousand and One Nights!' The judge's shadow flowed out from a pair of white tennis shoes, while the wife's head intersected the angle of a planter, giving her shadow an extravagantly sculpted coiffure.

Thinking back on it now, Nilo regrets his decision. He doesn't know what he'd been thinking. The hotel's been shut down for at least a year. They weren't supposed to be taking guests any more. The caretaker lowers his head as the water drains away, disappears. Nilo returns to the topic of pumpkins. He asks how long it'll be before they can harvest the pumpkins. The caretaker sighs and answers that if the weather cooperates, it'll take forty days, fifty at most. Under his breath, Nilo goes over the list of where things are kept: keys, check-in forms, skin cream, fish food. The caretaker sighs again, decides to take action. He grabs hold of the pool ladder. At the third step, he hops down and sloshes across the tiles. The water comes up to the top of his boots. He swishes his soles around trying to come across something – an arm, a leg, a torso. They look at each other, Nilo standing at the edge, the caretaker down in the pool: it doesn't make any sense whatsoever. No sign of the judge. Nilo blinks a few times. At this point, even he doesn't understand why he had the caretaker drain the pool.

The next several hours elapse as though part of a long drawn-out match punctuated by hard-won points. Nilo goes back to searching the rooms, the orchard, the storage shed. Afterwards, he gives up. He falls asleep in the deckchair with his mouth half open and the book on his chest.

In the late afternoon, a sound wakes him up. At first it's far away, indistinct, then comes echoing through the mountains, getting closer and closer. It's a car honking. From where he's lying, without getting up, Nilo watches the caretaker walk out to the front gate. There's the horn, the pop-pop of the motor, the smell of exhaust. A red VW Beetle sputters across the expanse of lawn overrun by vegetation. It parks. The judge gets out. He looks excited. He explains how he went into town the night before. He made the acquaintance of two *absolutely remarkable* individuals. He bought the Beetle from one of them. And a house from the other. Paid for the Beetle in cash. Wrote two cheques for the house. He announces all of this enthusiastically, banging on the rusty hood with joy.

2

It was supposed to have been just a temporary stay, but the days go by, and the judge doesn't check out. Every two weeks, he settles the bill for his room, drinks, meals. Always in cash. His wife visits on the weekends.

She's trying to convince him that this whole thing is ridiculous. The judge invokes the fresh air. The river water. His wife says that if it were only a matter of these things, then all he had to do was go to the country club. During the week, they communicate by cellphone. She's the one who calls. It's hard to hear, the reception's so bad, the judge tells Nilo. His son never calls. His daughter and her husband promise to visit. But they never show up.

One afternoon, the judge says he saw a hog lying in the middle of the road. It looked like a bull. It was pink. *Absolutely remarkable.* They stared at each other for a while, until the hog got up on its hooves and with a heavy shuffle disappeared into the undergrowth.

When he tells of this encounter, contrary to all those stories involving men and animals, stories of tenderness, mutual understanding, tales of awe, of wild beasts lying in wait, primal encounters, the judge announces that he'd like to eat that hog. Living at the hotel are: a half-dozen hens, a skinny horse, ducks, two cows, a rooster, a stuffed parrot. Not a single pig. Nilo offers to have some excellent pork sent over from Redenção. The judge says that he's not talking about any old hog, he's talking about *that* hog.

This conversation occurs on the concrete risers that sometimes serve as spectator stands alongside the tennis court. It's a hot day. Nilo sends the caretaker off to enquire at the neighbouring farms. He knows that one of them raises livestock but can't remember which. Or is he imagining things? He's feeling worn out, in a fog. A faded white line divides the court in half. Sitting next to him, the judge wipes the sweat from his brow. He says they need to fix the air conditioning in his room. Ever since the judge arrived at the hotel, they've spent the afternoons together in conversation. Nilo and the judge compare various ailments: rheumatism, sciatica, lower-back pain. His knee aches. When he tries to remember things, his mind spins in place. He concentrates harder. Certain episodes fail to cohere. There doesn't seem to be any cause and effect. Nilo makes an inventory of what the judge is wearing: a New York Knicks cap, tennis shoes, white socks, a gold watch. Indiscernibly, without the slightest sound, or without any sound that he can make out, an airplane crosses the sky. Nilo raises his hand to his forehead, like a visor.

When the plane vanishes, he tells the judge that it reminds him, the story about the pig, that is, of the fox that used to prowl around the building where he stayed in London for a time, during the period in his life that, now that he thinks of it – Nilo blinks – seems to explain everything that came after.

3

In retrospect, it was rather childish, some kind of strained and awkward attempt at camaraderie: Nilo and the red-headed English major plotting how to catch the fox that kept on overturning the garbage cans outside the Goldsmiths residence hall where he'd been staying that summer. They weren't exactly friends. Nilo didn't have any friends. In those days, he had a certain distaste for the company of others. He was single-mindedly driven by tennis. He was always training, never went out. Whenever he ran into the red-headed guy, in the cafeteria, he kept to his usual telegraphic mode of making conversation, nothing too personal. At night, from the second floor, he'd watch the fox knocking over rubbish bins as it circled the building.

One day, in passing, they happened to mention the fox and soon began discussing the best way to trap it. They considered spreading glue on the welcome mat. Stuffing a piece of meat with sleeping pills. Building one of those Rube Goldberg contraptions in which the fox's paw would trip a mechanism that would knock over a line of dominoes, the last of which would propel a toy car that would drop onto the on/off switch for a fan whose wind would inflate the sail of a little boat that would, after crossing a puddle, slice through a wire with its saw-shaped prow, making the net plummet, and they'd capture the fox.

One morning, Nilo bought a postcard. It depicted a generic scene of Piccadilly Circus, with the fountain and the statue of Eros in the background. In the picture, there was snow everywhere and the statue was shrouded in fog. Later on, after returning to his room, he took another look at the card. He regretted his decision. He'd chosen the wrong one.

He flipped it over anyway and wrote a note to his fiancée. But he couldn't decide whether or not to mail the postcard. He was getting sleepy. Feeling exhausted. He'd been training five to six hours per day. In his spare time, Nilo would go to see apartments and houses in the area around Kilburn. His days were numbered at the residence hall. His fiancée was arriving soon, and they'd have to find a larger place. His fiancée was a violinist. That year, she'd watched from the sidelines as he jumped from 492nd in the world rankings to 385th and then to 310th. But the win in Buenos Aires and what had come after – the sponsorship offer, the invitation to play in Europe, the temporary stay in London – had taken them both by surprise.

One day he was jumping rope when a young man wearing a bandanna approached him. Whenever he didn't go to train with his coach on the grass courts at West Heath Lawn, he'd use the university facilities. It was good, in a way, because then he didn't have to cross the city. Goldsmiths was in New Cross and having to go all the way to Hampstead every day wasn't exactly thrilling. It didn't make any sense that the sponsors had set him up with this housing at Goldsmiths. It was an austere building with few amenities and not so conveniently located. Had the other housing options already been taken by better players? The bandanna guy asked if he wanted to hit a few. They walked out of the gym, chatting about rackets, grips. To warm up, they rallied, alternating between the far corners. When they started keeping score, he served a series of aces – the bandanna guy was pulled wide, skidded off the court.

So Nilo decided to rein in his serve. Pace himself. Dragging the games out with easy rallies. Letting the other guy think he stood a chance of winning, so he'd give it his all.

On the way back to the residence hall, he passed a line of trees and two other tennis courts. Someone called his name and Nilo recognized his red-headed neighbour waving from the stands overlooking one of the courts. Towel around his shoulders, he climbed the metal bleachers and sat down. He hadn't known that his neighbour was interested in tennis. The redhead said that actually he didn't have any interest in the sport. On the court, two girls were engaged in an aggressive match. The one with the ponytail and wine-coloured skirt spun her racket, stood at the ready. When the ball came: she slammed it violently, crying out. The red-headed guy said he had a theory. They sat in silence until Nilo asked: What's your theory? The redhead explained that there was a way to tell how big the tennis players' pussies were based on the way they cried out. It worked for every single girl. There was a science to it, he said. He could provide more details if Nilo wanted. When their attention turned back to the court, the player in the wine-coloured skirt was on the ground. She seemed to have fallen on her arm. She was sitting near the baseline, her racket lying halfway to the net. A small group had gathered around her.

The following week, Nilo competed in a tournament in Brighton. The week after that, in Oxford. Then he went to Paris. He always spent most of his time at the hotel. Everything turned out as expected, the matches never really posing any serious challenge. In Paris, he struck up a friendship with the maid, who brought him extra towels without his having to ask. In the evenings, he called his fiancée. They talked about: the competition, the conservatory, his parents, her parents, metro stations, parks, the launderette.

Back in London, he took a shower and headed down to the cafeteria. The meal service had already ended, but residents could still use the kitchen. The stove was next to a large window. Nilo heated up a can of Indian chicken curry. He thought about how he liked playing tennis. He'd spent most of his childhood and adolescence doing it.

But suddenly he wondered if he'd go on liking it.

Then he heard a noise. Through the glass, he saw the fox dragging plastic bags along the ground, scattering trash all over the entryway. He believed that if he managed to emulate what he most admired in the players he envied, he'd be able to create an uber-style. But nothing was really that simple.

When he got outside, the fox was no longer there. Nilo took a walk around the building. He pissed in a bush. Two hippies passed by. To the sound of his urine splashing onto the leaves, he thought: If the fox got away, then pissing on the bush would even the score. A fox is not a pig. The fox is more elusive. A pig and a fox are not the same at all.

4

O ne night, Nilo met up with the coach and his wife at a pub. He spotted them from a distance. They were leaning against the bar with a girl he didn't recognize.

As he got closer, he had the feeling he'd seen her somewhere before. He said hello. They were introduced. She was a friend of the wife's.

They asked if he wanted a drink. As he leaned forward to order a shot of whisky and an apple juice to chase it down, Nilo remembered who she was. The tennis player from Goldsmiths. He mentioned the coincidence and asked if her arm was all right. She said yes. It had taken a month to heal, but now it was better.

A long conversation ensued. She recounted how as a teenager she had competed in a few tournaments. She'd considered going pro, but life had taken her in other directions. She'd studied English at university. She'd taken a diving course in New Zealand. That's where her father and her grandparents were from, she said. Her great-great-grandparents were English. They'd emigrated around 1850 or so. Then, at the beginning of the century, she explained, her father had made the opposite trip and returned to England, just before the war. Another group joined them, more friends of his coach. She pointed, it was his birthday, the guy in the ridiculous sports coat. They discussed the coat, started referring to the birthday boy as 'the guy in the ridiculous sports coat'. She switched from beer to whisky. Bursts of laughter broke out, toasts – he'd lost sight of his coach. She was talking about various streets, museums, parks, all the places he still hadn't gone to and needed to visit. She showed him a picture. That's my favourite park, she said. She was in the photo, from the waist up, eyes closed and leaning against a bridge. She told him she didn't think she'd ever really stopped playing, stopped taking it seriously, she meant. But looking back on it, everything seemed to make sense. She'd started getting more involved with her classes at university. She'd met a girl who played tennis a lot better than she did. But it was impossible to know what really made the difference in her decision to give up trying to go pro. Maybe it hadn't been either of those things at all. Like they say: I started getting into linguistics and I was spending less and less time playing tennis, until it just got swallowed up entirely. Or maybe: I was meant to stop playing tennis precisely so I could start getting interested in linguistics – it was fate. Or it was that I had to stop being interested in tennis so that I could get to know another girl who was so much better than me and not be totally devastated by it. When I read about people who've died, I think to myself, so that's how someone's going to write about me some day? With one fact explaining another, and my every inspiration? As if anyone could know anything about a life. He'd had too much to drink and didn't know whether he'd really been following it all, but everything came back to him on the bus ride home. He stuck his middle finger down his throat, tried to vomit, because he'd feel better if he vomited. He heaved, but couldn't make anything come up. He leaned his head against the window and the pool in the university gym loomed larger at night. That was the impression he had, as he plunged in while everyone else was in their rooms sleeping, or out at parties, freshman mixers, smoke-filled apartments. He sat at the edge of the pool with his legs in the water. He couldn't see to the bottom. It was as if somewhere on the other side, there was an inverse world in which a confused old man, a perfect stranger, was searching for him. It didn't make any sense whatsoever. The gym was dark, but there were points of light outlining the pool. Its surface glittered coldly.

The phone woke him up in the morning. It was an estate agent. He said there was an apartment Nilo had to see, close to Regent's Canal. They agreed to meet at the place in two hours.

Nilo emerged from the tube station. It took him a while to find the street, but soon he realized that he'd passed by it. Bergholt Mews. At the end of the block, there was some kind of garden with a tree in it.

From a distance, he saw a man, probably the estate agent, a short guy with greying hair wearing a blue suit and gloves. The man handed Nilo the keys. He said he had to go – he was holding a handkerchief over his mouth, it looked as though he had a toothache. Without ever taking the handkerchief from his mouth, he instructed Nilo to leave the keys in the drawer of the table on the ground floor when he was done. If Nilo liked the apartment, the man said, he knew how to get in touch.

The building had two storeys. The apartment was on the upper floor. Nilo walked up the stairs. The entry hall was dark but well maintained. He turned the key. Outlines of formerly hung paintings marked the wall in the hallway. He wandered around the living room, looked out the window. The place wasn't very big, nor was it small. Everything was in perfect condition. The rooms felt nice and airy. The street outside was quiet.

When he went back to the residence hall, he'd call his fiancée. Then he'd call the estate agent. But first he sat down in a corner of the living room. He couldn't really say how long he'd been there, or when he'd started crying. Not a steady sort of weeping. It was a spasm, two or three sobs, as though some prolonged discontent had traversed his body and finally reached his throat. In two weeks, his fiancée would be in town. He probably wouldn't be able to pick her up at the airport, he'd be training. They would agree to meet at the apartment. He'd take a shower in the locker room. Then start thinking about his fiancée: she'd have set down her luggage already, been through all the rooms, the kitchen, looked out the window in the laundry room, seen the yard, and now she'd be sitting at the dining-room table, in front of the meal, checking her watch. He wouldn't have arrived yet, but soon he'd join her, and he'd tell her about the fox. ■

VALDIR PERES, JUANITO AND POLOSKEI

Antonio Prata

TRANSLATED BY DANIEL HAHN

ANTONIO PRATA
1977

Antonio Prata was born in São Paulo.
He has published nine books, including *Douglas* (2001),
As pernas da tia Corália (2003), *Adulterado* (2009) and,
most recently, *Meio intelectual, meio de esquerda* (2010). Prata
also writes for television and contributes a literary column to the
newspaper *Folha de S. Paulo*. 'Valdir Peres, Juanito and Poloskei'
('Valdir Peres, Juanito e Poloskei') is a new story.

A t first, everybody on the street had the same purchasing power, and belongings per capita comprised a bicycle, a football, a box of Playmobil, some building blocks and other odds and ends. With the release of the sticker album for the '82 World Cup, however, we did notice a slight change in the distribution of wealth: some got five little packs a day, others were entitled to ten, but really nothing that might threaten our socio-economic balance. When all was said and done, what with suffering at the lack of the rarest ones – Sócrates, Maradona and Paolo Rossi – and disdaining the duplicates – Valdir Peres, Juanito and Poloskei – we all learned the law of supply and demand, and we understood the pleasures and hardships of the middle class. Until the day Rodrigo showed up with the remote-control jeep.

T he father of Rodrigo, my neighbour in the house to the left, was a tennis player. From the ages of twelve to nineteen, he never lost a match, and people in the know said that he was going to be one of the greatest players of all time, but on his twentieth birthday he had a motorcycle accident, injured his shoulder and was never able to compete again. Since then he'd spent his days at home, smoking pot and listening to prog rock. The family was supported by his wife, an ophthalmologist. None of the neighbours had much confidence, then, when Rodrigo's father called them up, each of them in turn, to talk business.

Every night for a week, the same scene was repeated. He would receive the potential business partner in the TV room, offer them a beer and then strike up a chat about football, which seemed to be merely the warm-up to his main subject. Then, quite casually, he would ask the neighbour if they'd seen the Corinthians match the previous Sunday. Whatever the response, he would add: 'Actually I didn't see it myself, but I'm going to watch it now.' The expression of curiosity on his interlocutor's face was his cue to raise the cloth – an old towel on top of the television set, under which was hidden a rectangular silver object. 'This is a video-cassette player,' he'd explain, pointing at the novelty his brother-in-law had just brought back from the USA. 'It records programmes and plays films that you can buy or rent on any street corner nowadays in the United States.'

The demonstration would begin with the previous Sunday's game, it would take in a few scenes from *Star Wars* and had as its climax, appropriately, *Deep Throat*, brought over by his brother-in-law from the same trip. 'It won't be long,' he'd say, 'before everyone will have a video-cassette player. Everyone! And what's the most lucrative kind of film in this industry?' the ex-tennis player would ask, fanning himself, none too discreetly, with the cover of the porn tape. If each of his neighbours were to come in with ten thousand cruzeiros (the price of a fridge in those days), they could open up an 'adult films' rental shop, and within the year, he swore, they would be rich.

None of the inhabitants of the street took the bait. Some out of modesty, others because the idea had come from a guy who spent his days stoned, sitting in the living room of his house, listening to Jethro Tull and playing solos on air guitar. One night that week, I heard the father of Henrique, my neighbour from the house to the right, commenting to his wife: 'Well, that gizmo is actually pretty cool, but it's just one of those gringo things. Take it from me, the craze isn't going to catch on here.'

Rodrigo's father, however, wasn't discouraged: he managed to get money from his brother-in-law, raised a bit more from the bank, persuaded his wife to sell the car and opened the rental place. Six months later, at Christmastime, he wasn't yet rich, but he did have enough money to give his son a 4×4 remote-control jeep.

On the twenty-fifth of December, while the adults were eating the leftovers of the Christmas turkey, the children would be out on the pavement premiering the gifts they'd received the night before. I was focused on trying to detach the hair from a Playmobil figure, when I heard the buzzing sound – the sound a bee would make, if it were the size of a cat. A metre away from us, facing us off like an animal all set to pounce, was the jeep, about forty centimetres long.

It backed up, turned towards the left and began to circle us. When it had returned to where it had started from, Rodrigo appeared from behind a tree, the remote control in his hands and an undisguisable expression of pride on his face. He walked over to us, deep in concentration, the tip of his tongue poking out the side of his mouth, as he made the jeep do bootleg turns. When he was standing in front of us, he looked up from the controls, looked right at us with an air of infinite superiority, and just said: 'It's American.'

We contemplated the toy in solemn silence, while Rodrigo contemplated the toy's power over us. It was Henrique who had the courage to ask the question that was in the minds of everyone there: 'Can I have a go?' It was the cue Rodrigo had been waiting for. 'No, you don't know how to do it, you'll break it.' Having said that, he turned his back and walked off home, the car at his side, like a well-trained dog.

The jeep would have been an isolated event on the street – the rise of one particular family, who would soon move to another neighbourhood, leaving behind them a few memories and a touch of envy – if Henrique's father had not also begun to earn some money.

Henrique's father was a university lecturer, but he'd left the faculty two years earlier to take over a carpet shop, which he'd inherited from his grandfather, a man from Lebanon. At first he struggled to understand how the whole business worked and he nearly had to shut the place down, but after a year spent working himself to the bone, sales began to improve. He opened a branch in the new shopping centre, in the Zona Norte, and the first sign of his prosperity reached the street six months after the Christmas of the jeep, on Henrique's birthday.

It was a late afternoon, in June. Rodrigo and I were competing for a sticker of Fillol, the Argentinian goalie, while others watched us, standing or sitting on their bicycle seats. That was when we heard the buzzing, much louder than the noise Rodrigo's jeep had made – it was the sound three bees would have made if they'd been the size of three cats. When we turned, we found ourselves face to face with Henrique, in dark glasses and a beige uniform, sitting on a little electric motorbike, a faithful copy of the one used by CHiPs, the highway patrol from the television series. Without a word he accelerated straight past us. He went as far as the parkland at the end of the road, which we used to call the Bush, then returned, calm and haughty like Jon Baker or Frank Poncherello, the cops from the TV programme. Rodrigo pretended none of it had anything to do with him, but when he slapped his hand down to claim the sticker, Fillol stuck to the sweat on his palm.

From then on, no one was interested in the jeep. All we thought about was having a go on the CHiPs bike. Sometimes Henrique would let one of us ride it, but only sometimes, and even then he would run alongside. 'Not too fast, it'll break!', 'Careful with the pothole!', 'Only as far as the tree, then give it back!'

Henrique's reign lasted several months, and there didn't seem to be anything to threaten it before Christmas, but at the start of the eighties the porn industry was storming ahead, which meant that by September, on a perfectly average Wednesday, there came Rodrigo's response.

It was around noon, and we were conducting the funeral of Fonseca, the Australian parakeet belonging to Ernesto, a red-headed boy who lived at the end of the road. Australian parakeets didn't have the status of dogs and cats, not even of turtles or hamsters, and Ernesto had organized the ceremony less out of any attachment to the bird, who had been found lying stiffly at the bottom of his cage that morning, than for the amusing possibilities of the burial. The funeral moved on foot from Ernesto's house to the Bush, some forty metres away, where a little grave awaited us, already opened up with twigs and ice-lolly sticks, in a bed of violets. The deceased was in a shoebox, with Henrique's bike standing in for a hearse. Ernesto walked alongside, his hand on the handlebar, controlling the speed – a privilege Henrique had granted him, I don't know whether out of respect for his bereavement or as a guarantee that the deceased would travel by motorbike.

We were already nearing the Bush when the electric murmur of the little bike was overwhelmed by a loud roar, so loud that it would be useless to try and compare it to the humming of bees, even if they were as big as tigers: what we were hearing was the unmistakable din of an internal combustion engine. The cortège stopped, we turned, and found ourselves face to face with Rodrigo, in helmet and gloves, on a red Fapinha mini-buggy.

(To say that a mini-buggy was to childhood what a Ferrari is to adulthood is inaccurate, because once we've grown up not everyone is interested in cars, while at eight there wasn't a single boy who didn't dream of having a Fapinha; it would be no exaggeration, then, to say that there was not, nor will there ever be, an object more coveted by every man born between the sixties and eighties of the last century.)

All it took was for Rodrigo to come past the funeral, and that was enough for the glory days of Henrique's motorbike to be brought to an end, but Rodrigo wanted more. He'd been suffering over the downfall of his jeep and the sight of the other boy from head to toe in his CHiPs outfit more than three months earlier: not only did he give everyone a ride on the back of the little car, almost crushing the brand new mini-buggy, but he also offered up the passenger seat to transport Fonseca, the ex-parakeet. Henrique followed behind, alone on his bike, inhaling the exhaust fumes. After that he was quiet for weeks, kicking gravel, breaking twigs, cutting worms in half and squashing ants. He knew the competition had come to an end. What could his father buy? A mini-helicopter? A mini-submarine? There was no place left to go, they had hit the ceiling: the only path to tread, from now on, was downward.

On the twenty-third of December, after dinner, Henrique turned up at my place, nervous. I was still at the table and my mother had just gone to the kitchen carrying the plates. 'I've got a plan,' he whispered, glancing inside, afraid to be heard, and gestured for me to follow him out to the street.

We stopped outside Rodrigo's house. I reminded Henrique that our neighbour was away. He had gone with his family to spend Christmas in Chile to see his first snow. Rodrigo smiled slightly. 'Precisely,' he said, taking a broom handle from its hiding place in the bushes and taking aim at the front door: an iron frame with four rectangles of tinted glass, one above the other. 'If we break them, we can get in.' I didn't understand. The space left by the glass was big enough for us to slip into the house, but never enough for us to bring out the buggy. 'It's not the buggy,' he muttered between his teeth. Only then did I understand: what my friend was planning was an attack that would have symbolic impact. He had lost the war, he knew that, and his revenge would be to capture, a year after the start of hostilities, the thing that had first sparked the conflict, which awaited us on the upper floor of the house, in Rodrigo's room, at the back of a cupboard: the remote-control jeep. Perhaps Henrique was going to hide it under his bed, or perhaps he'd smash it up with a hammer and bury the remains in the Bush, I don't know: the important thing was to steal it.

I was scared to take part, and even more scared to try and stop him and look like a coward, so I just stood there, while he made an assault on the glass in the door using the broom handle like a battering ram. The first time, nothing happened. The second, again nothing. Then he stepped back to the pavement, gathered momentum, and this time, yes, this time he got what he wanted. Or nearly: as the glass smashed into thousands of tiny shards, the noise reverberated down the street and we raced off, each of us back to his own home. I don't know how, but we were found out, the grown-ups made the connection to me as an accomplice and the cost of fixing the door was split between my parents and Henrique's.

The following month, Henrique's family, who now had carpet shops scattered across the city, moved into a penthouse apartment in Morumbi. Not long afterwards, Rodrigo and his parents also left, for a house with a pool, in Jardim América – they had by that time seven porn rental places in São Paulo, two in Rio de Janeiro and another in Brasília.

A week after Rodrigo moved, an estate agent turned up on the street, and there was a couple with him. He showed the house to the potential buyers, and on the way out I saw him hiding the key in the fuse box. Late that night, without waking my parents, I slipped out of bed, took the key and entered the house. I walked across the hall, in the dark so as not to attract the attention of the neighbours, up the stairs, went into my friend's room and opened the cupboard in which the jeep had been kept. I knew how unlikely it was, almost impossible, but what did I have to lose? I found a single blue sock, a bald Playmobil figure, eight stickers of Valdir Peres, three of Juanito and seventeen Poloskeis. ∎

AMIS

BARKER

BARNES

BOYD

ISHIGURO

MARS-JONES

McEWAN

RUSHDIE

SWIFT

TREMAIN

2

BANKS

DE BERNIERES

HOLLINGHURST

KENNEDY

NORFOLK

OKRI

PHILLIPS

SELF

SIMPSON

WINTERSON

CUSK KUNZRU LITT MITCHELL O'HAGAN PEACE SEIFFERT SMITH THIRLWELL WATERS

The world's
most accurate
literary crystal
ball is back!

SPRING 2013

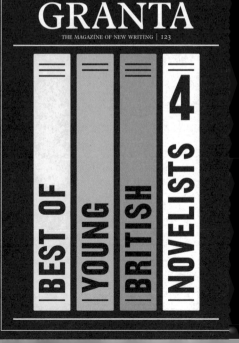

GRANTA
THE MAGAZINE OF NEW WRITING | 123

BEST OF YOUNG BRITISH NOVELISTS 4

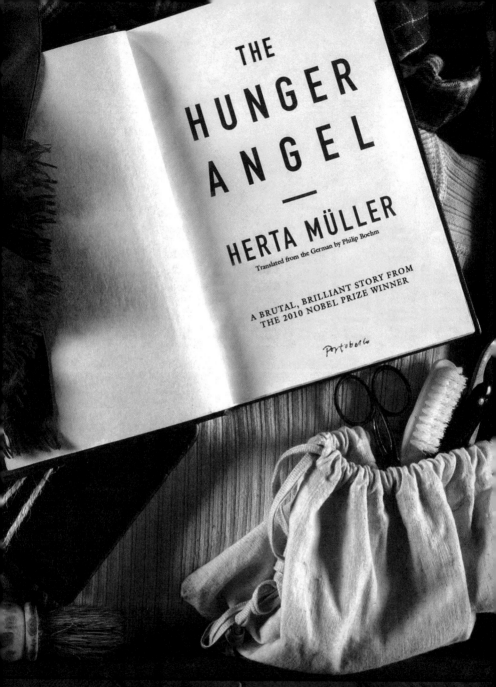

THE
HUNGER
ANGEL

—

HERTA MÜLLER

Translated from the German by Philip Boehm

A BRUTAL, BRILLIANT STORY FROM
THE 2010 NOBEL PRIZE WINNER

Portobello

'A work of rare force'
Times Literary Supplement

PORTOBELLOBOOKS.COM

GRANTA

TOMORROW, UPON AWAKENING

Antônio Xerxenesky

TRANSLATED BY INA RILKE

ANTÔNIO XERXENESKY
1984

© Stephanie C. L. Fernandes

Antônio Xerxenesky was born in Porto Alegre.
His first novel, *Areia nos dentes*, was published in 2008 and his
collection of short stories, *A página assombrada por fantasmas*, in 2011.
Xerxenesky has collaborated with several newspapers, magazines
and websites, including *Estado de S. Paulo*, *Suplemento de Pernambuco*
and Blog do IMS. In 2007, his short story 'O desvio' was adapted for
television by the screenwriter Fernando Mantelli. English translations
of his work can be found at wordswithoutborders.com and the
online edition of *Two Lines* magazine. 'Tomorrow, upon Awakening'
('Amanha, quando acordar') is taken from his story collection.

There is a clear distinction to be made between Christmas celebrations and those of the new year. The former are family occasions, or, for those without family, sad get-togethers with friends (and even then only close friends, the ones regarded as family). But New Year celebrations, being held in a spirit of renewal, an atmosphere of 'from now on everything will be different', of 'put it all behind you, here comes 2011', are all about good riddance, and nobody really wants to celebrate that sort of thing with people as permanent as family. Seeing in the new year is a ritual to be undertaken with friends, lovers, casual acquaintances. The city of Porto Alegre empties out completely, leaving only beggars in the streets, while the lower-middle, middle-middle and upper-middle classes flock to the Rio Grande do Sul and Santa Catarina beaches, where they celebrate the turn of the year as if it were a carnival compressed into a single day. Which explains all those crazy stories that do the rounds, like: 'I screwed two chicks at New Year,' or: 'Then we all went skinny-dipping,' or: 'I took acid and lay on the sand and watched the fireworks.'

He, for his part, had had no such experiences. At nineteen years of age he felt he had missed out on every opportunity for a good time, breaking free, getting some kicks. He had never even travelled on his own (that is, without his family). So in the new year he would make sure things were different, and now was a good time to start. The way he spent this New Year's Eve would be a symbol of what was in store, an introductory ritual to the adventures he would have in his twenties, making up for his boring teens and a childhood which, if not sad, had certainly been dreary.

That was the plan. He had rented a house in Imbé (with financial help from his father); a small town with few buildings and a cold, brown sea. It was a bit far away from his friends, who would be on the neighbouring beaches, but he was taking his girlfriend Juliane. His very first trip alone with a girl. Even if this escapade was still far removed from the kind of kicks his friends went on about, in him it aroused sentiments of epic proportions. To him, aged nineteen, having sex was no routine occurrence – each time was new and amazing and special. He didn't like to admit it, but Juliane was his first lover. She was three years younger than he was, but seemed infinitely more experienced – if not more experienced, then at any rate more relaxed about sex, and consequently more relaxed about the world in general.

They arrive at Imbé on 30 December, after some tense moments in the car because he isn't sure if he has taken the right road. They leave their bags in the rented house (pretty, despite hideous furnishings and a musty smell). Darkness falls.

They go out to meet some friends who are having a barbecue on the next beach, Tramandaí. The evening goes well. More friends arrive. One guy opens the boot of his car and connects a sound system, turning the volume up loud enough to provide party music for an entire neighbourhood. Juliane drinks beer. So does he. He keeps glancing at his watch: the truth is he can't wait to say ciao to his friends and to the horrendous noise, and go home to bed with Juliane, get down to some full-blown intimacy and fall asleep together in the small hours (so that he'd know what it felt like to sleep next to a woman).

It is 2 a.m. by the time they return to their rented house in Imbé. He drives nervously, opens the front door nervously, draws Juliane to the bed and scrambles out of his clothes nervously, almost shaking with nerves, like a teenager taken to a brothel by his uncle (an experience his friends claim to have had but not he, and now it's too late).

They wake up at noon. It is the 31st, the last day of the year. Tomorrow will be 2011. They have lunch (they've brought packets of instant noodles). She wants to go to the beach. He prefers going to the supermarket while it's still open, to stock up on beer and sparkling wine for tonight, not to mention the pork for the traditional *pernil*, the grapes and the lentils. So that's what they do. He takes his time going round the shelves, determined not to overlook a single ingredient of the good-luck rituals, because all rituals matter. Everything is a symbol, and he more than anybody else needs to define his symbols for the year to come, his year of change.

He drops his purchases off at the house and walks to the shore to meet up with Juliane. She told him earlier that she would stay on the nearest beach, the one at the bottom of the road. But finding her isn't as easy as anticipated, the sand is packed with people and parasols and dogs and children and beach chairs and corncobs and empty beer cans and soda bottles. There's a competition going on (not official) for the car with the loudest sound system. Three women in bikinis are dancing around a Celta – much to the dismay of the owner of the Corsa, whose music has attracted just one pot-bellied man holding a cup of maté.

He spends half an hour looking for her. Each time he spots a head of blonde shoulder-length hair he waits for the person to turn round in case it's Juliane, but it never is. He gives up and returns to the house. The first thing he sees upon entering is her pink, sunburned back (she didn't use suntan lotion and her fair skin can't take the sun). He tells her about his search on the beach, to which she smiles and says: 'We must've just missed each other – while you were looking for me, I picked up my stuff and came home. The sun's too strong out there.' And she's right: the sun *is* too strong, in spite of the clouds which do nothing to cool the air, only trap the heat.

They while away the time with a game of poker, then go to bed. Come six o'clock, he gets up, puts the groceries on the kitchen table and starts making supper. She opens the fridge and starts drinking. Night falls, as ever. They eat the roast pork. He has overdone the pepper, and the rosemary tastes a bit strange, but she doesn't comment on this. They clink with beer (the sparkling wine is for later on, at midnight). They discuss whether or not to go down to the beach to watch the fireworks, whether or not to jump over the waves (which must be done seven times in succession for good luck in 2011). Is she wearing white panties? he asks. All the papers have been going on about white being the lucky colour, so wearing no panties is preferable to wearing black ones. She claps her hand to her forehead and says: 'Silly me! I forgot all about taking a shower!' and runs off to the bathroom.

He has brought a book with him to Imbé, something warmly recommended by an uncle of his, a professor of literature. The title is somewhat pompous – *Tomorrow in the Battle, Think on Me* – and the novel is rather long. There's not much point in starting it now, as he will have to stop when she comes out of the bathroom. So he switches the TV on, puts his brain in neutral and watches the new year celebrations taking place around the globe. His eyelids droop.

He is not sure whether he dozed off, but has the feeling that a long time has elapsed. It's eleven o'clock. He can still hear the shower running.

He goes over to the bathroom. Thinks to barge in and surprise her. Instead, he knocks on the door timidly. 'Everything OK?' No answer, and a shiver runs down his spine. He turns the handle and the door won't open. Locked? He tries again, and the door gives way (it just needed a little push). Juliane straightens up, startled. She has been hunched over the toilet bowl. 'Go away!' she says. 'I don't want you to see me like this.' He asks her what's wrong, did she have too much to drink? There are traces of vomit on the seat and on the floor around the bowl. 'I don't know. I feel terrible.' He says not to worry, that he's there to help. She doubles up again and disgorges another torrent into the bowl. He takes a wad of toilet paper and wipes up the spill. Her skin is still wet from the shower. 'I don't know what's wrong with me,' she repeats, as if to say it's not her fault.

'It's OK.'

'No, really, this has never happened to me before.' He suggests possible causes – the sun, the beer, the roast pork (the pepper, the rosemary). He asks if she has any allergies, but she doesn't seem to hear, because she doesn't answer.

She cleans herself up. He helps her to the bedroom, she lies down. She asks him to bring her a bucket, and he goes off in search of a bucket all over the unfamiliar house, eventually finding one tucked away in a small, dark, cobwebby space, presumably the maid's room.

She vomits again, in the bucket this time. Thirty minutes left of 2010.

'Could be an allergic reaction,' he says.

'But I'm not allergic to anything,' she replies.

'How about giving your parents a call?'

So then she explains – feebly, her voice choked from the strain of throwing up. She told her parents a lie, said she was going on this trip with a girl as they wouldn't have let her go with a boyfriend. Parents from the backwoods, you know how it is, they think a girl of sixteen's less safe with a boyfriend than going off with her mates to some wild party where she'll be hassled by all sorts of guys. No, he can't call her parents, they mustn't hear his voice or they'd know she was lying and never let her go on a trip ever again.

'What if I take you to the hospital?' But she has no health insurance, she's underage, they don't know where the hospital is, her parents would end up finding out (they always do).

She is dripping with sweat. No respite from the heat even at night, that's what the summers are like down south, in December. He gets up to switch on the fan: a breeze might do her good. No sooner has he done this than she's fast asleep. The effect was so sudden that for a terrified, insane moment he thinks she might actually be dead. Then, seeing her chest rise and fall as she breathes, his fear is assuaged.

Bursts of noise can be heard outside. The new year is almost upon them. Another fifteen minutes to go. Juliane opens her eyes wide and looks about her in terror, as if she has no idea where she is, which bed, which room, which boyfriend. She lurches over and vomits once more in the bucket. He holds her head fondly, and she lies back again. 'What can I do to help?' he asks in a voice choked like hers, as if he's on the brink of tears. Juliane, sounding more dead than alive, just begs to be left to sleep. She closes her eyes and falls asleep instantly. Ten minutes to midnight. Taut with nerves, he gets up to wander about the house. On the sofa he finds his book. The story begins as follows:

'No one ever expects that they might some day find themselves with a dead woman in their arms, a woman whose face they will never see again.'

He throws the book on the floor, as if it had delivered a shock so powerful that, had he not released the pages immediately, he would have been electrocuted on the spot. Although it makes no sense whatsoever, he takes this to be an omen and rushes to the bedroom, convinced of Juliane's demise. She's still sleeping and breathing. He begins to weep, shedding one small tear at a time. He goes back to his book and reads on, driven by the need to know what the opening sentence will lead to, what the novel is about – and may it have no bearing whatsoever on his own life, please. An abrupt change of subject, an explanation, anything like that would be a relief. But reading on brings no relief, each sentence renders him more nervous than the last.

The fireworks, intermittent at first, begin to explode en masse, like gunfire in battle. He puts the book down again and returns to the bedroom. Juliane is still asleep, her mouth smeared with greenish vomit. It's midnight, and it's 2011. He goes to fetch the book and sits down beside her to read. He has no idea why he does this, he could just as well turn on the TV and watch the firework displays in Copacabana, but then that would only depress him further. He could try and get some sleep, but – what a joke, what a horrible joke – he is sure, as sure as he is that the sun will rise in the morning, that he wouldn't get a wink of sleep, not with that deathly pale girl lying there. 'A moribund girl,' he tells himself, immediately regretting having thought in such terms. How could he possibly sleep, given the possibility of waking up with his arms wrapped round a dead woman? So he carries on reading, obsessed with reaching the end of the novel, unable to stop, compelled to read every single line and go wherever the narrator takes him – it's the only way Juliane will stay alive. Something has lodged in his mind, an absurd superstition, which is ridiculous because he's not superstitious and never will be, but he puts his faith in it anyway, because if he doesn't he'll suffocate. What it boils down to is this: if he manages to finish the book, all will be well. The dead woman in the man's embrace will remain forever captive in fiction.

He reads on feverishly, running his finger along the lines so as not to miss a single word. Juliane sleeps on, moaning softly from time to time. Looking up from his novel, he recoils from the sight of the body lying on the bed. Hours go by, his eyes ache and grow heavy, the lines begin to dance and swirl on the page. A drunken brawl breaks out in the road. Leftover fireworks are set off. Cars race by at a hundred kilometres per hour with music turned up full blast.

Page 300 – 5 a.m. already and dawn is about to break. He laughs out loud at the idiocy of his superstition, and can't think how he could have got so carried away. But he'll keep on reading, because it is imperative that he finishes what he set out to do.

It is the first day of 2011. In 2011 he will be twenty, and officially an adult. Perhaps this is what adulthood comes down to: utter loneliness. Deceiving yourself by inventing superstitions and other nonsense might work for some, but evidently not for him. The life he faces is not going to be easy, life is never easy for the kind of person who doesn't believe in the supernatural or in God or in spirits, who wants to distance himself from his family and strike out on his own, who's not at ease with sex, and who's fazed by having a moribund girl lying on the bed beside him. It won't be easy for someone who doesn't watch much TV, who has trouble sleeping, who takes everything to heart to the point of not getting any sleep at all. Nor will it be easy for someone with only books for company (not that he knows that yet, he just suspects it will be so). Books never bring peace of mind.

Yet he carries on reading.

He finishes the book and puts it on the bedside table. He lies down beside Juliane, but doesn't take her in his arms. He just lies on his back, staring at the ceiling. It's broad daylight outside. Juliane wakes up with a start, as from a nightmare. He asks her if she's all right (in the hoarse voice of someone who's been up all night) and Juliane says yes, she's feeling much better. She gets up, embarrassed about the mess and the vomit and the stink and how she looks half dead, and says she's going to take a shower. He stays where he is, closes his eyes and thinks: Now I can sleep at last. ■

RAT FEVER

Javier Arancibia Contreras

TRANSLATED BY JETHRO SOUTAR

JAVIER ARANCIBIA CONTRERAS
1976

Javier Arancibia Contreras is a writer,
journalist and screenwriter. He was born in Salvador,
Bahia, after his family emigrated from Chile during the
dictatorship. He has lived in Santos, São Paulo, since adolescence.
Contreras is the author of two novels: *Imóbile* (2008),
which was shortlisted for the São Paulo Prize for Literature,
and *O dia em que eu deveria ter morrido* (2010), for which
he was awarded a literary grant from the São Paulo state
government. While working as a crime reporter, he wrote a
book on playwright Plínio Marcos, *A crônica dos que não têm voz*,
which was part reportage and part biographical study.
'Rat Fever' ('A febre do rato') is a new story.

As I lie on the old spring bed, inherited from Mother along with the house, I get the feeling that night is advancing too slowly. I follow the passage of time on the clock on the bedside table, and I think about how medicine doesn't bring about drowsiness but rather it has the opposite effect, overwhelming the body with stimulation. In truth, this is more likely due to the constant pain I've felt since the accident.

I'm in the bedroom I lived in for twenty-odd years, but despite the familiarity of the childhood toys arranged in orderly fashion on shelves, the unaltered position of the furniture and the recognizable smell of the bedclothes, I can't stop thinking about how strange the situation is, in particular that it's the first night I've spent here since I left home.

No silence is absolute, and though the flat is remote, it has its own noises. Not the sounds of life you get in the city – televisions, traffic, music, arguments – but rather something that belongs to the house itself, like the creaking of its wooden structure. At least that's what I think, as the heat starts to conquer every pore in my body and make my mouth and throat suddenly dry. I may be feverish. But it's so sultry in the small hours that there's no way of telling. Everything around me, myself included, is warm and sticky.

With one leg broken and the other covered in haematomas, my movement is rather restricted. I should have brought a pitcher of water with me when I decided to have a lie-down in the bedroom, but quite apart from whether I'd have been able to do so in my condition, I never would have had the foresight. Perhaps I would if Mother were still alive, but it's because of her death that I find myself in this situation.

Raising my torso squeezes my abdomen and causes me so much muscular discomfort that I let out a high-pitched wail, but performing that first manoeuvre doesn't even come close to the pain involved in getting my legs out of the bed. Once I've managed it, the sense of relief feels the exact opposite of the pain, and it gives me the impetus to get to my feet and press my crutches to the floor.

I was in the final stages of recovery and decided to sign myself out of hospital and leave right away. I'd been interned for over a month after all. I lied when I told them I'd hire a private nurse, but not when I said I'd be staying at the home of relatives, albeit with no relatives actually living there. With the help of the janitor, it took no more than an hour to grab some work stuff and a few belongings from my flat, before getting a taxi to the back of beyond, where I am now. Satisfied I'd make it worth his while, the driver carried my bags and helped me up to the house, and I was finally able to install myself in here. It's an extensive property and the borders are rather haphazard, meaning the neighbours are quite far away.

The musculature of my arms has to be completely rigid and firm to absorb the jolts when I walk. I start to move slowly, first to the bedroom door, which is only ten feet away but seems impossible to get to. I hold on to the doorpost, sweat pouring down my face and soaking my back. The kitchen is at the opposite end of the house and getting there in my condition is like scaling a mountain. It's dark in the corridor, the bulb has gone, and so I struggle over to the light switch in the living room. Exhausted, I switch the light on, and immediately hear a strange sound, like a sharp whistle or a knife scraping against stone. I look about me but don't see a thing. I take one of the crutches and check whether the sound repeats itself when I put pressure on the floorboards inside the door, but I immediately feel pain shoot up my leg. At the dining table, I pull out a chair and sit down in relief. I look over at the kitchen and think how I should have picked up some shopping before installing myself in here. I'm soon back up on my crutches, and when I finally reach the kitchen I practically have to hug the fridge so as not to fall over. I open the fridge door and confirm the worst, that the contraption no longer works. There's a bottle of water but also fruit withering and rotting on the shelves and other bits of food in a dreadful state, including a worm-eaten piece of cheese, the grubs slumbering in a glass compartment, and a half-opened milk carton giving off a nauseating smell. I walk on a little further and find practically nothing edible in the cupboard that's supposed to serve as a pantry. Leftovers, things that had been opened by Mother and are now spoiled, limp, turned green. I lean my left crutch against the side of the fridge and take out the bottle of water. The taste is musty, but that's the least of my worries. I have to find a way of getting food and water, as well as the extra supplies of medicine I forgot to buy. The lack of a phone signal is worrisome, as is my certain knowledge that for quite some time Mother has had no landline. I know this because I did telephone her a few times when I first left. She would answer, my being stuck for words would render impossible any chance of us starting again, and then from one day to the next the number simply ceased to exist.

It's clear I haven't properly prepared for coming here but I've been feeling disheartened since Mother died. Mainly due to having spent so many years without seeing her. Perhaps it was because of that, as well as the partisan stares and insults my presence caused at the funeral, that everything around me became so abstract as I sped through a red light after the funeral.

Sitting back down on the chair in the lounge, I search through all the things I brought from my apartment, laid out on the dining table before me. My laptop, dictionaries and grammar books, the book I'm working on in its original version, a large travel bag full of clothes and shoes, a diary with notes and phone numbers and a sixteen-millimetre film can – a useless souvenir I once acquired in a junk shop along with a projector, and which today serves as a container for the drugs I consume while I work. Contrary to appearances, I am not a writer, playwright, scriptwriter, columnist, journalist or anything of the sort. I am merely a translator. But not one of the trivial ones who translate from boring, insipid languages like English. I translate directly from uncommon languages, grammatically complex and unmelodious languages like the Scandinavian ones. What brings me most pride and massages my ego is that I'm considered the only proficient and qualified professional in the country capable of translating directly from the most mysterious, dialectic and literary of all the Slavic languages, Russian. While I know that, aside from a few tiresome academics and those of the literary milieu, most people couldn't care less, I consider translating from such a language to be a work of art. I feel as though I'm writing the book itself, through the act of rewriting it. On the other hand, even though I have a clear sense that my extensive literary knowledge would allow me to write better than any of the creeps who currently enjoy prestige in intellectual circles, I have great difficulty expounding my own ideas. This is because there was a brief moment in life when my desire to become a writer was stronger than my feeling that nothing could reach or even come close to what had already been written. But then a phrase came to me and went, disappearing inside my head, and it has nagged, trapped and tormented me ever since.

I pick up the book by the young Russian author in the original and read its strange title out loud: звук выскабливание каменным ножом or, in Westernized form, *Zvuk vyskablivanie kamennym nozhom*. I delight in the guttural phonetics of the words as I stamp them upon my voice, even laughing with pleasure. A sort of electricity runs up my spine and a sense of stimulation flows through my blood. I switch the computer on and get down to work right away because my deadline, which my editor felt the need to remind me of when he visited me in hospital, is not as far away as it might be: an unforgivable lack of respect for the complex syntax of the greatest mother tongue of the Eastern world. However, this is not really a problem, as performing such an unusual translation will give me much more pleasure than will the money the fool pays me for doing it.

I open the book and smell its pages, the same ritual I've performed for years, and then read the opening lines out loud and realize they are potent, shocking even, which brings me extra delight and satisfaction.

The dead man's blue eyes still sparkled in the early hours of the morning. The pale body, its brown uniform plastered with dust and blood, is different from the others on account of the man who existed inside it having spent several hours in a state of utter horror, still alive though cut to pieces by shrapnel from the bomb that decimated the whole platoon. When the paramedics arrived at the battle scene, Lazar Ganchev tried to say something, his mouth agape and trembling for lack of air, his eyes protruding like those of a beheaded pig, his face all blood and bones, but all that could be heard was his raggedy voice, panting, calling out countless times for his mother. Until the end came. Mothers may not be physically present at war, but they are always there in the imminence of death.

I sweat a great deal as I start to work and once again think about the fever that has possibly invaded my body. I soon look over at the film can thrown on the table and think for just an instant before taking out the little wrap of cocaine. As cigarettes and drink do for many people, cocaine has always helped me work, and only work. It's a rule I've been strict about for a long time, because method and euphoria are complementary extremes for me, like a balanced risk. This all started when I did a few German translations of Freud's studies and writings on the drug for science magazines. I think of all the trouble that warped genius spread about the world, as I rack up two lines straight on the tabletop and energetically snort one of them.

Which is when I hear the scraping sound again. I also have the feeling that something is happening behind me. I turn my body agilely without thinking about the position of my legs, and let out a howl of pain. My eyes squint so tightly the sockets practically turn inside themselves, blurring my sight for a few moments. When my vision finally regains its composure, I look into all the corners of the room but there's nothing there.

I decide to get up. I grab the crutches and walk three paces into the middle of the room, from where I have a broader view of the place. I still don't see anything, so I walk over towards the corridor, go a bit further and, for the first time since coming back to the house, I feel compelled to go into what used to be Mother's room. Like my own, the room is exactly the same as it's always been, tidy, unaltered in its arrangement of trinkets, the coat stand to the right of the dressing table, the chest at the foot of the bed, where I sit down. Mother was always orderly, organized, accustomed to doing her household chores. That the house remains spotless even though she's dead doesn't really surprise me, even after all these years. Years that reinforced our estrangement and overcame me, made me old, bald, bland, all of which I'm reminded of when I see my scraggly appearance in the mirror atop the dresser. I found out from the funeral director that Mother died here, lying down, probably in her sleep. I now realize I didn't even get a chance to ask about or even interest myself in the *causa mortis*. I try to think of her, but the images I have are remote, distant, like photographs left forgotten at the bottom of a drawer. It's a horrible feeling. It's almost as if she never really existed.

Going back into the living room I look at the dining table and have it confirmed that I am not alone in the house. Someone has finished off the cocaine while I was in the bedroom. I open the film can. The rest is still there but the second line has vanished from the table. I notice a few letters have been tapped at random on the computer, after the translated passage – *onuyftsew*. I check everything else on the table. It's all there. I sit down and try to think in an objective and rational manner. There is no one at home other than me. I myself must have snorted the second line amid the euphoria of translating the book. I myself must have knocked the keys when I heard the piercing sound behind me, turned and smashed my legs against the table.

Though I consider rationality to be a virtue, disbelief blows hard in my ear.

When Lazar Ganchev caught sight of the giant columns outside Moscow's Lomonosov University, his eyes clouded over. His beating heart and trembling hands felt vindicated. Ganchev would have to promptly drop out of the law course he'd given so much time to, in order to go to war. After informing the rector that he was giving up, he left the place feeling the exact opposite of how he'd felt on his arrival. Anger and a general sense of rancidness upset his stomach and took hold of him with increasing force. There were still fifteen days to go before the official date of his call-up and Ganchev knew they would perhaps be the last days of his short life. Rather than cause him fear or anguish, this thought produced a feeling of revolt and indignation in the young man. He thought about the possibility of deserting, of fleeing, but he was terrified of being branded a coward. My

God, he thought, trying to justify himself, are there not enough homeless and unemployed in the country to send to the trenches? Ganchev walked all around the town centre while he thought about what he'd say to his mother. He had found out about his call-up and pulled out of university without saying a word to her. He thought of telling her of his plans to go and study in America, but he was unsure whether she'd oppose him, humiliate him and forbid him from fleeing. He also knew that if he were to go through with the plan, he'd never see her again, though that would probably also be the case if he decided to go to war. The only difference was that in one scenario he'd be alive and in the other he'd be dead.

I feel myself nodding off, the stuffy weather adding to my sense of immobility and draining me of energy. The heat inside me, rancid and strange, has been overwhelming and gradually destroying me ever since the moment it set in, I no longer remember when. I don't hesitate to open the can and rack up two more lines of white powder. My work is nocturnal. Always has been. At some point in my life I tried to invert the hours, but failed. Mornings and afternoons tire me, distract me, lead me into doing all the usual things that end up ruining any chance of interpreting the writing. I require night because night commands silence. And silence out here, despite the house's peculiar sounds, is almost holy.

I snort another line and, just as happened before, I hear a noise behind me. Not the same sharp whistle, nor anything similar, but a sound that's no less shrill and horrible. I am so startled I stand up quickly, using my crutches for support. I go into the middle of the room, straighten myself up so as not to fall, and only then do I see it. A monstrous creature, a rat about a foot long. It has a coat of lead-coloured hair, practically black, dirty, wet and bristly, tufts coming up as far as a face that's pocked as if it were raw, with a long snout full of folds and pits all mixed up with its whiskers. The animal stops trying to hide and comes out of the shadows, ignoring the silence to put on a show of authority. Its eyes are red, protruding, intense, shrill, excited, and when it opens its mouth and reveals its gums, I notice its sharp, crooked, rotten teeth. I remain on my feet, standing still, for with one leg broken and the other unable to make sudden movements, I've no choice. I wait for the creature to adopt a position before deciding my next move. The rat stops making its strange noises and just stares at me. Now that it has revealed itself and quickly shown me its powers, I realize it is studying me. Like me, it doesn't know what to do. It takes me a while to think of an idea, then I move slowly towards the kitchen, as if walking under water, and grab the worm-ridden cheese. Without making any aggressive movements, I throw the piece of decomposed cheese over towards the rat. The animal retreats but doesn't, I notice, seem to be afraid. Then it heads for the cheese, allowing me to see for the first time its long tail, which had been tucked away under its body. It sniffs the cheese, moving its snout from one side to the other, vigilantly, not daring to take a bite, but what it does next surprises me. With its huge nails, sharp like a knife, it pounds the cheese and worms, smashing them to smithereens. Then, with its hind legs, it starts to further destroy what remains. I can't figure out what it's up to, but it never stops sniffing at what's left of the cheese. And then its intentions become clear. It moves quickly towards the dining table, circles round the chair where I'd been sitting, sticks its claws into the wood and, without too much trouble, climbs up onto the chair. It leans upon its front legs then rocks back on its hind legs and springs forward up onto the table. Then the rat snorts the cocaine. Snorts it and eats it, as it doesn't quite have the skill to sniff it all up. With its snout all filthy and slobbery and speckled with white powder, the monster squeals again in a show of victory. I act without thinking. If I'd thought things through I wouldn't have done it, but only afterwards do I realize my mistake. My arm jumps the gun, lifting the crutch up off the floor and hurling it, with all the force my body can muster, in the direction of the animal. I don't know how I do it but I hit it full on, though I also take out everything else on the table, computer, film can, bag, everything. The impact sends the rat flying off the table and smashing into the wall on the other side of the living room, where it falls to the floor, stunned and spilling blood. I've lost my means of support and so I inevitably collapse too, and when I hit the wooden floor the pain in my legs is so overpowering I lose all feeling of any kind.

I awake screaming. All eyes in the funeral parlour flash upon me and only then do I realize that I must have dozed off in my seat, my head propped up against the wall and my eyes shadowed behind my sunglasses. An old lady, I've no idea who she is, whispers to another, a long-lost great-aunt I amaze myself by being able to recall. 'What an awful man!' I overhear the old lady uttering into my great-aunt's ear. A tall, stout man with a huge scar across his face – and only because of the scar do I know he's my godfather – nudges a short guy with his elbow and nods in my direction, pointing out who I am. He doesn't even know me, but he gives me a dirty look as he straightens his tie. I lower my eyes and do likewise, evidently having loosened it at some moment before falling asleep, which must also have irritated everyone. I decide to leave the hall. Outside the day is clear, the sun is full, and I think about it being the wrong kind of day for burying someone. I walk around a bit outside and come upon the office of the funeral parlour, damp on its walls and in a state of disrepair. A tall, incredibly thin man comes over to me and asks if I'm a relative of the deceased. I tell him I'm the son and he looks me up and down before offering me a coffee, which I accept. We speak very little, he doubtless thinking it bad manners to interfere with a son's grief. I remember that the person who told me about my mother's death on the phone was a distant cousin, but he didn't even take the trouble to tell me how it happened. He must have been made to do it by the others. He just said that she'd died and that the funeral was scheduled for today. The conversation had been a mere formality. But the funeral director has a loose tongue. He tells me that Mother died at home, in bed, probably in her sleep.

When I look back outside, the coffin is being taken by procession to the family plot. I should have been one of the pall-bearers, but nobody called for me. Even the distant cousin is involved, probably in my place. I watch from afar as the stonemasons fill up the grave and then, just when I'm thinking of heading over, I realize that everyone will reproach me for having forgotten to buy flowers. And yet it wasn't a lapse, much less a lack of consideration, but rather because I know Mother never liked flowers. Doubtless no one else here knows that. As they doubtless don't know what made me leave home. Just as they doubtless don't know why I never went back.

I leave the place quickly and walk to the car park, taking my jacket off and unbuttoning the top of my dress shirt as I go. My clothes are totally soaked in sweat and I start wondering whether the fever that periodically takes over my body might somehow be inherent in me. I'm dizzy and pale when I get in the car. I wait for a good while, breathe deeply. Then I leave, accelerate and, in an instant, as if the diving equipment of my memory had suddenly broken, Mum's almost secretive voice enters my head, as if talking to herself, speaking the phrase that has nagged, trapped and tormented me. Only now do I recall that it came from her mouth following the death of my father, a death I have no memory of: the only thing that makes life bearable is that it comes to an end, son.

And at that, I hear the sound of tyres screeching on tarmac, the smash, the shattering of glass, and I sense twisted iron entering flesh. ∎

GRANTA

FAR FROM RAMIRO

Chico Mattoso

TRANSLATED BY CLIFFORD E. LANDERS

CHICO MATTOSO
1978

Chico Mattoso was born in France but has
lived in São Paulo ever since. His first novel, *Longe de Ramiro* (2007),
was shortlisted for the Jabuti Award. His second novel, *Nunca vai
embora*, was published in 2011. Mattoso was one of the editors of
Ácaro magazine and has written for numerous other magazines
and newspapers. He currently lives in Chicago, where he studies
screenwriting at Northwestern University. 'Far from Ramiro' is an
extract from his novel of the same title.

Morning invaded the room. Ramiro tried to protect himself with the sheets, but when he looked, it was still there, as if to say: I didn't ask to be born. Neither did I, he murmured, and covered his head with the pillow. He managed to sleep a bit more, but then the light came again, sharp, penetrating the cotton padding. Ramiro rubbed his eyes and got up. He staggered to the window. Grabbed the shutter. Jerked it, tried to push it back onto the track. He began to shake the window, and that was when the shutter yielded and opened fully. Sunlight and city noise blasted in. It became impossible to go back to sleep.

Still groggy, Ramiro could only emit a guttural yawn. Lucidity returned slowly, accompanied by uneasiness. Hand on his belly. An involuntary belch. A desperate run from the bedroom, followed by a disastrous stumble over a magazine dropped at the entrance to the bathroom. Ramiro crawled to the toilet, but when he got there the nausea had gone away. A weak sound came from the plumbing. Someone dropped something on the floor above, and outside a car braked abruptly and gave rise to a long chorus of horns.

It was autumn. A meagre autumn, one that held the leaves on the trees and refused to abandon the warm embrace of summer. Ramiro missed the cold. In the cold, the days were more defined. In the cold, the birds calmed down. In the cold, everything sought accommodation, there wasn't that Babylon of heated bodies bumping and tripping into one another. But now it was hot, and Ramiro's skin was sticky, and the prospect of taking a shower seemed just as inviting as the desire to go to the window and hurl insults at the pedestrians below.

He could see the backs of several buildings from the window. Service stairs. Clothes hung out to dry. A few balconies, with women of about forty charring their breasts in the sun. One day Ramiro saw a boy throw a cat out of the window. He witnessed the entire scene, the cat thrashing about, the boy trying to escape the scratches, the fall down seventeen floors until the crash. The cat landed on its feet. The boy – he could hear – was beaten so badly that the police had to be called. One thing or another happened, couples slapping each other, old people talking to themselves, a man in a tie who every Friday climbed to the terrace and bellowed like an orphaned gorilla, a dishevelled lady who spent the day at the window smoking and staring at nothing.

By that time, life in the hotel had become so routine that it seemed as though Ramiro had always been there. It had only been three months, but it could have been three days, or three years, or three centuries; looking back was like listening to a fairy tale. Once upon a time Ramiro. Once upon a time Ramiro walking downtown. Once upon a time Ramiro walking and wanting to buy a sound system, or rather, torn between buying a sound system and continuing to save money so he could wander around Europe. Once upon a time Ramiro passing by a hotel and having his attention caught by its flickering facade and stopping in front of that vertical aquarium guarded by a pair of rhinoceroses in coats and ties with communication devices. Ramiro approached the glass. Inside, people were moving with a submerged slowness. There were old women with no wrinkles, gringos with moustaches, well-behaved children counting the stains on the sofa, young receptionists with blue badges helping conference participants; there were velvet walls, cab drivers in hats, prostitutes attempting discretion, a decorative fountain, and many, many employees with no apparent job function, each one wandering around as if expecting something terribly important to happen. That's how it was: Ramiro looked, went in, approached the reception desk, and, almost without thinking, smiled at the attendant, opening a formal dialogue that culminated in the signing of a document and the approach of the porter, who tipped his hat and then noticed that Ramiro wasn't carrying any luggage.

Three months. Three months without setting foot in the street, three months wandering through the service areas of the Royal Soft Residence. Three months of silence, and insomnia, and yawns, Ramiro dragging himself through the halls like some hostile ghost, not speaking to anyone, not thinking of anything at all, calling home just often enough to keep his mother from committing suicide or calling the police or renting a helicopter and showering the city with flyers bearing his photo. It was uncomfortable. Ramiro would say everything was fine, that his trip had been unexpected; his mother would implore him to tell her where he had disappeared to, that his friends also wanted to know, and the people from the newspaper weren't sure if they could count on him, and the back pain, and the brother out of work, and Tati, poor Tati who was left in the lurch – and how could Ramiro not heed even his girlfriend's appeals? I'm fine, he would reply, I'm fine, and his mother would yelp at the other end when he repeated these words: I'm fine, trust me, I'm fine.

He didn't have any clothes – when he entered the hotel he had been wearing a T-shirt and Bermudas, which had transformed into useless rags – so Ramiro opted for a bathrobe. Besides being comfortable, it proved effective in warding off company, once even provoking rebellion in an elderly lady who declared herself incapable of eating her asparagus in the presence of an 'undressed man' in the dining room. There were other incidents, but none worthy of note, and little by little the garment started to seem normal to the guests and employees, who came to view Ramiro with the same sleepy arrogance they dedicated to one another.

An undressed man. Still dazed by his stumble, Ramiro spent a few seconds hesitating between thinking about the shutter and jumping in the shower. Clearly, the prospect of bathing was much more attractive, not only because of the burning sun out there but because the shutter awoke in Ramiro a vague desire for destruction, as if all the world's evil were packed into the rectangular framework of the window in his room. The shower seemed the most appropriate action for that moment – and surely would be, were it not for the incident the night before.

It had been during his shower. When it started, Ramiro had even thought it funny: it was a game, a harmless joke. Gradually, however, the amusement gave way to a peculiar kind of terror. When the water began falling, Ramiro felt that he was soaping parts of a body that was not his. The legs were not his legs, the arms were not his arms, the chest was not his chest – not even the dick seemed familiar. He continued to bathe and felt as if he were invading someone's privacy, touching unbidden a strange body, and this induced horror and disgust, Ramiro trying to take away his hands but realizing that they too did not belong to him – and soon all that was left were the eyes, Ramiro transformed into a spectator of himself, or rather, of the other, seeing like one of those cameras skydivers wear on their helmets. But then he looked around, saw the bathroom, the robe, the bottles of shampoo, and began to understand that it wasn't he who was invading another's privacy but the opposite: through the eyes of the intruder, Ramiro saw the invasion of his own space.

The discussion alternates between the origin of Bilica's nose – Armenian, Turkish or Lebanese – and establishing a criterion for deciding who'll go and get the beer. It's difficult. Besides the abstainers and the recently arrived, two other categories try to avoid the task: the wealthy, who shirk responsibility by tossing large bills in the kitty instead, and the lovers, who fight violently in a corner and thus prevent any approach or demand. Fifteen people are yelling at once, some loudly requesting silence, others laughing at some joke, two or three beginning a peanut war while, in the middle of everything, someone coming out of the bathroom declares that the toilet has stopped working again.

Bilica, the host, is shut in the bedroom with his girlfriend, which is sufficient excuse for the provenance of his nose to come back into play. The argument is interrupted when Egídio, holding an extremely strange piece of metal, comes into the room and announces to those present that now the bathroom is available only for washing their hands. Then the doorbell rings and Vanessa and two girlfriends arrive with bags full of beer, and the euphoria is such that no one asks why they're dressed the way they are, all three in green, wearing hats that look like remnants from a carnival float.

Sitting on an ottoman, Ramiro struggles to find a comfortable position. Someone offers him wine. Only when he says thanks does he realize he hasn't opened his mouth for two hours. There he is, in the home of old friends, surrounded by people he knows, and even enjoying himself, appreciating one person's joke, another's sarcasm, the funny story that Pedro always tells about some distant uncle, but all this time he hasn't felt the need to say anything at all. Sometimes he thinks about Tati, wondering whether she'll get off work in time to stop by the party, but then his thoughts wander and before he knows it, his mind is on things as diverse as the latest earthquake in Asia, king-size mattresses and the odd growth that has appeared on his index finger.

It's still good to think about Tati. They're approaching one year together, but there's still the old quiver, the weird sensation of imagining that, at that very moment, she's somewhere in the city, breathing, imparting to things her soft manner, making everything seem absolutely natural or necessary. On the other hand, for a while now, thinking about her releases in him a vague nostalgia, like a river that gradually turns into a swamp. To Ramiro, it is more and more uncomfortable to wallow there, and perhaps this is why it's so hard to maintain his concentration, why the growth on the end of his finger seems so large, why the matter of the earthquake causes him so much anguish.

When he gets up for a beer, Ramiro sees that the argument over Bilica's nose has ended. The topic under discussion now is more difficult to determine, since, in the midst of the confusion, a classmate of Egídio's has taken out a guitar and started to bang out some Tropicália classic. Damned guitars, thinks Ramiro as he goes to the kitchen, hearing the guy asking for silence as he prepares the audience for the show.

The beer is warm. Ramiro rummages through the refrigerator but finds only soft drinks, dead batteries, sliced bread, hamburger meat. Lacking an option, he decides to open a warm can. The drink goes down roughly. He feels like putting ice in the glass, but somebody will laugh at him, and Ramiro will have to answer in kind, and then one of those laborious dialogues will begin, full of taunts and witticisms.

It's not worth it.

In the living room, they prepare for the celebration. There will be no surprise. Bilica is going to come down the stairs, with the flushed face of someone who's just got laid; he's going to listen to the murmur, catch on to the whole thing, casually enter the room; then come the shouts, the clapping, the birthday boy feigning surprise, hand on heart and an appreciative sigh. Of course, that's part of the game, but there's something unpleasant in this play-acting, at least to Ramiro. Maybe it's the certainty that a few moments after the hugs, the presents, the laughter, when everyone is scattered about the living room and the party has returned to its original state, someone is going to bring up the subject – and everything will begin again.

Having a dead friend is often equivalent to having a special stamp on your documents, the kind that attests to some distinction. People suffer, cry, ask themselves why, and after finding no answer they begin, perhaps as a kind of defence, to try to make a precious thing of it, transforming suffering into a badge of honour, petty as any other. Two months earlier, at Milena's party, Ramiro experienced the first demonstration of this phenomenon. Someone mentioned Nestor's name, and after a brief silence a long rosary of memories began. Soon, everyone was trying to recall a more extraordinary story, a funnier incident, a more unusual situation they experienced with him, and suddenly it had turned into a veiled competition in which, through closeness to the deceased, one was guaranteed a transcendental kind of virtue.

It was going to happen again. One spark was all it took: the name of the dead person, uttered a single time – then comes the silence, the pleated mouths, the genuine sadness, all quickly buried under avalanches of sentimentality. What would the dead man say if he knew he'd become a household saint? Probably he would take a drag on his cigarette, look up, blow a few smoke rings, and, with the tranquillity of the disembodied, decree: 'Bunch of fuckers.'

And he'd guffaw, and clap Ramiro on the back and invite him to get drunk at a bingo parlour or watch girls at the bus station or maybe board a subway car and allow himself to be swept up, at least for a few minutes, in the illusion that it's possible to forget oneself. But now Nestor is far away, and Ramiro finishes downing his third can of beer and gradually feels he's regained his lucidity. Egídio brings more peanuts, Pedro begins another unlikely story and everything seems small while, on the ottoman, two of Bilica's female cousins fight fetchingly for more space.

The noise goes on. The guy with the guitar tries to show off his eclectic taste, strumming Bob Dylan for one of the girls who came with Vanessa. They make a curious couple, he striking poses, she in that weird outfit, exchanging ambiguous glances that will probably lead nowhere. Perhaps Ramiro should call Tati, convince her to put off her work till tomorrow – because sometimes it seems like a lie, that there's no swamp at all, that he loves her exactly as he did before and is merely hiding his true feelings under a mountain of pride and cowardice. Yeah, call Tati, or maybe forget her and sit down beside Bilica's cousins, or get out of here and slip into a movie theatre, or simply get another beer and let the time go by. But then someone hears a noise, and everyone scrambles to a corner, and the lights are turned off, and Ramiro is squeezed between a fat guy with a beard and a bookcase full of books, old notebooks and computer parts. It's hard to breathe. Someone hands him a whistle and a bag of confetti and, fingers to his lips, asks Ramiro to keep quiet.

Damned shutters. Leaning against the wall, his gaze running over his fingernails, Ramiro notices how the light reveals the imperfections in each object. His nails are dirty. As is the lampshade. Cars honk their horns down below, and perhaps there's nothing to do but close his eyes and tell everything to piss off.

To piss off would mean calling the management and asking for a new room. The girl would attend to him with a distracted air. Ramiro would summon his best baritone voice, the manager would come on the line and the move would be effected in minutes: Ramiro would abandon 501 to find the comfort of a new dwelling, where the shutters glided freely and the act of taking a shower didn't lead to morning terrors and paranoid fears of annihilation. But Ramiro won't do it. He won't let go of his old room, this setting for infrequent masturbation, irregular dozing, harmless meandering mind games, all impelled by a kind of permanent catatonia.

Room 501 was similar to the majority of single rooms in the Royal Soft Residence. As Ramiro had opted for an apartment in the rear, the space that at the facade was taken up by small balconies – duly decorated with battered ferns and colourless violets – was here replaced by an annexe, which allowed the installation beneath the window of a reclining easy chair and a rack for shoes. When not in bed, Ramiro would sprawl on the easy chair, losing himself in mental exercises among which were the making up of names (Ficner, for example, or Garbeliades, or even Plaucio or Cintileria) and the attempt, using the strength of his neurons, to control the flight of the insects flitting around the light bulb. There was also what Ramiro called 'concretist erection', which consisted of imagining some object and, through the force of concentration, trying to become aroused by it – the previous week, for example, he had achieved surprising results mentalizing a Xerox machine.

He needed to empty his head. He needed to sit in the chair, turn his attention to the curvature of the doorknob, the navigation of moths, that small dirty ball that persisted in forming in his navel – and, there, it was done, thought disconnected from body until it was extinguished for good. Thus Ramiro avoided the thin lips of his father, or the flaccid skin of his grandmother, or the day he fell out of his bunk and broke his chin on the wooden floor. His mother, her obsession with hats, the dental braces Roger lost in the neighbour's yard, Nestor with his anxious way of lighting a cigarette – everything would crumble until a single image was left: Tati. They were on a bus, going to the movies, she took his hand, and said, you have a woman's nails. He looked at his nails, and she explained that he must have taken his mother's hands, and then Ramiro raised his eyebrows and observed that he had long ago ceased taking his mother's hands. She laughed, and coughed, and said that people in her family commented that her laugh was exactly like her grandmother's. How is it possible, she asked, to inherit a laugh, especially a laugh she had never heard? Ramiro didn't know what to answer. He took her hand, bit it, she punched him on the arm, and at that moment the bus braked abruptly and they realized it was time to pull the cord.

The cord. A hand pulling the cord. The fingernails of the hand, dirty like the edge of a lampshade, the morning light drenching the room, and there in the middle is Ramiro and his muddled brain like a grimy wad of cotton. Ramiro pats the robe's pockets, where he finds a crumpled cigarette. He is sticking the cigarette in his mouth when the phone rings.

It must be the reception desk, the girl with the shrill voice announcing discounts at the panoramic bar, or advising that the fitness centre is going to undergo renovations. Ramiro doesn't answer. As always, he goes to the bed and presses the pillow against his ears. He remains that way, staring at the telephone, a smile on his lips, but then realizes the protection is not enough. The ringing of the telephone vibrates through the furniture, the walls, the built-in wardrobe. Ramiro tightens his grip on the pillow, to no avail. He gets angry. Goes to the phone and yanks it out of the wall. Advances towards the window, ready to throw it out, but then checks himself, opens the minibar, deposits the phone inside, behind the sports drinks.

Ramiro sighs. He sits on the bed, throws his body back, his feet touch the carpet, looking for his slippers. Finding one, he puts it on his right foot, while his left foot explores the nearby area, traversing the imperfections in the rug, bumping into a bottle cap, plunging into a small mound of crumbled cracker. Can it be that Ramiro's feet look like those of some relative? What about his arms? And lungs, pancreas, intestines? He lifts his hands in front of him and what he sees are feminine nails, dirty, inherited from he doesn't know who, from his mother, his grandmother, a gust of wind, and it's time to get up and leave and put an end to all this. Ramiro finds the other slipper.

The morning takes hold of the room, and now he leaps up and tries to bring order to his thoughts. He raises his hand to his mouth. Where the devil did that cigarette get to?

It didn't seem as if she was going to go to sleep. She cried, sighed, wiped her face on the pillow, giving the impression that soon she would turn and try to change the subject, talk about the college or about film or last night's storm, her voice at first choked up until resuming its normal firm, delicate tone. But she didn't turn, and Ramiro went on stroking her hair, and when he looked she was almost snoring and there was no longer any alternative but to turn out the light and observe her body profiled in the half-shadow; she was sleeping more and more deeply, while her eyes were becoming less swollen.

When Ramiro turns on the lamp, he's able to see a bit more. Her purse is thrown behind the door; she arrived so distressed that he didn't even have time to ask questions. You don't know, she said, and then Ramiro found himself in the difficult position of having to listen to a horrific story and balance shock and resignation, desperation and serenity. Ramiro felt none of that, the matter was grave but his head was somewhere else, and when she told him her friend had been the victim of a flash kidnapping, the only thing that occurred to him was the headline he'd seen in the newspaper a few days before, ENERGY CRISIS REDUCES FLASH KIDNAPPINGS, and that was so absurd that he felt like interrupting what she was saying to tell her about it. Of course, that would have been totally inappropriate, she was very upset, and besides, it had not only been a kidnapping; the thieves had abused the girl badly. Ramiro berates himself for being so insensitive, he hasn't known Tati for very long, she isn't quite real to him yet, and perhaps because of that it's easy to think of headlines and funny things and stare at his girlfriend's breasts, counting the seconds before tearing off her clothes and biting her neck and squeezing her thighs and so on.

She sleeps, and Ramiro watches her, and it's strange to see her like this – she whose body is beginning to let itself be known, the supple skin that makes him believe in chance and happiness. Ramiro thinks about waking her, but to do so would spoil something, like smudging a drawing. The truth, he muses, is that Tatiana is a very strong name, a name for a fat, powerful woman full of vigour, who leads armies and enslaves husbands. It's not a name for someone who is sleeping. Not a name for someone who is crying and saying she wants to live at the beach and who ten days ago was only a drunken girl waiting in line for the bathroom, who took Ramiro by the arm and asked him, a complete stranger, to help her vomit.

Ramiro observes her and sees an animal. A beast. A beast that breathes. He knows that soon he's going to be hungry, that he'll have to get up and face the chaos in the living room, push aside the boxes to find the telephone. He knows that the noise will wake Tati and that she will come, groggy, looking like a zombie, to hug him before babbling something and locking herself in the bathroom. Ramiro will stay on the sofa, gazing at the mountains of boxes, thinking about putting some order to it all. It's been more than a month since he moved in, but it seems as if he arrived yesterday – or is leaving tomorrow. He's living in quarantine, as if his body needs time to adjust to the new home by inhabiting it gradually, without shocks or jolts. It's evident that this is only an excuse, but Tati usually finds it amusing and calls Ramiro a bum, and it's good to arouse in her that kind of superiority, that ingenuous way of raising her eyebrows and curling the corner of her mouth. On second thoughts, Tati isn't really that strong a name, Tati is a very fragile and subtle name, and who could have known that a name like Tatiana could house so much delicacy, *Tati, Ta-ti*, and then she moves as if to awaken, but it's only her body seeking a more comfortable position.

Ramiro continues to lie there. I have more to do, he thinks, pondering the need to get up, take a shower, put on decent clothes. He looks at her face, feels a twinge of envy because he's not sleeping. That's so petty, she's only napping – and Ramiro feels guilty once again and briefly reflects on how unstable his moods can be.

Everything is so stupid. It's stupid that he has yet to get out of bed, it's stupid to continue thinking about it, it's stupid to realize that now Tati is murmuring something and to believe that, if he brings his ear close to her mouth, he'll be able to understand some of what she's saying. If he were alone or, rather, if he weren't afraid of waking her, Ramiro could start to cough, or light a cigarette, or open the closet door and make faces in the mirror, laughing and feeling sorry for himself. But it must already be past two, and the sun is blazing out there, and the noises of the city seem to invite him to a commitment that cannot be postponed. It's more or less at this moment that she starts to awaken.

First comes a twitch. Then a click of the tongue, a light grumble, and she turns on her side as if she were going back to sleep. She moves slowly, her body limp, re-encountering herself. She stretches her neck. Unfolds her arms. Yawns. She opens her eyes, widens them, and for a moment seems startled and lost. She props herself up on one elbow. Wipes the sweat from her forehead. She looks at Ramiro, puts her hand on his hair, her index finger curling around the fringe. She tries to say something, her voice doesn't come out. She clears her throat. She tries again, and this time the voice emerges slowly, slurred, almost childlike. She says: *Ramiro*. But now it is he who appears to have fallen asleep. ■

DISCOVER
NEW WORLDS OF WRITING

'Provides enough to satisfy the most rabid appetite
for good writing and hard thinking' – *Washington Post*

Have *Granta* delivered to your door four times
a year and save up to 29% on the cover price.

Subscribe now by completing the form overleaf,
visiting granta.com or calling toll free 1-866-438-6150

US
$48.00

CANADA
$56.00

LATIN AMERICA
$68.00

GRANTA.COM

GRANTA

THE MAGAZINE OF NEW WRITING

SUBSCRIPTION FORM FOR US, CANADA AND LATIN AMERICA

Yes, I would like to take out a subscription to *Granta*.

GUARANTEE: If I am ever dissatisfied with my *Granta* subscription, I will simply notify you, and you will send me a complete refund or credit my credit card, as applicable, for all un-mailed issues.

YOUR DETAILS

MR / MISS / MRS / DR ....

NAME ....

ADDRESS ....

....

CITY... STATE ....

ZIP CODE .... COUNTRY ....

EMAIL ....

☐ Please check this box if you do not wish to receive special offers from *Granta*

☐ Please check this box if you do not wish to receive offers from organizations selected by *Granta*

YOUR PAYMENT DETAILS

1 year subscription: ☐ US: $48.00 ☐ Canada: $56.00 ☐ Latin America: $68.00

3 year subscription: ☐ US: $120.00 ☐ Canada: $144.00 ☐ Latin America: $180.00

Enclosed is my check for $_____ made payable to *Granta*.

Please charge my: ☐ Visa ☐ Mastercard ☐ Amex

Card No. ☐☐☐☐☐☐☐☐☐☐☐☐☐☐☐☐

Exp. ☐☐☐☐

Security Code ☐☐☐☐

SIGNATURE .... DATE ....

Please mail this order form with your payment instructions to:

Granta Publications
PO Box 359
Congers NY 10920-0359

Or call toll free 1-866-438-6150
Or visit GRANTA.COM for details

Source code: BUS121PM

SPARKS

Carol Bensimon

TRANSLATED BY BETH FOWLER

CAROL BENSIMON
1982

Carol Bensimon was born in Porto Alegre.
In 2008, she published her first work of fiction, *Pó de parede*,
consisting of three stories. In 2009, Bensimon's debut
novel, *Sinuca embaixo d'água,* was shortlisted for the São Paulo
Prize for Literature, the Jabuti Award and the *Bravo!* Prize. 'Sparks'
('Faíscas') is an extract from a new novel of the same title.

All we did was take the BR-116, passing beneath bridges that showed slogans of cities we hadn't the slightest intention of visiting, or which told of Christ's return or counted down to the end of the world. We left behind the suburban streets whose beginnings are marked by the highway and which then disappear in an industrial estate or among the abandoned shacks along a stream where stray dogs crawl and rarely bark, and we carried on, on until the straight road turned a corner. I was driving. Julia had her feet on the dashboard. I could only look at her occasionally. When she didn't know the words to the song, she hummed instead. 'You've changed your hair,' I said, glancing at her fringe. Julia replied: 'About two years ago, Cora.' We laughed as we climbed into the hills. That was the start of our journey.

My car had been out of action for some time, under a silver waterproof cover, like a big secret you just can't hide or a child trying to disappear by putting her hands over her eyes, surrounded by junk in the garage at my mother's house. Initially, my mother was desperate to resolve the situation. It's a bad business leaving a car off the road for so long, she would say, although she understood very little about business and even less about getting rid of things. She lived in a house that already seemed too big when there were still three of us. When you opened certain wardrobes in that house, you could see the entire evolution of ladieswear from the mid-sixties onwards. Lovely jackets, pretty dresses that didn't fit my mother any more. I was direct about the car. I said: 'Maybe I'll come back.' I could sense her breath crossing the ocean and almost capsizing before returning to dry land. Perhaps it was a mistake to offer hope to a single mother, given that I wasn't even considering the possibility of moving home at that point. We never spoke about the car again.

Three years later, I was back and found the garage fuller than ever, so much so that I could barely see the terracotta floor tiles for the bags full of papers, the boxes of all sizes. There were balls of dust, an electric heater, a small bicycle, a minibar missing a leg. I got the impression I could have written WASH ME in the air with my index finger. I pushed open the wooden concertina doors and let in the light. I stood looking at the street for a while. It was no longer the same street, I mean, it was the same street, but in place of the houses belonging to my childhood friends – where were they now? – an apartment block had been built. It scared me to think that one person's aesthetic preferences could be summed up in that white, seventeen-floor mastodon, which stuck out on the block like a naked woman in an order of nuns, or a nun at the First Brazilian Meeting of Polyamorists.

Apart from that, there were other subtle changes to that section of the street. They did not date from the last three years, however, the three years I had spent away from Porto Alegre and that house, during which time I had rarely imagined my return and the exhausting list of comparisons that would almost certainly stem from it. For some reason, what I was trying to do was rebuild the street of my adolescence and my difficulty in achieving that made me think about those little books you get in Rome where, by superimposing two images, you can see something that was once grandiose where now there are only remains of columns, marble blocks or a sizeable area of grass.

Then I went back into the garage. I pulled the waterproof cover off the car. It was very clean. A strange, metallic blue body in the midst of all that dusty chaos. The battery, though, or whatever it was, had gone to pot.

Even though the car was unfit to drive right then, I adjusted the back of the seat and stayed sitting there. I very nearly put my hands on the wheel. But cars weren't my obsession. You ask me what model just went past and I'll never be able to say. It was their mobility that appealed to me, mobility as an end. And I was thinking how obscure that is when you are first presented with a car, how, at eighteen, with your driving licence in a flawless plastic sheath and that ridiculous photo with the haircut you'll regret later, all you want to do is cruise along open roads at dawn without ever getting anywhere. Or rather, your anywhere is an album to be heard in full, your anywhere is a river you watch as you smoke, with as many friends as you can fit in the back seat. The curious thing is that keeping these habits beyond their expiry date makes them seem, in the eyes of others, to be nothing more than a sign of eccentricity in someone who never knew how to grow up.

My mother entered the garage as I was reminiscing. In the rear-view mirror, I saw her running her fingers over the dust-covered boxes, head bowed, giving the impression that she was reading what might be written there, as if until that moment she had ignored their contents or didn't even know why they were piled up in her garage. I got out of the car and waited for her to approach. She gave me one of her out-of-context smiles. 'Won't it start?' It was quite common for bad news to come out of my mother's mouth accompanied by a smile. Not out of spite, quite the opposite; there was some notion of compensation in it.

'I think it would have been a miracle if it had,' I said.

We agreed that it probably wasn't anything serious, nothing a mechanic couldn't sort with the turn of a spanner. We stayed standing there. I looked around me. Funny I couldn't remember that tiny bicycle. No one other than me had been a child in this house.

'Is Julia going with you?'

'Mm-hmm.'

'I thought you'd fallen out.'

It was a bicycle with stabilizers and there was a bell attached to the handlebar.

'I thought you weren't speaking any more. You had a fight once, didn't you?'

'Yes. But it's fine now.'

I asked what was in all those boxes. My mother raised her eyebrows and looked down. They were papers she had collected from the office. She opened a box, as if she needed to illustrate what she was saying. I saw part of a beige folder labelled INVOICES 2002. The box was probably full of them, right to the bottom. Only the years changed.

'Do you miss the office?'

She thought about it.

'I miss having an obligation to leave the house.'

I rang Julia four days later from a petrol station. The sky was blue, it was Saturday, the clouds glided until they scattered into pieces. I asked her to wait for me in front of the hotel. The attendant soon finished filling my tank and I left.

All great ideas seem like bad ones at some point.

Julia was staying in one of those little hotels in the city centre. Not the kind that has decayed to the point of being considered elegant, but something a bit more functional, near the bus station, frequented by executives in suits that are too broad for their shoulders. There were half a dozen of those right at the entrance, laughing loudly as they milled about the red carpet, rather worn in the middle but new-looking at the edges. A cluster of fake palm trees too, whose plastic leaves looked more rigid than Tupperware, gave a tropical welcome to those arriving by car at the main door. Julia was waiting for me next to one of the palms. She was wearing a denim jacket buttoned up to the neck and burgundy skinny jeans. She had radically changed her hair; it fell to her shoulders in a slight wave and a substantial fringe hung over her forehead, almost covering her eyebrows. Never in a million years would you guess that this girl had grown up in the depths of Rio Grande do Sul.

She was biting her cuticles. That hadn't changed. When Julia saw me, the tip of her finger was released from between her teeth, she nodded, grabbed her bag by the handle and walked towards me. I got out of the car. She was from Soledade, Capital of Precious Stones – all cities in the interior feel the need to proclaim themselves capital of something and naturally the reason for their singularity is a compulsory source of pride for their residents. So there was no one in Soledade who didn't see in an amethyst coaster or a rose-quartz obelisk the most beautiful, sensitive art.

I received a lengthy embrace and a 'Paris was good to you', a subject I thought best to hold at bay with a stock smile. A few metres away, a man wearing the baggy gaucho trousers known as *bombachas* was watching us with a certain sad interest.

For a few moments, I imagined what it would have been like if she had been there too, in the small apartment on the Rue du Faubourg du Temple, from which you heard a babble of Chinese voices going on about what may well have been their regular business, but which assumed a tense quality due to the fact that I couldn't make out any variety in their intonation. Julia would certainly have liked the grand boulevards, the gilt detailing on the facade of the opera house and a pastry in six perfect shiny layers sitting in the window of a patisserie just as much as she would a metro station in urgent need of renovation or an argumentative beggar raising his finger to an old lady. She was an adaptable girl, who took the best from whatever she was presented with. Put her in any city in the world and, within three months, she'd be calling it home.

We carried Julia's bag to the back of the car and positioned it in the boot, at which point there was time to exchange a few banal questions and answers about how our lives were going. Paris is lovely, Montreal is freezing, the course is great. Then we got into the car. The previous day, I had bought a road map of Rio Grande do Sul. I hadn't taken a GPS with me because receiving any kind of instruction would go against the idea of the trip. I wanted a map on which we could circle the names of towns with a red pen, a map that starts tearing at the folds on long journeys. Julia looked at it with a faint smile and shut the door.

'Where are we off to first?'

I replied that we were going to Antônio Prado, up in the hills. Julia began to unfold the map.

'But you've never been there, right?'

'Neither of us has been there.'

My attempt to say something of consequence ended with the click of my seat belt, which only made it sound more ridiculous. To prevent any echo, I added, almost without breathing: 'And your parents?'

She laughed.

'Oh, they're quite furious. Hurt, actually.' Julia looked at the map, like someone flicking uninterestedly through a magazine in a white waiting room. 'But I don't care about that as much as I used to, you know? They went to live by the beach.'

'I know.'

'It's nice there, but there's nothing to –'

We were interrupted by three successive knocks on my window. I looked round and recognized the guy in *bombachas*. He was the only person left after all the initial hubbub, other than two employees in kepis, the kind chauffeurs wear, but which definitely seemed to suggest something else, perhaps two boys dressed up for a carnival dance at the Friends of Tramandaí Society. I lowered the window.

'Those boots you're wearing are for men,' he said, pointing into the car, his finger withdrawing and returning twice. From his expression, my boots seemed to have ruined his day.

Slightly shocked, I looked at my feet to check what I was actually wearing, and saw it was my Doc Martens, for which I had paid a small fortune in one of the brand's shops in Paris. Those boots were iconic in almost all counterculture movements, but it was too much to expect that such a symbolic connotation would penetrate the weary carcass of someone who, at best, had seen boots like this protecting the feet of the military police as they shot rubber bullets into the tents of the Landless Workers' Movement. That's the problem with fashion: you depend on others. If they don't get the message, all your efforts go down the drain.

I let out a short, resigned laugh.

'I hardly think you're a fashion expert.'

So I was sitting there confronting his prematurely wrinkled face, when I felt Julia place a hand on my leg and heard her say quietly that we should get out of there. A few minutes later we were leaving the city on the BR-116, a noisy grey line following the train tracks, cutting the suburbs down the middle, which, like any exit route from any big Brazilian city, makes apparent the country's determination to emulate the United States, although what becomes even more apparent is the failure of that mission.

I was still in shock over the incident with the man in *bombachas*, even though I had the strongest convictions about fashion and style, about gender and the rule book of life. But reading *The Second Sex* or whatever doesn't make you immune to idiotic opinions. To be honest, the thing I found most discomfiting was not knowing exactly what Julia thought about it all. It's true that she had unleashed her anger once we moved off in the car ('I can't believe he knocked on the window just to give his opinion on your boots!'). It's true that she had made it clear I shouldn't pay any attention to the words of a stranger ('What an accent he had, my God!') and, on top of that, she thought very differently ('I love your boots'). But that effusiveness ended up producing the opposite effect: it increased my distrust.

Meanwhile, outside, the buildings by the edge of the road seemed as though they were being consumed by soot, broken down by a kind of urban erosion, in which two seconds were equivalent to hundreds of years. Some of them held advertising boards showing amateur models in rather grotesque positions, desperately striving to look attractive. If someone appears at one of those windows, I thought, I won't be able to help feeling a twinge of commiseration.

'You'll never guess what was going on in that hotel,' said Julia, and I was prepared to continue with the subject, whatever it was, until we recovered our Reserves of Intimacy, frozen some years earlier. 'No idea.'

'A meeting of chinchilla breeders.'

She started laughing like one of those people who chuckle alone as they walk, and you're never quite sure whether it's because they have earphones in (what could they be listening to that's so funny?).

'They were negotiating pelts with a *Serbian*. Actually, it was two Serbians, father and son. And the teenager was the expert.' Julia picked up my iPod. 'How do you plug this in?'

'With that cord there,' I pointed. 'But carry on, please.'

'It only gets better.'

'I can imagine.'

The unnuanced joy of an indie band dribbled through the speakers like a viscous liquid. I thought: glad we kept the good tunes for when we're leaving the city limits. Then she continued her story about the chinchillas, which was particularly long and juicy. She had followed almost the entire transaction from a distance, leaning against the entrance to the convention room as the breeders took turns in front of the Serbians. They were carrying suitcases, which they opened on a large table, and they were overflowing with pelts, kind of like chinchillas in plan, chinchillas in 2D, get it? said Julia, to which I replied, yes, unfortunately I could picture it. 'So the boy picked up the pelts one by one and smacked them. Sometimes he blew. I think that was how he worked out whether it was a good or a bad pelt. Then each one was given a label with a value. They were separated into piles. So many dollars for this pile, so many dollars for the other, and in the midst of it all there was a red-haired interpreter, trying to make them understood, but occasionally someone would get carried away and bang on the table, and she seemed completely lost.'

I had been up into the hills many times, when I was a child and my parents still had a bit of energy. In those days, money came in without them having to make much of an effort and turned into articulated Ninja Turtle figures and five-star hotels. I never asked for a sibling. My father was an ENT doctor, an *otorrinolaringologista*, twenty-two letters long, five fewer than *inconstitucionalissimamente*, although he insisted his profession was the longest word in the Portuguese language.

'Cora, listen. *Inconstitucionalissimamente* is an adverb.'

'So?'

'So, it's not even in the dictionary.'

'But it exists.'

'It exists, yes, but it's a word whose only use is to be long, understand?'

I really liked having that conversation over and over again.

It was funny the way that my father's professional success gave me the false impression that otorhinolaryngology was booming during that period of my childhood, like pet shops and private security firms today. Not that the whole city was suffering from tonsillitis, sinusitis and tumours of the ear canal, but everyone who woke up one day coughing or half deaf seemed to have my father's number on their fridge door. Because of this, whenever someone mentions the difficult days of frozen savings, the dollar through the roof, all I can think about is how we had it easy in my house at the start of the nineties. This contributed to a curious feeling that I always lived my life upside down; the decline of the majority was my most prosperous period and, when things started to improve around me, I was already in free fall.

When I say the three of us went to the hills frequently, I'm of course talking about the resorts of Canela and Gramado. Few families attempt anything more than that. On those trips, my father was the guy who drove with his arm hanging outside the car, and my mother was the woman who thought that that posture wasn't correct or safe. My father was the guy who saw a stall and wanted to drink sugar-cane juice and eat cake, and my mother was the woman who reminded him that my aunt and uncle were expecting us for lunch.

Julia and I stopped to eat at a place by the roadside. It was begging to be visited, a pastiche of German architecture, the front of which was overcrowded with flowerpots and garden gnomes and rugs made of squares of hide. We got out of the car and inhaled the fresh mountain air, as if we had spent the last six months in an airless cave. Two signposts fixed in the gravel ('Give us a try!') left no doubt that they also served lunch and snacks as well as offering cheese, salami, honey, phonecards and batteries to take away. I took a few steps forward and looked at the valley below us, speckled with wooden houses. Chimneys were smoking, dogs were barking, children were running around, a girl whose outstretched arms, open palms and short steps gave the impression that she was wearing a blindfold. Julia came up to me, dragging her feet over the gravel.

'Perhaps we should look for something outside the town. When we get to Antônio Prado,' I said.

'Like cabins?'

I nodded.

'I second that.'

Between the ages of eighteen and twenty-one, I think we must have planned the famous Unplanned Journey a hundred times. And when something like that is repeated so often, with minimal variations, it's natural that everything compacts into a single powerful memory, the setting for which is determined at random – it only needs to have happened once in the place in question – while its dramatic charge comes from the sum of all the nights that eventually led us to the idea of the journey, plus the number of years separating us from those nights. In my case, the memory is this: Julia and me lying on the rug in her spartan room on the third floor of the exclusive Maria Imaculada all-girls residence, where she lived the whole time she was at university. We're looking at the ceiling. To my left, there's a record player that Julia's family was thinking of throwing away, and the vinyl that's spinning once belonged to her brother and brought great delight to the small parties where her parents served Coca-Cola and a boy who was more devious than the rest adulterated his friends' plastic cups with palm cachaça. *Houses of the Holy*, Led Zeppelin's 1973 album, lived in between Pink Floyd and Metallica in a typical teenager's bedroom in Soledade, often smelling of the sweat of forgotten football shirts under the furniture. But then Julia's brother supposedly stopped listening to music after he got married.

The day we listened to *Houses of the Holy* lying on the floor, we got carried away again over the Unplanned Journey. There was an infinite number of uninteresting cities to be discovered, and that album seemed like fuel for our plans for freedom. But, yet again, we didn't leave the room, we didn't run downstairs, we didn't reach the car before the spark went out. To tell the truth, we stayed staring at the ceiling, even though the volume and tone of our voices betrayed a good deal of excitement.

It was as if you'd spent months thinking about whether to dye your hair blue, and suddenly you realize that all that time spent deliberating, analysing, imagining, has ended up completely satisfying your desire to rebel. And so the trip was left for another time, a safe distance away from disappointment; after all, having blue hair was perhaps not such a great way to break from the status quo and uninteresting places were perhaps just uninteresting places, nothing more. I breathed deeply. It was mountain air, and we were there, five or six years late, but there, finally. We had survived a fight that was still hanging over us, Paris, Montreal, the madness of our families. That journey was another irresistible failure. ■

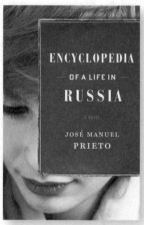
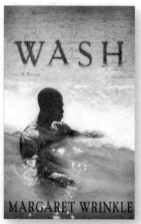

GRANTA

LION

Luisa Geisler

TRANSLATED BY ANA FLETCHER

LUISA GEISLER
1991

Luisa Geisler was born in Canoas, Rio Grande do Sul.
A columnist for *Capricho* magazine, she is the author of
Quiçá (2012), which was awarded the SESC Prize for Literature.
She now lives in Porto Alegre, where she studies social sciences and
international relations. 'Lion' ('Leão') is taken from Geisler's story
collection, *Contos de mentira* (2010).

Her mother would get off the phone soon. Mia sat down on the kitchen doorstep. She looked at her conquest with a smile. Her dandelion on fire. The long white seeds, each with its own flame, yellow and red and orange and grey and red and yellow. The smell of burned grass. The flame came together around all the seeds, reached the stem of the dandelion. Mia heard her mother say goodbye on the phone. She threw the stem inside, onto the kitchen floor, and trampled it with her small shoes.

When her mother got to the kitchen, Mia was in the garden. But the little stem was by the door, next to the stove. Mia's mother smiled with her mouth, but not with her eyes. She picked up the stem. She threw it in the bin, alongside burned leaves and napkins and a singed dish towel and a colouring book reduced to ashes.

In the garden, Mia foraged through carnation bushes. It would take her less than a day to find a perfect object. She was the girl with the short blonde hair. Eyes brown like the earth that clung to her knees. At school, Mia was the shortest in her class. Her size helped her squeeze in among the twigs. Her quick little arms between leaves and branches. She didn't always go looking in the garden. It was in the garden, though, that Mia would find the treasures.

Mia appreciated the rarities. Materials that were different and new. Her experiments had taught her that certain things didn't work, like spoons and cups. And then there were days that were urgent – days when experiments and novelties could wait.

It was always the same process. Wait for her mother to light the stove and leave the kitchen, have the object ready, go in, run. Wait. Leave, run. She'd already tried plants and money and colouring pencils, without any trouble. She'd got to know the whole neighbourhood in her hunt for objects.

It was in a red carnation bush that Mia found the cat. Yellow. Smelling of wet dog. Yellow eyes, yellow fur, brown streaks wrapping its body like swathes of fabric. Paws a yellow so light they were white. Eyes and pink nose outlined in black felt-tip pen. The black mouth opened in a miaow.

Mia and the cat swapped glances. Mia pounced.

A side staircase separated the garden and the kitchen. Mia sat on a step. With shins swinging, she held onto the cat. Perhaps just the paw, or the ear, Mia thought. Just a little bit.

That evening, Mia's mother had friends over. Once she'd put the water on to boil, she took a plate of biscuits through to the living room. Mia ran to the kitchen and lifted her head to spy on the lit hob. It was far back, close to the wall. She heard steps. Swiftly, she opened the oven door, shoved the cat inside, closed the door. A miaow. She turned in time to see her mother walk into the kitchen.

'Mia?' Her mother was smiling with her eyes and her mouth. 'What are you doing, love?'

'Nothing.'

'That's all right then . . .' her mother said. She walked over to the stove, turned it off and picked up the kettle. On her way to the living room, she sneezed.

'Bless you,' Mia said.

Her mother thanked her. Was her mother catching a cold?

'No, love.' Her mother scratched at her nose. 'It was probably an insect or something, it's so dusty. Spring makes my allergies flare up.'

'OK.'

'Do you want to come and have tea with us in the living room?'

Mia shook her head. Her mother smiled and headed to the living room, carrying the teapot. Mia pulled the cat, by its tail, from the oven. The cat clawed and wrestled and scratched and wriggled and quarrelled and quarrelled and scratched. Mia ran to the garden. She held onto the cat with both arms.

She discovered that the cat was mesmerized by a loose thread dangling from her shirt; she discovered that the cat would chase any piece of thread that moved. Later, she discovered that the cat liked to capture small things, trinkets; to chase not just threads, but any moving object. She discovered that the cat liked things that tried to escape. The better they were at escaping, the quicker, more daring they were, the harder the cat chased them.

When she heard her mother call her to dinner, Mia's clothes were covered in bits of grass and yellow hairs. She was so covered in cat that she answered, 'I'm coming,' and forgot to go. She was still lost in thought when her mother crossed the garden, with no smile around her mouth or in her eyes, sniffling.

'Mia.'

'Hello . . .' Mia said. An unthinking 'hello', like when you answer the door buzzer. The 'hello' of someone who doesn't know who it is they're talking to.

'Where did that cat come from?'

It took Mia a moment to answer.

'Hmmm?'

Her mother sneezed.

'That cat. Whose is it? Where did you find it?'

'I just found him.'

'Where?'

'Here.'

'Mia,' her mother said, 'we can't keep it. It might have an owner who's looking for it.'

'He might not have an owner.'

'Mia.'

'Mum . . .'

'That cat's not ours. I'm allergic; it's not good for me. Who's going to look after it?' She faced Mia. 'And who's going to take it to the vet? We can't keep it. Come and eat your dinner.' She sneezed.

Mia left the garden without a word. The cat stayed behind. The felt-tip pen outline opened in another yawn. Mia, though, remained silent. She was silent during dinner, and during her bath. Silently, she ignored her mother before going to sleep.

Her silence came to an end with an 'ah!' late the following morning. She'd found the cat again, asleep amid the pansies. Mia took the cat in her arms and carried him to the garage behind the house. The dark garage with its one high-up window and its shelves and boxes and the smell of mildew.

She played and prodded and kept one eye on the clock and she played and kept the other eye on the cat. She couldn't let any hairs fall on her clothes. The cat wasn't a dog. It kept still and it squirmed out of hugs and tried to fight and tried to scratch and fought and tore into little plastic balls after trapping them. Mia liked the cat more than she did any dog, more than the little balls he destroyed, more than anything. Ten to midday. Mia ran to have lunch. Her mother eyed her up between forkfuls.

'What have you been up to this morning?' The mother's eyes went from her food to her daughter.

'Stuff for school.' Mia concentrated on eating quickly. 'For class on Monday.'

'I didn't see you in the house.'

'Because I was doing it in the garage.'

'What were you doing?'

'I wrote a story.'

'What about?'

'A cat.'

Her mother went back to looking at her food.

When she went back to the garage, Mia looked for the cat everywhere. She found him and took him in her lap and passed her hand over his soft fur. She chatted to him in whispers. She told him about her mother. She told him how they'd be caught if they weren't careful, but she'd be there for him. She stroked his back. The cat stretched his tail upward, daintily, and Mia carried on stroking him down the length of his tail.

Mia went to school in the mornings, and in the afternoons she went to the garage. Always watchful. She brought back what was left of her school snacks for the cat. There were nights when the cat ran away, but Mia would go in search of him. She searched the whole neighbourhood, in trees, through parks, among other sleeping cats. She'd bring him back to the garage. She knew her mother didn't keep track of where she spent her time. If she had to go out to look for the cat, she left quietly.

Her mother stuck to her own routine. As long as her daughter was in the house at mealtimes, she didn't worry. The kitchen had been clean for days, she'd felt no more tingling in her nose and Mia was keeping on top of her homework. It had been days since she'd had to go out at night knocking on her neighbours' doors, asking if they'd seen her daughter. She said to Mia's father:

'Whatever it is that's keeping her busy, long may it last!'

He laughed loudly.

'Have you considered that it might be something worse? I wouldn't be surprised if Mia were building a missile in there, just waiting for The War.'

Her mother laughed. She laughed like someone who's heard a joke so many times they've forgotten why it's funny.

Mia sat with an old sheet on her lap and the cat on top of it. She was telling him about how she'd almost been found out the other day.

'I had a yellow hair on my clothes.' She stroked the cat's head. 'And I couldn't get it off!'

She heard the garage door opening. Her mother's voice.

'Mia?'

Leaping up, Mia stuffed the cat in a large box under the sheet. That was what the box was there for. Mia's mother saw her daughter in the garage. She asked if she was all right. Mia nodded. Her mother smiled.

A noise.

The yellow cat scrabbled out of the box and emerged from under a pile of fabric, smelling of wet dog. Mia looked to the door.

'Nobody came for him.'

'What if I told you they had done?' Mia's mother sniffled.

Mia was looking at the door. She looked at her mother.

'You can keep him, Mia.'

'But what about your allergies? And his other owners? And the vet?' Mia was flapping her arms as if she wanted to take flight. 'He's not ours.'

'We'll figure something out.'

Expressions of relief, like when you take your shoes off at the end of the day. Mia and her mum looked at each other, smiled. They hugged. Mia looked at the cat, hoisted him onto her lap. Her mother talked about a pet shop nearby, about schedules, about dinner. She left the garage. As soon as the cat's paws touched the ground, Mia started to glance about the garage. She wondered when her mum would light the stove again. ■

GRANTA

BEFORE
THE FALL

J.P. Cuenca

TRANSLATED BY CLIFFORD E. LANDERS

J.P. CUENCA
1978

J.P. Cuenca was born in Rio de Janeiro.
He is the author of the novels *Corpo presente* (2003),
O dia Mastroiani (2007) and *O único final feliz para uma história de
amor é um acidente* (2010), which will be published in the US in 2013.
His work has been published in German, Portuguese and Spanish.
'Before the Fall' ('Antes da queda') is taken from a new novel,
forthcoming in 2013.

He has never committed the indiscretion of admitting, especially to himself, that his desire to abandon the city was reciprocal – that it also desired to abandon him. To go away of one's free will would be quite different from being expelled, or, worse, being seen as someone in flight. Would renouncing one's native land not be the rejection of its people? Is it possible to run away without being a coward? Whatever the answers, the very questions were defeats that he was unprepared to accept.

It was necessary to maintain the superiority of the one who abandons over the abandoned, the lucidity of the lover who says farewell and who, starting from a bright and irresistible point in the timeline, decides to be alone. Guaranteeing such a status before his personal diaspora was an inescapable issue. He himself, the son of emigrants, had an example at home: he feared being forgotten by professional colleagues, by the press, by his ex-wives, by the retinue of female admirers who had never met him (precisely because of that), by bar-room conversations – the proscription of those who depart, the name that ceases to be remembered until finally it is never spoken again. Besides going away, he needed to be missed. Exactly what his family, upon escaping from the shipwreck of its circles of origin in the seventies, had been unable to do.

His fondness for the meagre social legacy accumulated over thirty-seven years contrasted with the ill-disguised disdain he had not only for his conquests but also for their arena: Rio de Janeiro. The city, as he was wont to repeat, making instant antagonists in bars, would be the cultural capital of the Extreme Occident if not for Buenos Aires, the financial capital of the Extreme Occident if not for São Paulo, and was moving, then in pre-Olympic times, towards becoming a slightly poorer and a lot more exotic Barcelona in the backwaters of the southern hemisphere.

More exotic and more expensive: the real-estate boom, which transformed shacks in the shanty towns of Rio's South Zone into boutique inns run by Frenchmen in the post-tropical Mykonos that the favelas suggested in the days of the new armed peace, was already part of an irreversible process.

If in the early years of the twentieth century the narrow streets and the thousands of tenements in the city centre, focal points of diseases like smallpox and the poor, were demolished to make room for Haussmannian boulevards surrounded by mansions and art-nouveau buildings (which would also be razed for the construction of architecture-free skyscrapers so dear to the economic miracle of the military dictatorship decades later), at the beginning of the twenty-first century the tearing down of shacks to emulate the Parisian hillside would be a political and aesthetic impossibility – even if their conditions weren't all that different from the tenements of a hundred years earlier: piles of garbage, inadequate sewers, violence, tuberculosis, urban chaos. Not by coincidence, the men and women expelled from the centre by the urban renewal undertaken by Mayor Pereira Passos from 1902 onwards were the same ones who cleared the tropical forest of the hills and transformed it into favelas. It was a vicious circle, an uroboros not of a snake but of a dog chasing its tail – a very common sight in the streets of Rio de Janeiro at any time.

In the 2010s, more discreet and effective than razing the shacks in the South Zone was militarizing the area, constructing ten-foot-high walls on the borders of favelas, and gradually removing the oxygen from their residents. Part of the initial process of asphyxia were reforms that camouflaged the improvisation, incarcerated the area and opened a pathway, albeit without widening the slopes and alleys that bled throughout the hills, for the arrival of new characters: officers of the Brazilian armed forces and their mafioso ramifications, contractors, real-estate agents, foreigners, new capitalists, banks, presses, bistros, abstract-art galleries, American Apparel, Japanese frozen-yogurt shops in place of the old shoemaker, students of design supported by their parents who occupied by themselves the erstwhile shack where a family of six used to live and was now a Luxury Loft, an Upscale Condo, an elegant cubicle with an oblique view of the sea, costing $350,000 for twenty-five square metres. It was Rio's version of gentrification, the occupation of a degraded urban area by a richer social class through displacement of its original inhabitants: Hackney, Greenwich Village, Williamsburg, Kreuzberg, Canal Saint-Martin, Vidigal, Cantagalo, Rocinha, Pavão-Pavãozinho, Chapéu Mangueira, Providência, Saúde.

'It's like art. It's hard to explain exactly what it is, but you recognize it when you see it,' Tomás Anselmo once said, pointing to the first Starbucks on the Rocinha hillside, inaugurated in the summer of 2015.

If in the beginning a small cup of coffee tripled in price, afterwards it was the rent and then the purchase of property. And the official light bill, the official cable TV, the official tax, the official outlaw and a cultural process integrated with development, which led Tomás to discourse for hours about how music, funk dances, mini-shorts clinging to the asses of girls in the favela, libertinage and the manner of screwing were being rapidly gentrified in the protected South Zone favelas, now invaded by the middle class. Even the favela dances and bars began to look like copies of those found at street level, in a kind of Möbius strip of gentrification.

The uproar was beyond normal. Although the new colonizers, whites and gringos (even Brazilians), were apparently sympathetic to the exoticism and disorder of the favela, deep down they harboured the hope of a general clean-up. On the other hand, the original residents could no longer hide their prejudice against the newcomers from down below and their irritation with the ostensive policing – they were still under the control of armed men, sympathetic to every type of arbitrariness against blacks and the poor. They had spent decades in a ghetto dominated by drug traffickers at war with the police and with rival factions, now only to lose their houses and street corners to people who never spent a moment in their lives doing honest work of any kind. They ended up selling their houses and leaving for obscure outskirts without asking the obvious question: Why is it that now, when life has improved, we have to go away?

Slackers, spoiled rich kids, idlers, soap-opera characters, gays, would-be artists, self-styled intellectuals, incipient suckers and spittle on the ground: 'Up their ass.' It was the same prejudice encountered in ultra-elite Ipanema at seeing Arpoador taken over by favelados on Sundays, or South Beach filled with Eurotrash tourists, or Key West with pot-bellied drunks disembarking from cruises paid for in ten instalments, or Greenwich Village crowded with suburbanites from Connecticut, or the cafes on Boulevard Saint-Germain dominated by ignorant Americans, or the country-club pool full of nouveau riche from the Barra da Tijuca. It was that same prejudice based on race, social class, money and culture that began to be found unabashedly in any favelado beginning in the second half of the 2010s.

The word 'community', a euphemism for favela used for decades by journalists, samba composers and sociologists, became synonymous with cultural patrimony deserving of protection, manifesto, patronage by the state, walls. It always was or may yet be too late: the favela is still at war. It discovered in itself the restorative nostalgia for the Rio de Janeiro of the golden years of the bossa nova and, for some, the military dictatorship – a longing for the past that, until then, was the exclusive property of the retired crowd living in carpeted apartments at street level.

In the North Zone and the outskirts, invisible to the media and rather less crystallized in Rio's for-export imagination, the process of expelling the original population was faster and less subtle than in the favelas of the South Zone, without the risk of unfamiliar intimacy. Under the pretext of revitalization, a word that in pre-Olympics times could justify all kinds of atrocities, removals and arbitrary displacements, tens of thousands of people were ejected from their homes to create unlimited space for the new absolute owners of those areas: developers and their armed political allies. Marks painted on doors sprang up like death sentences to determine which houses were to be demolished in forty-eight hours in the ghettos of Vila Autódromo, Jacarepaguá, Taquara, Campinho, Madureira, Maracanã, Olaria and the area of the docks.

Disrespect for residents' rights to resettlement; the immediate transfer of any justice-department official critical of the process; the use of tasers to rouse beggars; the beating of street workers, itinerant vendors and handymen by Municipal Guards prior to dumping them in human warehouses in the wheezing edgelands of the city in an operation the municipal government called, without irony, 'Shock of Order': these were some of the marks of that decade that cariocas chose to ignore, corrupted by the promise of a World Cup, an Olympics, four subway stations, expressways, a pair of museums and stadiums – the provincial desire to be Londoners or New Yorkers in the tropics, to emulate cosmopolitanism through an urban plastic surgery that never came to be but was widely depicted in colourful graphics in the newspapers.

In those early years of the 2010s, the city was beginning to be lost for good to some of its long-time residents. Whoever was unable to pay for the New Rio was swept away to the hot, dusky outskirts that continued to grow virus-like along the deteriorating railroad lines outside the Olympic beltway. The price of real estate inside the small pearl necklace delimited by the sea and the Tijuca Massif came to be regulated by the international market, out of proportion to the real purchasing power of its inhabitants in 2013: rent for a thirty-metre-square efficiency apartment in an overpopulated building in the shadowy concrete corridors of Copacabana was equal to that of a similar apartment in Paris or New York and twice that of one in Berlin or Lisbon.

In little more than three years between the first and second decades of the twenty-first century, the same economic process that doubled or quadrupled the price of housing transformed the real into the world's most over-evaluated currency. In those days Tomás Anselmo's financial adviser would phone him at 5 p.m., twirling his finger in a glass of whisky and soda with lots of ice, to say things like: 'Listen, my man, I'm going to move the entire investment into the Interbank Deposits and the return we'll put in that mutual fund; I've been talking with the people at Factual and they've been unclear about the market, so it's time to protect your principal and take out only the return from a fixed-yield fund.'

Less informed natives of every age proudly repeated the headlines in the *New York Times* and the *Guardian* about the country's growth and the rise in the cost of living – without suspecting, or deliberately forgetting, that the abundance of money was the same that financed risky loans, the business of celebrated super wheeler-dealers that drained competitiveness from industry. When, in November 2009, shortly after the archangel Gabriel announced the Olympic Prophecy, the *Economist* published an article stating that at some time 'subsequent to 2014' Brazil would be the fifth-largest economy in the world, surpassing the United Kingdom and France; that the only risk in Brazil thereafter would be excessive pride; that Brazil, unlike India, had no ethnic or insurgent conflicts; that Brazil, unlike China, was a democracy; and, further, that Brazil, unlike Russia, exports more than just oil and weapons, it was believed that the future of the country of the future had arrived.

Years later, Tomás Anselmo would say, with spiritless eyes: 'The issue of the *Economist* with the statue of Christ the Redeemer taking flight on the cover was the start of our defeat. They hung that magazine on office walls throughout the city like a painting on an altar. Most people never read the twenty-page special on the magic future of Brazil, but they had it framed. What weeks! What months! There were mornings in those days! They took that material as a theophany, as if it had been written not by a group of gringo journalists with tentacles linked to investment funds of Beelzebub himself but by an apostle in ecstasy transcribing the voice of God as it narrated paradise to him and ordered him to take the text to the seven churches of Asia. We believed at that moment that we were condemned to prosperity – and unfortunately that was not our last ingenuous act. Better if the *Economist* had reprinted in its pages on Brazil the apocalypse of St John, now that the old things have disappeared and so many people dry the tears from their eyes, of that there can be no doubt.'

In those perplexing times, Tomás Anselmo complained that the balneary of Saint Sebastian of the River of January had become not only more expensive, but also distant from the references of his infancy and youth. In place of the neighbourhood movie theatres and old bookstores where he spent his sleepwalking adolescence were evangelical churches and fitness centres. In place of the French copper lamp posts and orangish light, the new fluorescent light of Rio de Janeiro was mendacious in its attempt to hide the darkness in which the city will forever live. In place of bars and restaurants and nightclubs with names so old they had lost their meaning, like Penafiel, Luna Bar, Garage, Real Astoria, 69, Carlitos, Basement, Giotto, Bunker and Caneco 70, monsters of mirrored glass, the irrational multiplication of pharmacies and drugstores, several per block. In the emptiness of each of those spaces now occupied by shelves of shampoo and tacky modernistic entrances, Tomás saw an aquarium of tables and chairs en route to the oblivion that he himself so feared, until the last photo of each of those old haunts was finally burned.

And not only were the theatres and bars dying, but also old witnesses of time: in Rio de Janeiro even the statues in the squares were disappearing or being dismantled by thieves to melt down their bronze, even though the squares were enclosed by fences to ward off the sleep of beggars. In the Passeio Público, the little angel of the Fountain of Love, by Master Valentim, was wingless and armless. In Praça Quinze, General Osório's sword, cast from the bronze of cannons in the Paraguayan War, had disappeared. On the sidewalk of Copacabana, the glasses on the statue of the poet Drummond, sitting with his back to the sea, were gone. At least the theft of his glasses would prevent his seeing the ugly passing of cars and buildings to which he was condemned for all eternity.

A man imprisoned in himself, his feet stuck to the ground, his sight faded, he was the statue, decrepit before forty, with the feeling of waking up every day with the hangover that arises between two acts of a drama: *How did I end up here? Just what city is this?* Lost in a narrative of déjà vu illustrated with paranoid determination, the act of reconstructing that path, which would be the same as taking his feet from the ground or finally treading on it, seemed impossible. Tomás Anselmo didn't know how to begin.

In the years that preceded the fall, when Tomás Anselmo was not in the street sighing and taking inventory of his losses, he would shut himself at home with his wife, turn on the air conditioning and organize small orgies lubricated with champagne in Martini glasses. He stuffed himself with psychedelics and never wrote but recorded music on his recently purchased sound equipment: sparse bass, sharp guitar riffs built by infinite overdubbing, atmospheric beats, synthesizers to die for. And he would spend hours mixing the cuts and trying to classify his sexy-melancholy compositions: *chillwave, glo-fi, neo-fusion, landscaping, hyperglitch pop, minimal electro-shoegaze, weightless psych-ambient,* etc. When the parties ended, before going to sleep, he would delete from the computer the tracks composed specifically for that select and scantily dressed audience – that, then, was his public and his stage in the nearly five years when he didn't write.

An invitation to a night out with one of his few remaining friends (they called themselves 'the resistance') provoked the repetition of various phrases: 'Go out? What I really want is for everyone to go home' or 'The only purpose of a cabaret is for single men to find willing women. The rest is a waste of time in a foul environment!' And Tomás remembered that he had no reason to look for women outside his air-conditioned palace of fifty square metres, outside the peace of his domestic desert, and later would trot out the litany that his closest friends knew by heart, until they stopped listening to him: that the euphoria and self-absorption of the carioca in the 2010s was unbearable, that the revitalized and illuminated Lapa was a hotbed of tourists, stupidity and obscurity, that there was practically no music or theatre by a contemporary compatriot that made him want to leave the house, that the poets in the city were pyrotechnic punsters and the writers of prose were zombies, blind mimics of dead traditions, and that any table in the city occupied by artists seemed to him torturous vulgarity: limited thoughts, full of formulas and recipes, bowing down to the powerful, to the old prevailing ideas, to paternalism and the thirst for money.

At a table in Rio de Janeiro in the 2010s, the artists who wasted their time on Earth exchanging information about plans and intrigues could be divided into two large groups: those with government money stapled to their foreheads and those who had labels for TV networks or their advertisers stapled to their foreheads. Anyone who wasn't part of either of the two groups would be fighting for crumbs from those circles, orbiting them attentively and then conspiring savagely to become part of them through the collusion with the aristocracy that fills positions in the complex and swollen organizational charts of ad agencies, production companies, the network itself, newspapers and TV, or through public notices and fellowships and handouts offered through the three branches of government.

Not that Tomás Anselmo was pure and didn't know how to circulate among those schemes and extract from them some money, some fame and some easy sex. Just the opposite – very much the opposite.

Even so, to pay so dearly to live in that tomb of ideas with the atmosphere of a public bathroom, where a trip to a bakery in Leblon takes on the air of a Hollywood expedition, with paparazzi setting up portable offices on motorcycles, sending photos to Internet portals in real time of the latest celebrity who kissed her or his lover in public, where being any place, from a table at a bar to the Municipal Theatre, going along the beach, is to exercise their main vocation of seeing-and-being-seen, where all are foreigners in the city of their birth, divided into countless communities, zones, favelas, neighbourhoods, condominiums, fans, hills, samba schools, criminal factions, street corners, posts at the beach and tables at the bar, no longer made sense for Tomás and for a silent and growing minority who not only changed neighbourhoods but left the city for good, not for lack of money but simply because they could not bear it any more. Or so Tomás Anselmo wished to believe in the golden decade of the 2010s.

Despite the self-deception, Tomás knew that the country and the tree-filled city and the people saying goodbye were only one person: Tomás Anselmo. He, who had never renounced anything, who had always been the target of someone else's renunciation – a job, a woman – was finally haunted by the awareness of never once having given up.

But soon everything would disappear. ■

GRANTA

STILL LIFE

Vinicius Jatobá

TRANSLATED BY JETHRO SOUTAR

VINICIUS JATOBÁ
1980

Vinicius Jatobá was born in Rio de Janeiro. He has
written criticism for *Estado de S. Paulo*, *O Globo* and
Carta Capital. He has also contributed to the anthology *Prosas
Cariocas* and to the film guide *1968 Cinema Utopia Revolução!*.
Jatobá has written and directed several short films, including *Alta
Solidão* (2010) and *Vida entre os mamíferos* (2011). Currently,
he is at work on his first novel, *Pés descalços*, and completing
Apenas o vento, a collection of short stories, from which
'Still Life' ('Natureza-morta') is taken.

You see the house and its time, the house and the house alone, though your secrets, your fears and silences still exist there, locked away behind the denseness of the closed doors and shuttered windows, your fears and silences desperate for an opening to escape a winter that seems eternal, to leave behind the low rumble of trapped accumulation to which they are held captive and ownerless, and you see, you see the house, you don't flee from it or ignore it, you see that the only thing that seems to move in its atmosphere is dust suspended against a fine thread of sunlight, that time itself sleeps lazily on the stupefied clocks, you see the proud furniture relinquishing its strength to despondency, cracking and losing its exuberance and shine, the quilt on the silent bed becoming a filthy cloak where any trace of the smell of its owners is lost amid the dusty fury, the grime, the tears on the ceiling and the weeping in every corner

at first he didn't want to buy the plot and thought the whole thing absurd but I argued that nowhere in the world was so perfect for us to live as here, only here could we be eternally happy, as I'd dreamed of since childhood, and who doesn't want happiness, we'd build the house of our dreams here and live out the countless days that lay ahead of us, and Paulo just looked at me, silent, aloof, proud, his eyes condemning me as if it were inappropriate to want to be happy here, thinking me mad and crazy and fragile, and I loved him for it, even for that, for making me feel simple in his arms, paralysed under the stare of his dark eyes, all those cold nights together, squeezed against each other, submerged under the covers, yes, your madwoman, I'm your madwoman, I said in silence, and he there, staring at me as if buying a plot of land in a place as boggy and humid as Irajá was something really quite stupid, Paulo always so intelligent and learned and me so ignorant, as he would say shamefaced to his friends, forgive her for not speaking properly and not knowing anything about politics, yes, a little airhead, and I know I've only ever really understood my sewing machine, which was all I had in life besides God, my dear God, that machine has brought me pleasure, bricks and mortar, the two of us alone night after night, doing battle, dreaming, accomplices, keeping secrets that we still share, I knew it wasn't stupid to buy that plot and I said come on, man, are you made of sugar, for Paulo was always so clean and perfumed and he hated mud and dirt and always wiped his feet on the mat, even though the mat was so filthy it was like not wiping them, he wiped them more for the gesture, he furnished himself with gestures, and he went mad whenever his son, all smiles, took the dog into the living room, years later, when the sludge had gone and the house existed and the neighbours had multiplied, and then I went further, I said come on, man, this is where I want to have children, I said, and he ended up giving in, though not without first thinking it was all madness, a godforsaken shithole with no tarmac or anything out there in the back of beyond, but it was a simple matter of me having headaches for weeks and weeks until he changed his mind, feeling nauseous whenever he came close to me in bed in our little rented room in Cascadura and there I'd be, hearing the deep breathing of my heart, and there I'd be, feeling the smooth fabric of my nightdress touched along the line of my buttocks, and even then I had terrible headaches that only stopped when he finally gave in, I who was always excessively pretty and who always got the men worked up on the tram or the tramps in the streets where I walked, restless, as if I were inappropriately clothed, feeling myself naked in front of everyone but keeping a calm face for I was Paulo's woman, the man I love and the father of my child

the house, you see the house, with its abandoned backyard and the FOR SALE sign now rusted and cracked in the relentless heat, the wilted yellow leaves scattered about the yard and dancing to the circular motion of the wind, the old wooden dog kennel surrendering to the termites, the grass relentlessly growing, even in gaps in the tarmac, gradually invading a world it used to rule *it was mad to buy a plot so far away from where I worked as a horseback guard, riding through the Olaria bush until I was exhausted, until the stars cried out in the coal-black sky, a cool breeze cut through the stuffy heat of the thick scrub and I felt at one with the animal, breathing to the same rhythm as he and feeling content, lost to the music of the gathered night, and then trotting proudly along the trails of a morning, whistling at the girls and frightening away the boys who ran about killing whatever creatures they found, riding along the pathways, working and studying a lot, putting up with ten years of sleeping badly in that house that took shape without any help from me as money was so scarce, sleeping with pain in my back, lying there drained on the improvised bed and listening to Vera in the half-light pedalling away on her machine, sewing non-stop, sewing as if milking her subsistence from the ether, until I managed to get into the police and could finally buy a decent bed with an American mattress and I began to sleep peacefully and without any pain in my back, then I bought a suit to wear for my new job, an elegant suit like film stars wore, the American and English ones I so admired and that appeared in magazines, and I went about walking on air but always in the same dark green suit as I hadn't enough money to buy another one, that suit was my fortress, and as it tore I'd get embarrassed in front of my friends because of my wife's awful patching, but I resigned myself to it as there was nothing else for it with so little money, and what money there was went on the house, a man dependent on his woman for subsistence, depending on her sewing and tailoring to be able to live a little of the life I wanted to have but lacked the resources for, sometimes I found a note or a bit of shrapnel in the pockets of my trousers and she smiled at me in complicity, quietly, never saying a word, and that was the money I used to go out with my superiors, to get to know the world and see things and I felt guilty that she couldn't join in with what I saw, even though I didn't want her there in my world, even though I wanted to be free of her charitable stare, always planning to leave her but never daring to go through with it, always fantasizing about escape routes, until finally she got pregnant after years of silent suffering, years of thinking she was dry, that she was a desert, wanting it for years, and when I saw her full and expectant smile I knew I'd never leave her, she doubled the amount of sewing she did and put money aside, in a hole behind the wardrobe, for when the child came, she talked of her plans for extending the house and I listened in horror because I wanted to get out of there, a desire that would forever be frustrated for lack of courage, for loving her too sincerely, for admiring her without daring to admit it nor totally giving myself over to it as she did, she who was busy building walls in her mind, walls that would further and forever reinforce the foundations of that prison I wanted to leave without saying a thing, leave her to her mad dreams that grew in every sense and direction, go and live like the police in films, but I did worry about her, the image of her bent over the sewing machine all day disturbed me, I was scared of her stomach bursting and flooding the house, I feared showing signs of my wanting to escape, signs she hardly noticed as she made her little self-sacrifices, wearing the same threadbare clothes and eating second-rate meat, saving crumbs to build the castle of her dreams, ignoring the present and living in the future like a madwoman, shaming me with those charitable eyes, the thought of which made me feel sick when I was with the other women I slept with, Vera putting money aside and me running around with other women, lying, deceiving myself, rehearsing how I'd escape, spending what I didn't have, until one day*

the house, you see the house, its crockery lost in an ocean of reflections and deceptions, in a labyrinth of repetitions behind closed cupboards and drawers, the fine crockery used for the boy's wedding imprisoned with its hopes and best intentions, the knife that no longer hangs

I'd run through the bush and sit down in the mud with the toads, which leapt about excitedly, running away and invading the creeks, and when I got tired of chasing toads I'd sit on a rock and settle down to some fishing with my little cane and I'd catch a few tiddlers until night drew in behind the hill and then go running back to the house, running along as the afternoon slowly died and was overtaken by shadows, hearing noises like

*the laughter of ghosts getting louder until everything finally became night,
I'd go running into the living room and find my mother submerged in
the half-light, propelling the levers of the sewing machine with her feet,
the incessant creaking and bashing echoing about the house like voices of
the tortured coming out of the beyond, and she'd look at me and say good
God what a dirty little pig and she'd shoo me into the bathroom like she
did with the chickens when she fed them in the pen in the yard and I'd
throw myself laughing into the bath and become a fish, a toad lost in the
marshes, and Mum too, a little toad, a toad-pig, and I'd get her wet with
my furious splashing and I'd laugh because I was a fish at the bottom
of the sea, swimming with the whales and sharks, and Mum, is it true
that if you swim really deep you get to China, and she'd laugh, and later
I'd hide behind the kitchen door afraid of the screaming chickens, Mum
breaking their necks one by one and gathering their blood in a pan and
it was terrifying to see the bare chicken and its severed head staring at
me on the marble table and then, Mum, is it true that humans come from
monkeys, and she'd laugh and say go ask your father, he's the clever one,
I'm just a seamstress, but the next day I was older, watching the trams go
by with my dad, in Vicente de Carvalho Square, stealing sips of cold beer
from his glass and trying to inhale the smoke from the cigarettes I smoked
awkwardly, pretending I was interested in the panic of the people betting
on horse races and the results announced in Morse code by taciturn men
on stands, laughing at the mules and asses as they kicked out and neighed,
admiring the pretty girls coming out of church who stared at the ground
as they passed by in groups, accompanied by their aunts and helpers, Dad
telling me with wonder that one day hundreds of iron horses would cross
right through Irajá and into the town centre in under twenty minutes and
me thinking he was going mad, that the horse was too fine an animal to
stop being used just like that and anyway what would happen to all the
asses and mules and Dad saying that every house would keep one as a pet,
colleagues from school sitting around the bandstand waiting to go into the
cinema and admiring me from afar because I was drinking and smoking
with the adults, I'd stand at the side of the table as they played rummy and
watch them cheat and now and again I'd run to a far-off house carrying*

*the groceries of one of my father's friends, who'd decided to stay out with
his friends because our friends are all we have, lad, don't ever forget it, and
I was always glad to go to Nazário's house with his groceries as I got to see
his three daughters and Nazário would tell my father that I was helpful
but a fool, if he thinks I won't chop his balls off out of friendship then
he's very much mistaken, but what old Nazário didn't know was that I'd
already kissed all three of them in the backyard of the house and promised
to marry them all*

unclaimed photographs pile up in drawers, the last vestiges of
remembrance holding on until everything is finally destroyed,
because when the house loses the smell of its owners, and its objects
resign themselves to tedium, there will be no more memory and the
clock will become just a clock, the key just a key, the glass just a glass,
grease encrusting every nook and cranny in the old kitchen, a black
shadow spreading everywhere, rotting the air and staining the white
of the tiles, the old fridge robbed of its integrity by cavities of rust, the
penguin at the top offering a lost look of exile

*when Ana had left I took all his clothes and angrily threw them in the dirt
in the backyard so that the few neighbours we had could see that he'd been
thrown out of my life, out of my house, even though I knew he was the only
thing that mattered to me, Paulo, dear Paulo, watching me from behind the
wall, making kind and gallant signals that I pretended had no effect on
me, such pretty hands with long fingers, green and blue veins against his
pale skin, and smiling that soft smile that first charmed me, before a friend
gave me a little message from him, written in round, timid handwriting
and full of pompous words I was unfamiliar with but that lifted me up
to the clouds, my friends saying that if I didn't steal away with him then
they surely would, and my torturing him by withholding the only answer
I was ever going to give him, the man I chose to be mine the very moment
we started courting, and then finally getting engaged in the living room*

with an aunt watching, entwining our fingers in love and privation, his smooth voice whispering sweet nothings in my ear, words that stilled my beating heart, and I felt like the happiest most complete woman in all the world, and when my aunt left the room I squeezed his thighs and gave him longer kisses, and I felt him get excited, and I turned red and crazy, my world spinning and I let him see my legs just a little, wanting and desiring and worrying, imagining what it would be like, hearing stories from my older cousins, being given confusing and alarming advice, nobody knew how to love back then and they still don't, I bathed and felt my legs and my whole body, my hand ran all over my bristling skin and I let the water run down to my feet, happy seeing myself in the steamed-up mirror, torturing myself as I touched myself until one terrifying day I felt all that I'd only previously imagined those feverish nights, and right away I thought my cousins had lied, could it be so simple, a little that was a lot and that I wanted more of, that I wanted again laughing happily at life in our little room in Cascadura, hugging my man, and now this, dear Paulo with another woman, Ana tells me, thinking I'd die of shame and feeling ridiculously pregnant and hating myself for loving him the way I loved him, wanting to die when neighbours stared at me as I

the old record player thrown in the corner with a collection of old vinyls, a rusty gas canister and piles of ancient newspapers announcing the breaking news of bygone days, corroded and burned a dull yellow: the house, you see the house, abandoned to its fate, its stories silenced with no one to tell them to

a goddamn bullet in the chest, now is that any way to die, Pedro, for a man like Getúlio to end his days like that, in such a way, the life of the most prized and principled man this country has ever seen coming to an end like that, it's disgraceful, it's absurd, and I never saw Dad drink like he did that day, spitting and cursing, saying to himself that these days presidents killed themselves fucking hell, fucking hell, if presidents killed themselves then why not bakers, and mechanics and postmen, and chauffeurs and engineers, that presidents killing themselves really took the biscuit, and there were thousands of angry people ganging up together in the town centre, news of crowds gathering outside the Tribune's *offices and Son, now what, Son, what a fucking mess Son, you work for nothing in this country Son, you sweat blood in this country and it's all for nothing Son, if there's no longer room for people like Getúlio in this world then what's to become of the rest of us Son, I was no longer so young and by then I smoked my own cigarettes and drank beer from my own glass and Dad wanted Lacerda's head for what he'd published about Getúlio, that swine, that bastard, that Nazi, my father said, death to Lacerda and his family, may his children and grandchildren and great-grandchildren all die for what he's done, it's disgraceful, that's no way to die, but I didn't care, I saw people fighting in Cinelândia and Lavradio and I didn't care, I preferred talking to the whores in the brothels of Olaria and Madureira, fixing a car door would matter more to me than fixing a country, they could kill the lot of them for all I cared so long as they spared the whores, the world would be unbearable without the sad affections of a whore, if they killed the whores then I'd set the whole world on fire but fuck the president, he never whispered false sweet nothings in my ear for a few coins, fuck the president and his children and Lacerda and his children and the fact that they owned the country and that we were the doomed, that we worked for people who lived the high life without ever getting their hands dirty, I earned money as a typist on a magazine but I never read the news I set down, and Dad telling me things I didn't care about, Dad lost amid the confusion of the shouting and anger and running and fighting and broken bottles and people crying, Dad trying to imagine where it would all lead and saying to himself that Brazil was fucked, that Brazil murdered its own future every bloody day, a country with no enemies destroying itself, humiliating itself and humiliating everyone who dared dream beautiful dreams, that was what he said, that everything beautiful died young in this fucked-up country, the country had lost its innocence, said my father, and I didn't care, I didn't care, I didn't care about the future, what I did care about was reading mechanics journals and understanding the cars I*

so restlessly admired, hanging about the garage near home, watching the
people at work, the parts and the motors, I loved cars without ever having
seen inside one, loved them from afar, until one day the owner of the garage
asked me to go fetch some oil from Madureira and he gave me some money
and I bought it and then when it came to him paying me I said I didn't
want to be paid, what I wanted was to work in the garage and he laughed
and said very well, that I took after my father and that I could stay so long
as I didn't set fire to anything

dozens of old tools and apparatus abandoned in the loft, rubbish
accumulating in the corners of the living room, in the hallways,
dense dust encrusted in the indentations on plastic containers, in
the grooves of the furniture, the threadbare fabric of the sofas, the
sad and disorderly holes of the fan's rusted mesh covering, the sun
entering the living room and orbiting the dark clammy dust in a slow
and circular ballet

when I finally earned my first promotion and became a detective, I started
to earn a little more and Vera cut down on her clothes orders and was able
to read magazines and listen to the radio and I could buy the little wooden
horse Pedro wanted so badly, to run around the backyard like an animal,
leaping and getting dirty and falling and laughing, giving military orders
to huge armies that fought against the poisonous threat of the flowers in
the garden, killing the hordes of camellias with his wooden sword, a boy
who killed camellias would end up either an imbecile or a crook, to calm
him down I'd walk with him for hours, following the tramlines almost as
far as Olaria, and I tried to answer all the questions he asked me about
the stars and animals and machines and dinosaurs, making things up to
leave him satisfied when faced with the inexplicable, only heading home
once evening was drawing in and he sat on the sofa in the living room with
his arms folded, silently waiting to be brought his bread and butter and
milk like Lord Muck, milk just appearing in his glass while I had to steal

it from the cow, and Vera always looking at me with eyes full of hurt and nothing I could say would make her look at me the way she used to, a look that had always annoyed me but now that I didn't have it was all that I wanted, to win back that look, to be held hostage to her dreams once more, to have her include me in the future she imagined in her head and that no longer featured me, but I'd have to wince in shame for many years yet, face the disapproving looks of neighbours who'd witnessed the scandal of my clothes thrown out in the backyard, then one day I bought her flowers for the first time since we'd got married, with a note saying madwoman I love you, and she put the flowers to one side and went back to her sewing and I felt alone in the world and when I went to say something to her all that came out were tears, I wanted to thank her for everything she'd done for me and tears came out, I wanted to say what a blessing our son was and tears came out, that the modest house we now had was like a fortress to me and only tears came out, and faced with her silence I thought I'd lost her forever and all night I felt adrift in a bed that was a foreign country, until the next day when I found some shrapnel in my trouser pocket and I understood, the world became vast and expansive once more and I understood and I spent the whole day waiting to go home, and when I got off the tram I quickened my pace and when I got to my street I started to run scared that the house might no longer be there but it was, just as the table was there, ready with roast beef and potatoes, and the bed was made and fragrant and without a word being said I understood, I put my hands on her hips and she purred and I understood that I'd won back what I thought I'd lost forever

the floor bestrewn and lustreless, termites gnawing the corners of the floorboards and hiding in the door frames, fearful, lazily devouring what will soon no longer exist

Mila was lying on the ground as if she were asleep and I came sneaking out from behind the wall to give her a fright, laughing, screaming with all my might, and I screamed again, startling the pigeons on the telephone lines, a

terrified flock that made a shadow as it flew away over the backyard, but nothing, Mila kept lying there on the ground pretending she hadn't seen me, pretending to be asleep just to alarm me, I poked her under the tummy with a small stick and nothing, she's good at pretending, the little devil, if only Dad could see how good at pretending she is, this dog's an artist, we should take her to the circus and earn some money because she's an artist, once I made her hold her breath for half an hour, but she was very wise, she learned that Chinese trick, and she was stubborn besides, and Dad told me Mila had died, but that was impossible because only that morning she had run with me and played with me and even bit me and she'd eaten too and she'd done a poo in the living room so it wasn't possible, she was dead like when we played cops and robbers and so I told her the game had finished, which was why I didn't like the Chinese because they only played for real, and now how could I get my dog to stop playing the game, but Dad said she wasn't going to wake up again and that dying meant going to sleep forever and I told Dad that I wouldn't like to go to sleep forever and he went quiet and fetched a bread sack and put Mila in it and at dawn he went out and I ran to the door and asked if I could go with him and we went out into the dark night walking in silence, I played with the lantern and the fireflies and the sounds around us were strange, the world seemed to be plotting against us ever making it home again and we got to the river and we threw Mila in the river and when the sack hit the water it started to sink and disappear and Mila had turned into a fish, she would bark at the other fish and lead them to the riverbed to help me when I went fishing, when we got back home I asked Dad if I'd die too and Dad said that everything dies one day and that's just the way life is, so everything dies, and he said yes, that was the price for being alive and that was why every day was very important, and in bed I closed my eyes and tried to imagine what it would be like to go to sleep forever and I got bored because it was boring and the next morning I told Dad that if I died he was not to hurry into throwing me in the river but rather be patient and wait because I'd find a way of waking up

the deaf and mute telephone battling to hold on to the memory of
dear numbers that now give nothing when dialled

my son going about hand in hand with that dumb ugly north-eastern hick,
a fifth-rate nurse with parents who looked dumb and poor, living among
people of that sort, God, I was poor but I was never dumb, dying of shame
having to appear in photos with these people, his having chosen them
seemed to be some sort of revenge against me, falling in with such people
just to wound me, them being in the house I'd built through honest labour,
eyeing everything with curiosity, wanting to open all the drawers with their
dozens of hands and smiling at me as if we were part of the same family, me
hardly disguising my fear that they'd steal the crockery, that their dozens
of hands would make off with my cutlery and jewellery, that they'd spirit
away part of my fulfilled dream and the comfort of my things, I never
understood Pedro leaving home when he could have happily married the
daughter of the greengrocer, the pretty little Portuguese girl who was all
smiles and called me madam, and was elegant and beautiful and whom
I taught to sew after her mother asked me to and who went to church
every Sunday and had a big heart, not like that dumb ugly north-eastern
hick who dropped eggs on the floor and burned orange and cornmeal cake
and made gloopy rice and couldn't even season beans properly, a woman
lacking and uneducated, who went for walks on Sundays, didn't know
how to read her rosary and lay on the sofa pretending to read bright-
coloured fashion magazines, my son handing me her tatty clothes while
she wandered the streets making idle chit-chat with any man who'd talk
to her, and she was foul-mouthed and interrupted the men in conversation
and didn't know her place, a young woman who rather than stay at home
went out dressed in white to work with other men, left the house to sneak
about with who knows whom, doing who knows what, while my son got
home without a decent meal waiting for him, the bed doubtless crumpled
and neglected, those dishonest north-easterners, dirty like the blacks who'd
started to build wooden shacks on the hills and who came down to sit in
the squares and laze about, the government promised to clear vagrants off

the streets but just removing the blacks from the streets would have been a big improvement, communists are still people but where did so many blacks come from, and my son going about hand in hand with them, laughing with them, being mistaken for one of them, and becoming increasingly estranged from me, my Pedro, increasingly far removed from that lovely little boy who listened to my stories and watched me sew glassy-eyed and who asked me questions I didn't know the answers to, and to hide the shame of my ignorance I invented meanings, names, countries, did everything for him, gave my all for them, those ungrateful men incapable of giving me a kind look or word, my two boys living as if I no longer existed

the stagnant water in the iron pipes rotting and longing for skin, drying and creaking with hatred for the cold concrete, the house, you see the house and you see joyful moments clasping hands with sad ones, moments that wander around empty without their owners, withdrawing into the shadows

I left home and when I looked back all I saw was Mother's look of disgust, upset because I hadn't got married to Luisa like she'd wanted since we were young, condemning me for marrying for love just as she had once done when she fell for the son of a popcorn seller, fancy not having married Luisa, she used to say in church in front of me and Marta and hell, Mother, leave me be, I love her, I love her more than anything else in the world and she, angry, always looking at me accusingly when we still lived with her, relentlessly, treating me like an object, as if I'd somehow brought shame on the house, and asking me all the time if I knew where Marta was, if I was sure she was at work, and I'd say where else would she be, Mother, and she'd laugh and ask about the grandchildren that weren't on the way, and when would I at long last find my own home and get that woman out of here, that woman who was like a stain on her reputation, the same thing hidden behind every question, why had I changed the way I was with her, when did I stop being the man she'd hoped I'd become, making my life hell until one day I interrupted what she was saying and she slapped me and told me shut up while I'm talking, and I realized that if I didn't leave I'd lose the mother I cherished in my heart, that this woman was threatening the memory of the woman she used to be, that the bitter selfishness that caused her to mistreat us also buried, day by day, the happy image I had of my mother, the one who I talked to and chatted to about her past, I realized this while holding back the tears that poured forth into the night, wrapped around Marta's hips, trying to understand what had happened, what my mistake had been, and we decided to leave and rent a room and I quit the garage to go and work as an electrician, and Mother always said that I never got qualified in anything because of Marta, that Marta had been the end of me when in fact she'd been the beginning, that the problem with me was Marta when in fact she was the solution, and whenever I did a big electrical installation there was a great hullabaloo, there's nothing so wonderful as the first time you flick the switch on in a house that's never had electric light before, it's as if a whole family's dreams light up, as if they've all been blessed, man's ingenuity made the bomb but it also made the lamp, and when we finished the project at Armazém Matias in Madureira and we turned the lights on and that huge arcade lit up and my father came hobbling over with his walking stick and gave me a hug and said that he always knew I'd bring light into people's lives, my being a policeman stopped you from becoming a crook, you'd have made a good crook, but you do right to make so much light, my son, and I felt like saying that it was electricity that made light but as far as my father was concerned it was me who made it, and when I asked he said the madwoman was still mad but that she loves you, she loves you, every year another screw comes loose, but she loves you

the long double bed, the indentation of its owners' bodies frozen with disuse, the springs that creaked now mute and glass-like, the dining room arranged ready for guests that never came, the unwound unworking clock finally laying to rest the changing of the seasons

I spent my days remembering and writing in school exercise books, jotting down ideas and concocting a past like my grandfather used to do, living out my unexpected retirement, condemned to using a walking stick but grateful for being alive, we fall off ladders without knowing what will happen when we hit the ground, falling is a question, and falling was the best thing that could have happened to me because the dogs were in power, the police now had to go after young people, boys were criminals, girls in skirts who smoked and read books were terrorists, the military set the agenda and we had to do their dirty work, better to fall off a ladder than fall foul of your pride, to be left to catch people for stealing rather than catch them for thinking, to go after people because of something they've done in the past rather than what they might do in the future, the future they want versus the future we want, I spent my days writing in exercise books to escape the misery that was destroying my country, pretending not to notice stories in the newspapers, news that was there but not there, the dungeons that lay behind the triumphant headlines, a country that outlaws the dreams of its youth is a country going backwards, God put that ladder in my path, when the ladder broke and I fell I felt peace, better to have a walking stick in my hand than a whip, which I'd used on horses in Olaria but people aren't animals, and I lived like this, accumulating newspaper cuttings and exercise books until one day I got a call, and the world went silent and the ladder became a curse, because that fall should have killed me so that I never had to hear what I heard, it wasn't possible and the man said it was, that he was sorry, a son has the right to become as old as his father one day and the man said he was sorry, and the phone went dead and I felt like going over to my exercise books and erasing them all, crossing them out line by line and then maybe time would reverse, or if I wrote that the ladder had killed me then maybe it would have killed me, it wasn't possible and when Vera got back from shopping and saw me I felt her world collapse, a devious ladder that led to rock bottom and destroyed us, and then later on, when I saw him laid out on a silver table, it was really him, I'd still had hope but it was really him, he seemed happy and serene, and the doctor said it was very sudden, and I said it wasn't possible, doctor, only yesterday we went around on the noisy trams watching the streets slowly going by, the lamp posts and the houses and the people of the world passing by and us seeing them for the first and last time, it was only the day before yesterday that he broke the radio apart trying to find where the presenter was hiding, and the day before the day before yesterday I helped him climb the tree to put a thrush back in its nest, and now sir is trying to tell me that this man laid here is my son, sir ought to be ashamed of himself because it's not possible, a son has the right to become as old as his father one day, the good doctor ought to be ashamed of himself and make my son wake up, but it was no longer possible, and when I heard Marta and Vera in tears in the corridor outside I wanted to defy my son's wishes and put him in a bread sack right away and walk through the night to throw him in the river, because Son you understand play but I understand death, throw the bag in a deep river so that he might lose himself freely and go back to his childhood, go back to his dog, go back to his childhood and his fish, leave this world for a better one

the animals in pictures on the wall too scared to run away, their stories abruptly interrupted, dry waterfalls and dead fish, Napoleonic wars suspended for lack of will for victory, an immense and doleful moon denying romance to a couple watching a river that no longer runs, sitting on a bench in a sad square

and they ran down the corridor, the girl with the Indian face and the tanned little fat boy and that was that, Paulo in his corner wrote and read his newspaper and got cross because his grandson stole his walking stick to play with the dog, and Marta came and went, taking the grandchildren away and bringing them back again, and they grew and grew, the girl staring at the hardly used sewing machine until one day she asked if we could get it going and I taught her to thread the needle, she needed help stepping on the pedal because her legs couldn't reach and she laughed as she ran the sewing line over the fabric, playing with the giant scissors and the buttons that she stuck onto pieces of cloth like little faces and landscapes while the boy spent more time with his grandad, watching grandad bash his typewriter and going through the drawers of cuttings he kept gathered in the old storeroom, and one day I saw him sneak one of the exercise books into his rucksack and I didn't say anything, he took the exercise books and sneaked them away and brought them back again, and they grew bigger and bigger, and Marta had grey hair by then and a new husband, and they came and they had lunch with us at the weekends, until they left to go and live in Petrópolis and ended up visiting less, increasingly it was just Paulo and me, we watched telly and played cards, neighbours came by to talk badly of other neighbours, friends from church talked about the youth of today, the clothes the girls wore, on Thursday nights the living room became a policemen's club, Paulo told stories about outlandish crooks, everyone boasting, until one day Paulo told no more stories, the typewriter went silent, the drawers of paper remained closed, a good man deserves a good send-off, his was peaceful and serene, and I was left alone in the house, waiting for the day to come, awaiting the unknown hour, the second chosen on a whim by time for me to depart, sitting in the armchair and winding up my watch and listening to the radio and thinking about when my time would come, that life is made up of expectations but old age has only one, it gets disguised as several others but it's always there, waiting, it's our breath, it's our false step, and it's time to hand things down, to tidy up the sewing things because somebody will use them one day for some special occasion, the daughter's first social outing, the shirt button that comes off just before an important meeting, patching up little mishaps gives life its spice, the boy by now a man comes here and takes the exercise books one by one and asks me to talk about old times and asks me what his father was like and I tell him that he was a good man and that the lights on the Armazém Matias are the most beautiful in the world and that many couples have fallen in love in cars fixed by him, your father was a good man who fixed things that were broken, that was your father, a man who kept on believing, gave the fridge another chance, the radio, the cooker, he was a machine's best friend, today people throw things out at the first sign of any problem but he brought things back to life, that's what's been passed down to you from your father, that there's a trick to doing everything, that no problem's too big for a monkey wrench, and the lad laughed and went on his way and left me on my own, and so I patiently await my end, because I've a hernia, swollen shoulder and sore leg, because eyes that could once see through the eye of a needle can now hardly make out faces, I go outside the house and take care of the pepper trees and the lemon verbena, I sit in my armchair and listen to the sound of the presenters on the radio, biding my time until He says enough is enough, Amen

the house, you see the house, the last days of the house before it falls to the ground and goes back to being the dust from whence it came and where a building will be raised upon its last remains, the house and its furniture and its pictures and its papers and its fabrics, orphaned, silenced and still. ∎

GRANTA

APNOEA

Daniel Galera

TRANSLATED BY STEFAN TOBLER

DANIEL GALERA
1979

Daniel Galera was born in São Paulo but
has spent most of his life in Porto Alegre. He co-founded the
publishing house Livros do Mal, which then published his collection
of stories *Dentes guardados* (2001) and his novel *Até o dia em que
o cão morreu* (2003). His second novel, *Mãos de cavalo* (2006), has
been published in Argentina, Italy, France and Portugal and
is forthcoming in the UK. *Cordilheira* (2008) won the Brazilian
National Library's Machado de Assis Prize. In 2010, he wrote the
graphic novel *Cachalote* with illustrator Rafael Coutinho. 'Apnoea'
('Apneia') is part of a novel in progress.

He sees a bulbous nose with shiny pores, like the skin of a tangerine. A strangely adolescent mouth between the chin and cheeks that are covered in fine wrinkles, skin sagging a little. A trim beard. Large ears with even larger ear lobes, as if their own weight were stretching them out. Irises the colour of watered-down coffee in the middle of lascivious, laconic eyes. Three deep, horizontal furrows on his forehead. Yellowing teeth. An abundance of blonde hair breaking as a single wave on his head and flowing to the base of his neck. His eyes run over all four quadrants of the face in the interval between breaths and he can swear that he has never seen this person before in his life, but he knows that it is his dad because no one else lives in this house on this farm in Viamão and because lying on the right side of the man sitting in the armchair is the bluish dog who has been with his dad for years.

Why that face?

His dad gives the faintest hint of a smile. It's an old joke and has a set response.

The same one as always.

Now he notices his dad's clothes, the tailored dark grey trousers and the blue shirt soaked in sweat at the armpits and around his bulging stomach, the sleeves rolled up to the elbows, the sandals that he seems to wear against his will, as if only the heat stopped him from wearing leather shoes, and also the bottle of French cognac and the revolver on the little table beside his reclining chair.

Sit down, says his dad, nodding towards the white two-piece imitation-leather sofa.

It is early February and whatever the mercury says, it feels like the temperature here near Porto Alegre is over forty degrees Celsius. Arriving, he saw that the two *ipê* trees that stand watch at the front of the house were laden with leaves. They groaned gently in the still air. The last time he was here, back in the spring, the purple and yellow blossoms of their crowns were rustling in a cold wind. Still in his car, he passed the vines growing to the left of the house and saw many clusters of tiny grapes. He could imagine them sweating sugar after months of drought and heat. The farm had not changed at all in these few months, it never changed, a flat rectangle of grass beside the dirt road and a small, neglected football pitch, and in the road the annoying bark of Catfish, the other dog, the front door standing open.

Where's the pickup?

Sold it.

Why's there a revolver on the table?

It's a pistol.

Why's there a pistol on the table?

The sound of a scooter passing on the road is accompanied by Catfish's barking, hoarse as the hollering of an inveterate smoker. His dad frowns, he cannot stand the surly, noisy mongrel and only keeps it out of a sense of responsibility. You can abandon a son, a brother, a father, definitely a wife, there're reasons that justify all that, but you've no right to abandon a dog once you've looked after it for a certain amount of time, his dad had said to him once, when he was still a boy and the whole family lived in a house in Ipanema that had also been home at one time or other to half a dozen dogs. Dogs give up forever some of their instincts when they live with people, and can never get them back completely. A loyal dog is a crippled animal. It's a pact that we can't undo. The dog can undo it, although it rarely will. But man doesn't have that right, said his dad. And so Catfish's dry cough has to be endured. It's what the two of them do now – his dad and Beta, the old Blue Heeler bitch lying at his side, a dog that is truly admirable. Intelligent and circumspect, as strong and well built as a boar.

How's life, son?

And that revolver? Pistol.

You look tired.

I am, a bit. I'm coaching this guy for the Ironman. A doctor. The guy's good. Great swimmer, and he's not bad at the rest. His bike weighs seven kilos, tyres and all. One of those $15,000 bikes. He wants to do the qualifier next year and get into the world championships in three years' time, maximum. He'll manage. But he's so fucking boring. Just have to put up with it. I haven't had much sleep, but it's worth it, he pays well. And I'm still giving lessons at the pool. I finally managed to get the bodywork fixed on my car. As good as new. It cost two grand. And last month I went to the beach, spent a week in Farol with Antônia. The redhead, you know. Oh, right, you didn't meet her. Too late, we had a fight in Farol. And that's about it, Dad. The rest is the same old, same old. Why's there a pistol on the table?

What was the redhead like? You got that weakness from me.

Dad.

I'll tell you in a minute why there's a pistol on the table, all right? Christ, *tchê*, can't you see I'd like to have a bit of a chat first?

OK.

Fuck's sake.

OK. I'm sorry.

Want a beer?

If you're having one.

I'm having one.

His dad extracts himself with some difficulty from his comfy chair. The skin on his arms and neck has taken on a permanent pink tinge over the last few years as well as a texture that reminds him of chickens. He used to be up for a game of football when his elder brother and he were teenagers and was an on/off gym-goer until sometime in his forties, but since then, as if to coincide with his younger son's growing interest in all manner of sports, he has become a firm believer in a sedentary lifestyle. He had always eaten and drunk like a horse, smoked cigarettes and cigars since he was seventeen and enjoyed cocaine and hallucinogens, which all meant that nowadays he has some difficulty dragging his bones around. Walking towards the kitchen, he passes the wall in the corridor where a dozen of his advertising prizes hang, certificates in glass and brushed metal frames, mostly dating from the eighties when he was riding high as a copywriter. In the living room there are also a few trophies on the top of a low glass-doored mahogany cabinet. Beta follows him on this journey to the fridge. The bitch seems to be as old as her master, a living totem who follows him with a silent and floating gait. His dad's lumbering past the memories of now distant professional glory, the animal loyally behind him and the lack of meaning on this Sunday afternoon all awake in him a distress that is as puzzling as it is familiar. It's the feeling he gets sometimes when he sees someone anxiously trying to make a decision or solve a little problem as if the meaning of life depended on it. He sees his dad is right at the utmost limit of his powers, perilously close to giving up. The fridge door opens with a moan, glass tinkles, seconds later he and the dog are coming back, with a lighter step than when they left.

Farol de Santa Marta – it's over near Laguna, right?

Yes.

They twist off the caps, the gas escapes the bottles with a disdainful *pfff!*, they toast nothing in particular.

I regret not having gone more to the beaches in Santa Catarina. Everyone went there in the seventies. Your mum used to go before she met me. I was the one who started taking her south, Uruguay, places like that. The beaches up there disturbed me a bit. My dad died up there, near Laguna, Imbituba. In Garopaba.

It takes him a few moments to realize that his dad is talking about his grandfather, who died before he was born.

Grandad? You always told me you didn't know how he died.

I did?

Several times. That you didn't know how or where he had died.

Hmm. Maybe I did. I think I really did.

Wasn't it true?

His dad thinks before replying. He does not look like he is trying to gain time, he really is working something out, digging deep in his memory, or just choosing the right words.

No, it wasn't true. I know *where* he died, and I sort of know *how*. It was in Garopaba. That's why I never enjoyed heading that way.

When?

It was '69. He left the farm near Taquara in . . . '66. He must have ended up at Garopaba about a year later. Lived there for two years, something like that, until they killed him.

He looks at his dad and a snort of laughter escapes from his nose and the corner of his mouth. His dad looks at him and smiles with him.

Fuck, Dad. What do you mean, they killed Grandad?

Know what? Your smile is just like your grandad's.

No, I don't know what his smile was like. I don't know what mine is like, either. I forget.

His dad says that he and his grandad resembled each other not only in how they smiled, but also in much of their appearance and behaviour, that Grandad had the same nose, narrower than his own. His face was broad, eyes deep-set. The same skin colour. Says that Grandad's drop of indigenous blood had skipped his son but turned up in his grandson. Your athletic build, says his dad, you can be sure you got that from Grandad. He was taller than you, must have been five foot eleven. Back then no one did sports like you do now, but the way he chopped wood, tamed horses, worked the fields, it would've put today's triathletes to shame. Was my life too, until I was twenty. Don't think I don't know what I'm talking about. I worked in the fields with my dad when I was young and was amazed at his strength. Once we went looking for a lost sheep and we found the sick thing almost on the neighbour's land, two miles from the house. I was wondering how we would get the pickup there to take the sheep home, foreseeing Dad asking me to fetch a horse, but he heaved the creature onto his back, as if it were hugging him round the neck, over his shoulders, and started walking. Those sheep weigh about a hundred pounds and you remember what the land was like out there, just hills, and the ground all stony. I was about seventeen and asked to carry it for a stretch, I wanted to help, but my dad said no, it's sitting snug now, getting it off and on again is more tiring, let's keep walking, the main thing is to keep walking. There's no way I could have borne its weight for more than a minute or two anyway. You and he were cut from a different cloth. And you've got similar personalities. Your grandad was on the quiet side, just like you. A silent and disciplined man. He didn't rabbit on at you. He'd only talk when he needed to and get annoyed by other people when they wouldn't shut up. But that's where the similarities end. You're gentle, well-mannered. Your grandad had a short fuse. God, what an insolent old man he was! He had a well-earned reputation for drawing a knife at the slightest provocation. He'd go to a dance and end up in a fight. And to this day I don't understand how he got into fights, because he didn't drink much, he didn't smoke, gamble or get involved with women. Your grandma almost always went with him and, funny thing is, she didn't seem to mind this violent side he had. She liked to hear him play. He was one hell of a guitarist. Once my mum told me that he was like that because he had an artist's soul but had chosen the wrong life. That he should have travelled the world playing music and letting out his philosophical thoughts – that was the expression she used, I remember it clearly – instead of working the land and marrying her, that he squandered his true calling when he was very young and then it was too late, because he was a man of strict principles and to turn back would have been an affront to his principles. That was how she explained his short fuse, and it makes sense to me too, although I never really knew my dad well enough to be sure. I just know that he'd dish out punches left, right and centre.

Did he kill people?

Not that I know of. Drawing a knife rarely led to actually knifing someone. He did it more to show off, I think. Nor do I remember him ever coming home wounded. Except when he was shot.

Shot.

He was shot in the hand. I've already told you that.

True. Mangled his fingers, didn't it?

In one of those fights, he threw himself at a guy and the guy fired a warning shot at him but it brushed his fingers. After that he couldn't move his pinkie and . . . whatever the fuck that one next to it is called. This was on his left hand – his fingering hand. Weeks later he picked up his guitar again and soon he was playing as well or better than before. Some people said he started playing better. I wouldn't know. He came up with a crazy fingering technique for playing his *milongas* and *gauderiadas*. I don't think those two fingers are needed much.

What do I know. He certainly didn't need them at all. What really did him in was when your grandma died. I was eighteen. Life was never the same again after that, not for me or him. Peritonitis.

His dad pauses, takes a sip of beer.

Did the two of you leave the farm after Grandma died?

No, we stayed there a bit longer. For about two more years. But everything started to feel odd. Your grandad was really close to your grandma. He was the most faithful man I've known. Unless he was really discreet and had secrets . . . but that was impossible where he lived, a small little town where everyone knew everything. All the women fell for your grandad. That giant of a man, and brave and a guitarist too. I know, because I went to the dances too and saw single and married women throwing themselves at him. My mum would discuss it with her friends too. He could have been the town's Don Juan but he was faithful to the point of insanity. Plenty of little German blondes around there looking for some action, and wives wanting a fling. I certainly didn't hold back. And my dad would curse me. Said I was like a pig wallowing in the mud. Have you ever seen a pig wallowing in the mud? It's the picture of happiness. But your grandad's morality was based on this essential idea – it was almost maniacal – that a man had to find a woman who liked him and look after her forever. He and I fought a lot because of that. I even admired it in him while my mum was alive, but after she died he carried on nurturing a pretty absurd sense of faithfulness to someone who was no longer there. It wasn't exactly mourning, because it didn't take long for him to start going to dances again, stirring up trouble at barbecues, playing the guitar and getting into fights. He started to drink more too. Women swarmed around him like flies around meat and gradually he let down his guard to one, to another, but mostly he stayed mysteriously chaste. It was something I will never understand. And we started to drift apart, him and me. Not exactly because of our conflicting ideas about how to deal with women. But we started to argue.

And that's when you went to Porto Alegre?

Right. I went in '65. I had just turned twenty.

But why did you and Grandad argue?

Well . . . I'm not sure I can explain exactly. But he saw me as a loser and a womanizer, who didn't want anything from life and wasn't interested in the farm, in working or in moral or religious institutions of any kind. He was right, although he exaggerated a bit. I think that at some point he had just had enough and couldn't be bothered carrying on trying to teach me right from wrong. I wasn't actually such a hopeless case but your grandad . . . well. One day I felt the brunt of his famous short fuse. And the upcome of it all was that he sent me away to Porto Alegre.

Did he hit you?

His dad does not reply.

OK, forget it.

Let's say we exchanged a few blows. Oh, fuck it. None of this matters any more. Yes, he beat me. That's all I'm saying. And the day after that he said sorry, but announced that he was going to send me to Porto Alegre and that it would be for the best. I knew Porto Alegre, having visited quite a few times, and immediately knew he was right. From the first day there I felt big. I got a vocational diploma. In a year and a half I'd opened a print shop in Azenha. I was earning good money for writing ads for shock absorbers, biscuits and residential lots. *You didn't know that life could be so good.*

He laughs.

Now with added nuts – time to go nuts! And so on. They got worse.

OK. But Grandad was killed.

Right. From here on the story gets murky and I heard most of it second-hand. I'm not sure what happened, and maybe nothing specific triggered it, but about a year after I moved to the city your grandad left the farm. I found out when he called me. From abroad. He was in Argentina. In some back-of-beyond nowhere place, I don't remember its name. He said that he just wanted to go travelling for a while, but at the end of the call he sort of led me to believe that he'd left forever, that he'd send word from time to time and that I shouldn't worry. I wasn't worried. I remember thinking that if he ended up dying in a knife fight in some shithole, like the Borges character in that story 'The South', it would be wholly fitting. It would be tragic, but fitting. Anyway. I also thought that there was bound to be a woman involved somewhere, well, a 99 per cent chance of it, there's always a woman behind this kind of thing – and if so, that was a good thing. And over the course of the next year he only called me three more times, if I remember rightly. One of those times he was in the town of Uruguaiana. Another time he was in some small town in Paraná. Then he disappeared for about six months and when he called again he was in a fishing village in Santa Catarina called Garopaba. And although I can't remember exactly what he said, I remember feeling that something in him had changed. There was something childish about his voice. Some of the things he said were bordering on incomprehensible. His description of the place was incoherent. I just remember one detail from the phone call: he mentioned something about pumpkins and sharks. I thought my old man had lost his faculties or, even harder to believe, had started hanging out with hippies and got his melon in a muddle with some wacky tea. But what he was saying was that he'd seen the fishermen catching sharks by throwing pieces of cooked pumpkin into the sea. The sharks ate the pumpkin and the damn stuff fermented and filled their stomachs until they exploded. And I just said, Ah, got it, Dad, great, take care, and he said bye and hung up.

Fuck.

And he didn't call again. I started to get worried. Some months later, having not heard anything from him, I got on my bike one weekend, the Suzuki 50cc I had back then, and went down to Garopaba. An eight-hour trip on the BR-101 interstate, against the wind. We're talking 1967. To get to Garopaba you had to take a dirt road for ten, fifteen miles – in some places it was just sand – and all you saw on the way were half a dozen farmers' shacks and hills and scrub. Anyone you were lucky enough to come across was walking around barefoot, and for every motorbike or pickup you saw, you'd see five ox-drawn carts. It didn't look like more than a thousand people lived in the village, and when you got to the beach, there wasn't much more civilization to be seen other than one really white church on the hillside and the sheds and boats of the fishermen. Most of the houses were clustered around the whaling station and, although I didn't see it for myself, I heard they still hunted whale from there. They were starting to cobble the main roads around the fishermen's houses and the new square had been finished just weeks before I arrived. Small houses and farmsteads spread out around the village and it was in one of these little farms that I found your grandad, after asking around a bit. Oh, you mean the gaucho, one of the locals said to me. So I went looking for the gaucho and found that your grandad had set himself up in a kind of miniature model of the old family farm, some five hundred yards from the beach. He had an old horse, lots of chickens and a vegetable garden that now took up much of the property. He scraped together a living doing odd jobs and had made friends with the fishermen. He'd slept in a fishing shed until he found a house. I couldn't imagine my dad sleeping in a hammock, let alone in a fishing shed with the waves hammering in his ears. But this was nothing next to his spearfishing. The locals fished for grouper, octopus and who knows what else, diving around the rocks, and people even came from Rio and São Paulo, even back then, to do this kind of fishing near Garopaba. And your grandad told me how one day he went out in a boat with one of these groups and they lent him one of those tube and mask contraptions, a snorkel, and flippers and a harpoon, and he dived down and didn't come back up. A guy from São Paulo got terrified and jumped in to look for Dad's drowned body at the bottom of the sea and found him at the exact moment that he was harpooning a grouper the size of a calf. That's how they discovered that the gaucho was a natural at apnoea. He had always been a good swimmer, even in flooded rivers, but he hadn't imagined he could hold his breath so long. You should've seen your grandad back then. In '67 he was forty-five or forty-six, I can't do the maths, but it doesn't matter exactly, and his health was ridiculously good. He'd never smoked, would screw up his face in disgust at the idea, and he had the constitution of a criollo horse. He'd always been strong, but he'd lost some weight, and in spite of some signs of ageing, wrinkles, hair thinning and grey, and the marks of his years working in the fields, you would only need to polish him up and he'd be an ironclad athlete. His broad, solid chest. And just weeks before I arrived, a diver who was about his age, I think he was a military man from Santa Catarina, had died of pulmonary embolism when he tried to match Dad's dive time. I might be wrong, it's a long time since I heard the story, but it was something like four, five minutes underwater.

And why did they kill him?

I'm getting there. Relax, *tchê*. I wanted to give you the background. Because it's a good story, isn't it? Oh yes it is. You should've seen him back in those days. It's not normal for someone to leave one environment and fall into one that's so different and adapt as he did.

Don't you have a photo of Grandad somewhere? You showed me one once.

I don't know if I still have it. Do I? Yes, I do. I know where it is. Want to see it?

Please. I can't remember his face. If I could look at the photo while you tell me the rest of the story, I'd like that.

His dad gets up, bottle in hand, disappears into his room for a few moments and returns holding an old photograph with a serrated edge. The black-and-white image shows a bearded man, sitting on a bench beside a kitchen table, who is just starting to lift the metal straw of a gourd of maté to his lips, looking at the camera with a sideways glance, unhappy at having his photo taken. He is wearing leather boots, *bombacha* trousers and a woollen shirt with rectangular motifs. There's a supermarket calendar on the wall with a photograph of Sugarloaf Mountain and the light comes from above, from louvred windows that are partially beyond the top of the photo. There is no note on the back. He gets up and goes to the bathroom. He compares the face on the photo with the face he sees in the mirror. A shiver passes through him. From the nose up, the face in the photo is a darker and slightly more aged copy of the face in the mirror. The only difference worth noting is the beard, but in spite of it, it's like he is looking at a photo of himself.

I'd like to keep this photo, he says when he settles back into the sofa. His dad nods.

I visited your grandad a second time in Garopaba, the last time. It was June, during the *quermesse*, a festival they have there. There were concerts and dance shows. Everyone was stuffing themselves with mullet and whatnot. One night a singer from Uruguaiana got up onstage, a big lad, about twenty-five years old, and your grandad immediately turned up his nose at the sight of him. Said he knew the guy, he'd seen him play over in the borderlands and that he was rubbish. I remember liking it. He plucked vigorously at the strings, looked profound during songs and made rehearsed jokes between them. Dad thought that the singer was a clown who had a lot of technique and little true feeling. And that would have been that, except after the concert, when the singer was drinking mulled wine at a stall, a man thought it'd be a good idea to introduce the two of them, as they were both gauchos through and through. Gripping the guy's arm, he dragged him over to Dad and the two of them showed this immediate antipathy. Afterwards I found out that it was much more than a question of musical qualities, but at the time they pretended they didn't know each other, out of respect for the guy who was excited to introduce them. But the man was fool enough to ask Dad straight out if he had liked the singer's music, and with Dad, if someone asked, they'd get the truth. His honest opinion made the singer mad. The two started to argue and Dad told him to turn his mouth to the side because his breath smelt like the arse of a dead pampas fox. Quite a few people heard that and laughed. Obviously, the *indio* from Uruguaiana turned nasty, and it was just a little step from that to Dad pulling his knife. The singer backed off, the argument stopped, but the thing is I remember the reaction of everyone around us. They weren't just curious about the fight. They were looking askance at your grandad, shaking their heads. I realized that between my last visit and this one they had taken a dislike to him in the community. What I'm saying is no one wants to have a bad-mannered gaucho around who thinks it's cool to show his knife at any little thing. I told him to stop doing it, but your grandad didn't care, he didn't even realize his own stupidity. People here are scared of you, I told him, you're going to get into serious trouble. I went away and for a good while didn't hear from Dad. At that time I was pretty much stuck in Porto Alegre, working hard, and that was the time when I started to go out with your mum, too. We went out for four years and she left me three times before we got married, but anyway, I didn't visit Dad for a good while and many months later I got a call from a police chief in Laguna saying they'd murdered him. There was a Sunday dance in some community hall, one of those dances the whole village goes to. At the height of the party, the lights go out. When the lights come back on, a minute later, there's a guy lying in the middle of the room in a pool of blood with dozens of stab wounds. Everyone killed him; or in other words, no one killed him. The village killed him. That's what the police chief told me. Everyone was there, whole families, probably even the priest. The lights were turned off, no one saw anything. They weren't afraid of your grandad – they hated him.

They each take a swig of beer. His dad finishes his bottle and looks at his son, almost smiling.

Except that I don't believe that story, he says.

What? Why not?

Because there was no body.

But wasn't he there, stabbed to death?

That's what I was told. I never saw the body. When that police chief called me, everything was already more or less done and dusted. They said it took them weeks to find me. They looked for me in Taquara. Someone in Garopaba knew that he came from there. Eventually, they found someone who recognized the description of my dad and knew my name. By the time they called me, he'd already been buried.

Where?

In Garopaba. In the fishermen's little cemetery. Just a blank gravestone at the end of the plot.

You went and saw it?

I did. I saw the grave and sorted out some paperwork in Laguna. All very strange. I had a very strong feeling that he wasn't in that hole. There were weeds on the earth. I remember thinking, Shit, this ground wasn't dug the week before last, no fucking way. I didn't meet anyone who confirmed the story I'd been told. It was as if it hadn't happened. The story of the crime was, in itself, plausible, and the people's silence made sense, but the way I heard about it, the police chief's patter, that horrible stone without a name . . . I never really bought it. Anyway, whatever happened to your grandad, it was bound to happen. People go looking for a particular death, in most cases. He had his.

Haven't you ever thought of having the grave opened? There must be a legal way to do that.

His dad looks away in what seems to be irritation. He sighs.

Listen. I never told anyone this story. Your mum doesn't know. If you ask, she'll say that your grandad disappeared, because that's what I told her. As far as I was concerned, he really had disappeared. I left it at that. If you think that's terrible – too bad! The way I was back then, the life I led in those days . . . it would be difficult to make you understand it now.

I don't think it's terrible. Take it easy.

His dad fidgets in the armchair. Beta gets up and with a little jump puts her front paws on her master's leg, who grabs and holds her face as if he were muzzling her, leaning over to look her in the eye. When he lets go, she gets down and returns to lie beside the armchair. It is a small fragment of the inscrutable ritual of his dad's relationship with the animal.

And why're you telling me this now?

You haven't read that Borges story I mentioned before, have you?

No.

'The South'.

No. I haven't read anything by Borges.

Course not, you don't read a fucking thing.

Dad. The pistol.

Bueno.

His dad opens the bottle of cognac, fills a small glass and downs it in one. He doesn't offer any to his son. He picks up the pistol and examines it for a moment. He presses the button to release the magazine and then clicks it back into place, as if he were just wanting to show that the weapon is not loaded. A drop of sweat runs from his forehead, drawing attention to the fact that he is no longer sweating all over his body. A minute earlier he had been covered in sweat. He slips the pistol into the belt of his trousers and looks at his son.

I'm going to kill myself tomorrow.

He takes his time thinking about what he has just heard, listening to his irregular breathing coming out in short snorts through his nostrils. An immense exhaustion falls on his shoulders. He slips the photo of his grandad into his pocket, dries his hands on his Bermuda shorts, gets up and walks towards the front door.

Come back here.

Why? What do you want me to do after hearing this kind of shit? Either you're serious and want me to convince you to change your mind, which would be the worst thing you've ever laid on me, or you're having a laugh, which would be so cheap that I don't want to know – it's one or the other. Bye.

Come back, damn it.

He stops by the door, looking back at the sad floor of pinkish tiles and cement joints, at the luxuriant fern trying to escape from a pot dangling from a hook on the ceiling by thin chains, taking in the sweet, strangely animal, lingering smell of cigar smoke in the living room.

I'm not joking and I don't want you to convince me of anything. I'm just telling you about something that's going to happen.

Nothing's going to happen.

Get this into your head: it's inevitable. I decided weeks ago in a moment of utter lucidity. I'm tired. I'm fed up. I think it started with that haemorrhoid surgery. At my last check-up the doctor looked at the tests and looked at me like death itself, disillusioned with all of humanity. I had the impression that he was going to resign from my case like a lawyer. And he's right. I'm starting to get ill and I don't fancy it. I no longer taste beer, cigars are bad for me but I can't stop, I don't want to take Viagra to screw, I don't even feel *nostalgic* for screwing. Life's too long and I've run out of patience. Life after sixty, for someone who has had a life like mine, is all about being stubborn. I respect people who put in the effort, but I don't fancy it. I was happy until about two years ago and now I want to go away. Anyone who thinks that's wrong can live until a hundred if they want, good luck to them. Fine by me.

What a load of rubbish.

Forget it. I can't expect you to understand. We're far too different. Don't try to understand, you'll be wasting your time.

You know I won't let you do it, Dad. Why did you call me here to tell me?

I know it's unfair. But I did it because I trust you, I know you're tough. I called you here because there's something I need to do beforehand and I can't do it on my own. And only my son can help me.

Why didn't you call the other one? He might even find it funny, who knows. Write a book about it.

No, I need you. It's the most important thing I've ever had to ask anyone and you're the one I can count on.

Give me the pistol now and I'll sort out whatever it is you need doing. All right? Finished with clowning around now?

His dad laughs at his son's exasperation.

Tchê, lad . . . listen. What has to be sorted out is *because* of the other thing.

The suicide.

To me there's something gutless about that word, I'm avoiding it. But you can use it if you like.

What am I to do now, Dad? Call the police? Have you committed? Lunge and tear the gun from you by force? You really thought this would work?

It's already worked. It's as if it's already happened.

That's stupid. It's a choice you've got. What if I got you to change your mind?

It's not a choice. It would be easier for me, and much easier for you, to see it as a choice. My decision won't result in the fact – it's part of the fact. It's just another way of dying, lad. I took a lot of time to get to this point. Sit down, son. Want another beer?

He takes quick steps to the sofa and sits down angrily.

Look, think about it like this. Imagine what it would be like if you or anyone else tried to stop me now. What a hassle. Me trying to carry out my decision and you trying to stop me, who knows how, living with me, monitoring me, having me committed, medicated, your brother coming from São Paulo and your mum having to put up with me again. It'd be a ludicrous nightmare for everyone involved. Do you see how absurd it'd be? There's nothing more ridiculous than one person trying to convince another one. I worked with persuasion my whole life. Persuasion is the biggest cancer in human behaviour. No one should ever be convinced of anything. People know what they want and they know what they need. I know that because I was always a specialist in persuasion and inventing needs, and that's why I've got a wall full of little plaques over there. Don't try to talk me out of it. If you convinced me not to kill myself you'd turn me into a cripple, I'd live for a few more years – defeated, mutilated and sick, pleading for mercy. I'm being serious. Don't try to persuade me. To persuade someone not to follow their heart is obscene, persuasion is something obscene, people know what they need and no one can give us advice. What I'm going to do was decided ages ago, before I even had the idea.

I expected more from you, Dad. More than this retarded guff you're spouting. I'm disgusted by the idea of playing the victim – it was you who taught me that. And now you're acting all victimized.

Let me teach you something else right now: when you start to shit blood and go limp and wake up fed up with life every damn day, then you've got a moral obligation to act like a victim. Write that down. Oh, don't insult me, for fuck's sake. Bold as brass, are you now? Doesn't suit you. You're a sensible lad, even if you're a bit gutless. I've always been frank with you. I get you from tip to toe. I warned you about everything, and was I ever wrong? Eh? I said you'd lose your girl the way you did. I said you'd spend your life being the last resort of the desperate. But you're the intelligent one. The one who manages to think of others, even if you can't remember anyone's face. And that's why you're much better than me and your brother. I'm proud of that and love you for it. And now I need you to stand by your old man.

Fuck, Dad.

His dad's eyes are red.

It's Beta.

What about Beta?

His dad makes a vague gesture towards the front door and lets out an almost inaudible sound. The dog gets up immediately and leaves the house.

You know how I love that dog. We're very close.

I'm not doing it.

Why not?

I'm not set up to look after a dog. And anyway . . . Christ, I don't believe this. I'm sorry. I have to go.

Not to look after her. I want you to take her to Rolf, in Belém Novo. After I've . . . done what I'm going to do. Ask him to give her an injection. I've already found out, it won't hurt.

No, no.

She's already depressed now. She knows already. She'll waste away when she's on her own.

Do it yourself. You're the one who can't fucking choose anything.

I can. I'm not getting involved.

I haven't got the balls, lad.

No, no.

You have to promise me this.

Forget it, Dad. Impossible.

Promise.

I can't get involved.

Please.

No. It's not fair.

You're denying my last wish.

It's not happening.

You'll do it. I know you will.

I won't. You're on your own with this. I can't. Sorry.

I know you'll do it. That's why you're here.

You're trying to persuade me. A minute ago you said that was obscene.

I'm not going to persuade you. I'm done. It's my wish. I know you won't say no.

Pathetic old man.

That's my name.

Without warning a very old memory comes to mind. The scene is pointless and doesn't seem to be have been worth keeping as a memory, much less remembering at this inopportune moment. One morning before leaving for work, his dad was shaving in the bathroom with the door open and he, six or seven years old, was watching him. Once his dad had finished with the razor, he washed his face with soap, covering it with lather, and then rinsed it repeatedly. After the second rinse his face was no longer lathery, but his dad continued to splash his face with water, four, five times. He asked his dad why he washed his face with water so many times, since the foam had already disappeared. As if it was the most obvious thing in the world, his dad replied: It feels good.

My hand's shaking, Dad.

You're doing fine. You're a better human being.

Shut up.

Seriously. I'm very proud of you. No one else could do it.

I didn't say I would.

I could make you promise much worse things. Like making peace with your brother, for example.

I'll do that if you tell me you're pulling my leg. A few hours from now I'll be hugging him.

Good try. But the truth is I don't care. I wouldn't forgive him, if I were you.

Good to know.

Isn't it? I don't mind telling you now. But what I do need is for you to spare her. She's fifteen years old, but her breed can live to be twenty, or older. She's my life. Ever seen a depressed dog? If she's left here without me, I'll take all her pain with me. Can I consider it as promised?

You can.

Thank you.

No, you can't. I can't get involved.

I love you, lad.

I didn't say I would. I didn't. Don't touch me.

I wasn't going to touch you. I'm not even moving. ■

NOTICEBOARD

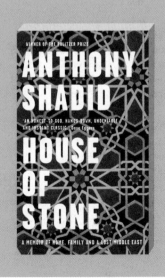

NOTES ON TRANSLATORS

Peter Bush is a freelance translator living in Barcelona. His translations from Portuguese include *Turbulence* by Chico Buarque and *Equator* by Miguel Sousa Tavares, which was awarded the Calouste Gulbenkian Prize for Portuguese Translation. Recently he has translated Ramón del Valle-Inclán's *Tyrant Banderas* from Spanish, and Teresa Solana's *The Sound of One Hand Clapping* and Quim Monzó's *A Thousand Morons* from Catalan.

Nick Caistor's translations include *Journey to Portugal* by José Saramago and *The Buenos Aires Quintet* by Manuel Vázquez Montalban. He is editor and translator of the *Faber Book of Contemporary Latin American Short Stories*.

Margaret Jull Costa has been a literary translator for over twenty-five years and has translated such writers as Javier Marías, Fernando Pessoa, Bernardo Atxaga and Ramón del Valle-Inclán. She has won various prizes for her work, including, in 2008, the PEN Book-of-the-Month Translation Award and the Oxford Weidenfeld Translation Prize for her version of Eça de Queiroz's *The Maias*, and most recently, in 2011, the Oxford Weidenfeld Translation Prize

for *The Elephant's Journey* by José Saramago.

Katrina Dodson is a PhD candidate in the Department of Comparative Literature at University of California, Berkeley, where she is writing a dissertation on Elizabeth Bishop, Clarice Lispector and questions of geographical imagination. Her work has appeared in *McSweeney's* and *Two Lines*.

Alison Entrekin's translations include *Near to the Wild Heart* by Clarice Lispector, *City of God* by Paulo Lins, *The Eternal Son* by Cristovão Tezza, which was a finalist for the International IMPAC Dublin Literary Award in 2012, and *Budapest* by Chico Buarque, which was a finalist in the 2004 *Independent Foreign Fiction Prize*.

Ana Fletcher has worked for PEN International and The Writer, a language consultancy. She holds an MA in comparative literature and translates from Spanish and Portuguese.

Beth Fowler won the inaugural Harvill Secker Young Translators' Prize in 2010. Her translation of Iosi Havilio's *Open Door* was published in 2011.

Daniel Hahn is a writer, editor and translator with some thirty books to his name. His work has won him the *Independent* Foreign Fiction Prize and the Blue Peter Book Award. He is currently national programme director of the British Centre for Literary Translation and is the consultant translator for this edition of *Granta*.

Amanda Hopkinson is Visiting Professor of Literary Translation at City University London and at Manchester University. She is currently writing *A History of Mexican Photography* and is translating Elena Poniatowska's *Leonora*.

Anna Kushner translates from Spanish, French and Portuguese. She is the translator of the novels *The Halfway House* by Guillermo Rosales, *The Autobiography of Fidel Castro* by Norberto Fuentes and *Jerusalem* by Gonçalo M. Tavares.

Clifford E. Landers has translated novels and short stories by Rubem Fonseca, Jorge Amado and João Ubaldo Ribeiro. A professor emeritus at New Jersey City University, he now lives in Naples, Florida.

Johnny Lorenz is an associate professor at Montclair State University. In 2012, he published a new translation of Clarice Lispector's posthumous novel, *A Breath of Life*.

Ina Rilke was born in Mozambique and grew up in Portugal speaking Dutch, English and Portuguese. She has translated works by writers including Erwin Mortier, Hella Haasse and Judith Vanistendael. She lives in Amsterdam and Paris.

Jethro Soutar is a translator of Spanish and Portuguese. He is also the author of two non-fiction books: *Ronaldinho: Football's Flamboyant Maestro* and *Gael García Bernal and the Latin American New Wave*.

Stefan Tobler is a translator of Portuguese and German and the founder of And Other Stories publishing house. Tobler has published translations by writers including Antônio Moura, Clarice Lispector and Rodrigo de Souza Leão.

GRANTA EVENTS

Celebrate Brazil's
Best Young Novelists

12–29 NOVEMBER 2012

UK	NORTH AMERICA	EUROPE
Bath	Boston	Amsterdam
Cambridge	Chicago	Berlin
London	Los Angeles	Brussels
	Miami	Paris
	New York	
	San Francisco	
	Seattle	
	Toronto	
	Washington DC	

VISIT GRANTA.COM/EVENTS

for a calendar of readings, parties and
conversations for the European and North
American launch of *Granta* 121: The Best
of Young Brazilian Novelists.

© FRANCOISE HUGUIER / AGENCE VU